Who Do You Say
That I Am?

Who Do You Say That I Am?

CONFESSING THE MYSTERY OF CHRIST

John C. Cavadini & Laura Holt

editors

University of Notre Dame Press

Notre Dame, Indiana

Manufactured in the United States of America

Library of Congress Cataloging-in-Publication Data
Who do you say that I am? : confessing the mystery of Christ / John
Cavadini and Laura Holt, editors.
p.   cm.
Includes bibliographical references and index.
ISBN 0-268-04401-5 (alk. paper)
ISBN 0-268-04402-3 (pbk. : alk. paper)
1. Jesus Christ—Person and offices—Congresses.
I. Cavadini, John C.
II. Holt, Laura.
BT203.W478   2004
232—dc22
2003025296

∞ *This book is printed on acid-free paper.*

This book is dedicated to Hans Frei (1922–1988)

whose "little book" on Christology
continues to be a huge inspiration to many

Contents

Preface

"But who do you say that I am?" This is the question Jesus asks his disciples on the way to Caesarea Philippi, and Peter readily supplies the familiar answer, "You are the Christ" (Mk 8:29). Equally familiar is the dissatisfaction Jesus expresses when Peter subsequently shows that he does not understand his own confession and would in fact limit the identity and ministry of the Christ to his own narrowly conceived notions of power and providence. The passage in the Gospel of Mark stands as a question to all of its readers, asking whether we are guilty of the same attempt to constrict the meaning and identity of the Christ to the scope of our own narrow preconceptions and ambitions. In every age Christians answering the question of Jesus must always be prepared to hear the rebuke of Jesus, "Get behind me, Satan! For you are not on the side of God" (Mk 8:33). Perhaps the tradition of reflection on Jesus' question can be regarded as a continuing attempt to forge an adequate expression of the faith to which the Gospel of Mark would call its readers, in every generation an attempt to resist the narrowing down that would elicit Jesus' rebuke even as shifts in culture and intellectual patterns require an ongoing development in the expression of the gospel's faith.

The advent of the third millennium of Christianity presented itself as an opportunity to reflect on this tradition of reflection and to advance it. What better place to take this opportunity than the Tantur Institute for Ecumenical Studies? Tantur, by its very mission and by the vision of His Holiness Pope Paul VI and Reverend Theodore Hesburgh, C.S.C., its founders, stands as a special reminder that Christian reflection on the mystery of Christ must retain the openness to resist confusing an adequate confession of faith with a reiteration of hopes that will prove too narrow and designs that will prove too constrained when Jesus asks us, "Who do you say that I am?" The call to reflecting on the central

Christian mystery in the presence of believers of the various churches is a call to openness and self-scrutiny, even as it is equally a call to maintain the integrity of the essentials of the faith we share. The location of Tantur in Jerusalem on the road to Bethlehem, at the confluence of the three religions of the Book, prompted us to engage our reflection in part by listening to how the other two religions of the Book might comment on the tradition of Christian engagement with the question of Jesus, "Who do you say that I am?"

The essays presented in this volume, then, were delivered at an international conference at Tantur, held in the last week of May, 2000. Such a conference is not possible without the assistance of many people, more people, unfortunately, than can be thanked in a short preface. Nevertheless, apart from the participants, I would like to thank the rector of Tantur, Reverend Mike McGarry, P.P., and his staff, particularly Issa D'Aboub and Vivi Seniora. I acknowledge as well the help of Kathryn Johnson, of Louisville Presbyterian Seminary, whose leadership of the "status quaestionis" discussion sessions gave all present the opportunity for on-the-spot synthesis and clarification of thought. The assistance of Laura Holt is acknowledged on the title page. I would like to thank the University of Notre Dame, and especially Reverend William Beauchamp, C.S.C., Executive Vice-President for Finance, for generously funding the whole conference. Donata Coleman's services in simultaneous translation were invaluable. Finally, Barbara Hanrahan of the University of Notre Dame Press, and Carole Roos, have expertly guided this work to its completion as a volume of essays. I would like to dedicate the book to the memory of Professor Hans Frei, who taught me, along with many others, the meaning of ecumenism even as he also taught the fundamental importance of correct articulation of the faith.

John C. Cavadini
All Saints' Day 2002
South Bend, Indiana

Who Do You Say That I Am?

Introduction

JOHN C. CAVADINI *&*

KATHRYN JOHNSON

In the first essay of this volume, Jaroslav Pelikan, as a historian of the development of doctrine, examines the christological creeds and confessions of the early Church. He sets the tone for the subsequent essays as he addresses the question of the relation between normative formulas and the mysteries which those formulas are meant to express. He explores what he sees as the persistent reliance of the conciliar confessions on a "combination of affirmative and negative formulas," studying the negations in particular, taking up one negation from each of the seven ecumenical councils, from Nicaea I's (325 C.E.) "Begotten *not* made," to Nicaea II's (787) warning, "If anyone does *not* confess that Christ our God can be represented in his humanity" they must be considered heretical. Pelikan identifies five functions for these kinds of negations:

(i)   the polemic concern to correct heresy;
(ii) the exegetical task of eliminating possible meanings of scriptural words or passages which were contrary to the Church's confession;
(iii) the devotional responsibility to shape private prayer and church liturgy;
(iv) the dialectical balancing of the connection and the distinction of the twofold proclamation of Christology with its constituent doctrines of the Trinity and anthropology;

(v)   the provision of a "lexicon of transcendence," an apophatic correction to the human desire to claim more knowledge than it can
possess.

It is the last which is perhaps the most profound and important. It implies that the confessions of the councils are not hopelessly distant, closed
formulas, the reified theology of a bygone era. Rather, in their attempt
to balance assertion and negation, they prove themselves the articulation
of a living faith. For in the very confession meant to state the boundaries
between their own position and alternative positions, they trace these
boundaries as the contours of mysteries never fully able to be expressed
in words. Thus, even as they articulate the faith in a normative way, they
invite reflection and development.

     In the second essay Morna Hooker reminds us that the confessions of
the councils cannot be taken, without any intervening hermeneutic, as
the teaching of the New Testament. We do not read anywhere in the
gospels or epistles that Jesus is "one person with two natures." To collapse the teaching of the New Testament too quickly into such a formula
is perhaps to misperceive the intention of the councils, narrowing them
in the way Pelikan has warned against, ignoring their delicate balancing
between scriptural and non-scriptural language. Conflating the teaching
of the New Testament too univocally with the teaching of the councils
also means that we may miss not only the answers, but the very questions
that were alive for the writers of scripture. From one point of view, the
language of Chalcedon is "utterly foreign" not only to our time but to
the language and ideas of the Christian scriptures. Valuable in its own
day as a response to particular issues, it poses a danger when regarded in
fossilized form as a comprehensive understanding of the biblical writings
themselves. For example, the question "Who do you say that I am?" was
raised for the first disciples by all that Jesus did and said, not directly in
the challenge from Jesus himself. As put in the gospels, the question
reflects already the change in emphasis from the "good news proclaimed
by Jesus to the good news proclaimed about him." Second, in prompting
an answer phrased in titles, the evangelists further encourage this latter,
christological emphasis. And, while titles are valuable summaries, they
are not the only way of expressing Jesus' significance. In the synoptic
gospels Jesus refuses to use titles of himself and instead employs the "enigmatic non-titular phrase, 'Son of Man,'" and the evangelists themselves

convey the sense of his identity most adequately in story. Even in the fourth gospel, where the continuity with Chalcedonian affirmations is strongest, continuity is still not identity. Finally, in exploring their new situation, the earliest Christians were often in dispute with their fellow Jews. The assumptions on both sides of the argument were Jewish, with both sides making arguments from Jewish scripture. When the communities separated and the shared context was forgotten, the Christian writings could be read in misleading, anti-Jewish ways. Indeed, the New Testament itself is today seen by many as anti-Jewish or anti-Semitic. Ironically, there is a cost to Christology in such forgetfulness, for New Testament responses to Jesus can be rightly appreciated only with an appreciation of their Jewish origins.

Gerald O'Collins, S.J., continues the biblical reflection on our theme. He observes that of the approximately 130 titles given to Jesus in the New Testament, only eight occur more than twenty times. (These are "Christ," "Lord," "Son of Man," "Son," "Teacher," "Son of God," "King," and "Lamb"). Sometimes these titles are paired, as in the Caesarea Philippi episode whose question gives title to this collection. Here, "Christ" is a "'low' or earthly title that refers to Jesus' human mission as God's designated Redeemer" and the "Son of God" is a "'high' title that conveys his true divinity." O'Collins's main focus, however, is on the titles from John 13:13, "Teacher/Master" and "Lord." While "Lord" can in Greek be simply a courteous address, it is clearly used frequently in many parts of the New Testament to convey a "'high,' divine sense." Examination of Pauline texts in particular shows a "new, christological monotheism" in which "Lord" (which was "*the* designation in the Old Testament for the one God") is used for the Son. "Teacher," on the other hand, is only used in the gospels and at first seems a low, human title. Because of the direct authority of Jesus' teaching, however, not as Wisdom's emissary but as divine Wisdom in person who shows a vision of cosmic generosity, this title, no less than the "high" titles, involves those who use it in life-transforming commitment. The titles for Jesus in the Bible are not simple descriptions. They are confessions, and their very claim to normativity involves the declaration of a mystery not fully available for description, but realized most fully in the life of transforming discipleship to which they call us. Indeed, O'Collins argues, the ways in which Jesus is named in Christian devotion have been among the primary means for "expressing and stimulating our knowledge of Jesus, our discipleship, and our worship of him." Biblical titles have been joined in later centuries by other forms of address. In their multiplicity, the titles bear witness to the inexhaustibility of Christ's mystery. The naming of Christ in all these ways puts us in a position "to know him, follow him, and pray to him and with him."

George Lindbeck's essay is the first not only to raise but also to examine the question of the relation between the biblical confessions and the credal confessions of the councils. He begins from the confessions of Peter at Caesarea Philippi, construed in traditional terms as the affirmation that Jesus is "equally and unitedly the messiah of Israel and the incarnate Son of the living God." Yet, he notes, by the time of Nicaea and Chalcedon, messiahship had disappeared from the credal definitions. To question the separation of these two great strands is a recent and uncompleted undertaking.

Formally, "messiahship singularizes incarnation and incarnation universalizes messiahship." There can be only one messianic age or person; yet without incarnation this messianic work in creation, redemption, and revelation need not be universal. Incarnation, on the other hand, need not be singular unless combined with messiahship. Yet at the same time overemphasized incarnation erodes the universal significance of salvation for the temporal and historical dimension of the world—the realm of narrativity. "Incarnational hegemony" has downplayed visible transformation in favor of a spiritualizing inwardness, a salvation both individualistic and undifferentiated. But many modern theologies "from below" have no more room for messianic themes than do objectivizing, "from above" incarnational perspectives—and in fact may actually exclude rather than simply ignore them.

Reconciliation of these two themes into mutually enriching integration faces no dogmatic barriers. Creeds and dogmas are affirmed by mainstream christological discussion (even in communions where they are not explicitly recognized as having "abiding and expansive relevance"), but *omission* of messiahship need not be seen as similarly relevant or binding. To be sure, early theologians (e.g., Justin) used the biblical language of messiah not chiefly to understand the person and work of Christ but either to argue from prophecy to Christ's divinity or to demonstrate Jewish culpability in rejecting him. But Christology from the medieval era onward has shown that dogmatic affirmations are separable from theological frameworks. This recognition helps Lindbeck reject the work of theologians such as John Hick and Maurice Wiles who repudiate credal affirmations because they reject the theological principles which framed them. "Unlike the picture of a closed dogmatic system which critics cherish," Lindbeck observes, "the historic doctrines of the Church, though vitally important, are rare and scattered points of orientation in a vast and open landscape full of dangers they do not warn against and of wonders of which they give no hint." This is in keeping with the characterization of the credal confessions articulated in the first essay by Pelikan.

In the next essay James Buckley finds in the Caesarea Philippi story an example of mutual rebuke that is corrective without breaking connection or destroying conversation. He invites contemporary theologians to a similar practice as a dynamic ascetic discipline of mutual illumination and correction. Using Hans Urs von Balthasar and Karl Rahner as conversation partners, he asks us to consider with them three aspects of the "late modern christological puzzle," questions about Jesus' particularity, universality, and unsurpassability. Without resolving the disputes between the two theological schools, Buckley invites his hearers to broaden their appreciation of devout and rigorous christological reflection within the community of Christ's disciples. He shows us that part of the normative openness (if it can be put that way) of christological confession is its empowering of legitimate debate within the confines of normative confession. A normative tradition which is normative precisely by pointing beyond itself in a normative way will have the character of a self-corrective discourse, responsive to the biblical texts and conciliar confessions, and responsive as well to the demands of discipleship and renewal which the confession that "Jesus is Lord" entails.

Continuing the systematic section of this volume, Jon Sobrino, S.J., begins the next essay by observing that "Never has the world been so unequal and so poor," yet the poor and the issues they raise are hidden from the world. Sobrino seeks in this essay to make a test of any christological proposal its impact on the visibility of the poor. A theology which puts the poor at the center, he declares, is the most universal. It is also the most real, resistant to the docetism which denies the broken world as it is.

The New Testament itself presents a variety of perspectives, but Sobrino lifts up especially the synoptic view in which Jesus' proclamation of the Reign of God was at the center, the starting point. While there are important continuities among the scriptural perspectives (e.g., on the radicality of the horizontality of human love) the nuances in (for example) the Pauline writings lost the stress on the demands of the Reign of God, Jesus' praxis, and his active defense of the oppressed. As Christology developed in the first decades of the Church, the relationship of Jesus with God the Father was emphasized (seen in the concentration on titles of Lord, Word, Son) at the expense of what had been equally important: the relation of Jesus to the Reign of God, his role as "Messiah" as this title indicated relation to the salvation and hope of the poor. Here Sobrino's essay raises in a different context the same issue raised by Lindbeck's essay. In contrast to the Pauline and Johannine strands of reflection, and to interpretations which by time of the christological councils had lost the centrality of the Reign of God, Sobrino insists that only by recovering that centrality can theology also recover both the historical Jesus who preached the Kingdom and the specific historical conflict which belongs to Christian faith—conflict on behalf of the poor.

While critical of the preference of "sin" over "oppression" as the name for the fundamental problem of human life (with the implied overshadowing of "liberation" by "liberty") Sobrino argues ideally for their reconciliation. Both the "justification of the sinner" and the "salvation of the poor" require mutual relationship since in both cases God is acting toward the weak, those who deserve nothing. And the option for the poor helps us to understand "justification by faith" since the justified sinner must love those of no value. Finally, Sobrino concludes, the poor of the world call the Church to see again the place of martyrs in a Church based on Jesus' martyrdom: the poor first are crucified, and the martyrs who defend the poor show the great love of God—they are martyrs of the Reign of God, of a creation living in the pain of the birth of human beings.

In the final contribution in systematic theology, Johann Baptist Metz, as a member of the generation of Germans "after Auschwitz," with all the particularity of horror represented in that phrase, argues that the critical revision of Christian theology required by this historical location must center especially on Christology. The doctrine which was the "leading edge" of anti-Judaism cannot be simply abandoned by Christians but must be reformulated in a way accountable both to Christians and to Jews. Such a theology will resist the temptation to "strong" categories which cover historical wounds with metaphysical accounts of salvation "blind to situations and devoid of memory." Metz looks for the origins of Christian forgetfulness of suffering in the history of theology.

He finds there, in the reduction of Israel to a "superseded presupposition in salvation history," also a loss of half the Christian heritage. While holding on to Israel's traditions of *faith*, the early christological dogmatic formulas show a Church whose categories of *thought* are indebted to philosophical systems in the Platonic tradition. From this influence came an assumption—that "ideas are always more fundamental than memories"—which loosens the "speculatively irreducible tension" between remembering and forgetting." Yet in truth the concept of God must be rooted in the remembrance of God. Christology after Auschwitz does not require rejection of traditional dogmatic formulas, but these dogmas must be in constant dialogue with the biblical narratives of discipleship: of conversion, resistance, and suffering. They must be opened up to a "dangerous and liberating remembrance in the Church." The essays of both Sobrino and Metz demonstrate some of the concrete historical situations which press what we have been calling the "normative openness" of the christological confessions toward development.

As the first essay in a cluster devoted to issues of Christology and interreligious dialogue, the contribution of Claude Geffré, O.P., calls dialogue among religions a "sign of the times" at the turn of the millennium, a new step in the religious history of humanity. Its appearance coincides with the expanding awareness of common responsibilities for the future which unites all the world's people into a single global family. Evident in most world religions, this impulse toward dialogue showed itself among Christians at Vatican II, which for the first time in the Church's history expressed a positive evaluation of non-Christian religions and also revised some of the traditional positions which would have made dialogue more difficult. This willingness to dialogue accompanies the growing awareness among Christians that the plurality of religions is not a provisional historical obstacle soon to be overcome by the Church's missionary efforts; theology must seek to understand how it could be God's will. This acceptance distinguishes the goals of interreligious dialogues from those of ecumenical efforts: the unity of the Church is a goal properly sought within history, in obedience to the Lord's command. On the contrary, the notion of a single global superreligion is a dangerous fantasy which invites disparagement of the irreducible riches of the world's religions.

The first rule of dialogue requires respect for the partners precisely in their difference. While Christian missionaries long operated by the Parmenidean principle of "like known by like," biblical tradition instead would suggest the recognition of the stranger precisely as stranger. The second rule requires faithfulness to self. Thus interreligious dialogue involves a paradox, for it requires reconciliation of absolute commitment to the ways of one's own religion with an openness to other convictions. Without falling into relativism, it must have an alternative to the absolutist views of truth which assume other views can be only error or partial or distorted forms of the unique truth on which it has the monopoly. Thinkers like Habermas have explored such understandings. On this view, truth is not exclusive of all other positions nor inclusive of all other truth; instead, it is understood as relative to the particular historical situation in which it arose.

Yet Christians must face honestly the questions which arise when the recognition of equality among partners necessary for dialogue is combined with faithfulness to the Christian message of incarnation. While it might seem legitimate to adopt a view of religious truth borrowed from other dialogical contexts, Christians must recognize their *exceptional* position among religions: they proclaim a message entirely relative to a historic mediation which coincides with the irruption of the Absolute; they claim as their founder, alone among all religious foundational figures, the very Son of God. Rightly, in Geffré's view, the Church after Vatican II has proclaimed both a positive judgment on elements of other religions while also proclaiming, with the whole Christian tradition, that Jesus Christ is the only mediator between God and humanity and that Christianity is the only religion to witness to the fullness of truth about God's mystery. The task facing the theology of religions, then, is to reinterpret the uniqueness of Christ as only mediator and the uniqueness of Christianity as the only religion of salvation in a way that gives positive value also to other religions. Dialogue partners from other traditions will bear witness to the condescension they have experienced from Christians when this task has not been accomplished.

Citing the work of Jacques Dupuis, Geffré affirms that, despite its ambiguity, the religious experience of humanity shows not only a human quest for the highest Reality but also the plurality of the gifts of God in searching for people. Thus, human history was a history of salvation well before the coming of Christ. Most contemporary theologians have come to reject an exclusive Christology in favor of forms of inclusivism, including theologies of fulfillment. But some have been tempted to adopt a pluralist view which involves a radically theocentric stance in which all religions revolve (like the planets in John Hick's "Copernican revolution") around the sun of the ultimate reality, who may or may not be called God. Roger Haight's recent *Jesus Symbol of God* provides an example of Christology, responsive to be sure to the recognition of religious pluralism, which so reshapes Christology that Jesus is the symbol of perfect mediation between God and humanity but not the constitutive or exclusive cause of the salvation of all people.

Geffré prefers to speak of the consequences of the "christological paradox," namely that at the very moment that we confess that Jesus Christ is the unique source of salvation in the incarnation, the Incarnation itself, as the manifestation of the Absolute in and by a historical particularity, invites us to resist absolutizing Christianity as a way of salvation exclusive of all others. The economy of the Incarnate Word is itself a sacrament of a larger economy, that of the eternal Word of God, which coincides with the entire religious history of humanity. Drawing his inspiration from Tillich's balancing of the "absolutely universal" with the "absolutely particular" in Christ, Geffré reminds us that at the heart of the preaching of the Incarnation is a *kenosis* or a kind of "creative lack" (*manqué*) or self-limitation. This invites us to a stance in dialogue which is not relativistic, but relational, which enables us to avoid confusing the universality of the mystery of Christ with the universality of Christianity as a historical religion. This self-limitation of the Absolute in the particularity of the Incarnation makes that particularity itself an opening to the other as other. The Incarnation is irreducibly, definitively, and absolutely such an opening. Perhaps we can say that this is another implication of a tradition which is at once normative, and which in its very normativity is an expression of openness.

David Burrell, C.S.C., in the next contribution, seeks to follow the path pioneered by theologians such as Jean Daniélou and Karl Rahner in exploring the potential of comparative theology to provide "mutual illumination," in his case among Christianity, Judaism, and Islam. At the start of this new millennium when people of different faiths at last are sharing the perspectives of their traditions, this approach will exemplify the insights to be gained from such comparisons for illuminating knotty problems within Christian life and thought—here, in particular, issues in accounts of revelation which have been controverted especially since the Reformation.

Burrell describes a triadic structure characteristic of the Abrahamic religions: each seeks to hold in a well-balanced tension of inner relationships an account of Revealer, Word, and Revealing Community. All the traditions understand the initiative of revelation, like creation, to be God's alone, by grace, so that the particularity of that revelation cannot be accounted for. Yet each tradition also insists on reception by free human agency. The revealing word, then, "will in one way stand over against the community which it shapes, yet that very community will also need to establish that word's coherence with respect to the intellectual world it inhabits, as well as employ the resources of the revealed word to illuminate the world in which it lives."

In the case of Christianity, the understanding of revelation is "internally tied" to God's choice of Israel. What is distinctive is the understanding of Jesus as healing presence of God's own revelation: the "word" of God is itself a *person*, and the revelation is of God's own self. For the believing community, then, to be Christian is to be transformed into "a comparable relation of filiation with God," to become "in the Son" God's children. Under the impulse of this confession, the common triadic structure becomes in Christianity a trinitarian divinity, "a divinity ready to receive into its rich inner life all those who believe in Jesus." It is in particular the role of the Spirit to effect the "divinization," the transformation of believers; "Jesus, as the Spirit of Christ," prays in the Christian prayer, allowing the Christian to "live by God's own life."

In Islam, the Qur'an stands in place analogous to that of Jesus: while Jesus for Christians is the Word of God made flesh, for Muslims the Word of God is made Arabic in the Qur'an. God's gracious transformation of the human creation, then, is also effected through the mode of revelation proper to that tradition. In each case, God's act of revelation is internally related to the community called forth by it: for Christians this is Augustine's "whole Christ," head and members; for Muslims it is the *umma*, the community of the faithful. In each case, the community is an organic unity "prior to the individuality of those who make it up"— an awareness which many modern Christians, especially in the West, have largely lost. For them, reflection on the parallel role of community in Islam may be a means of refreshing an attenuated dimension of their own life and teaching.

Islamic community is formed by the Qur'an in its ritual repetition, in which the word of God "becomes operative" in the lives of believers:

"If that operative Word is the same Word by which the universe is called into being, then allowing it to shape our perception and our action aligns us with the God-given order of the universe, thereby directing us how to return everything to the One from whom we have received everything." Attending to this analogous role in the transformation of community reinforces the insight that the Qur'an is not to be related to the Bible, and Muhammad to Jesus, but instead Word made Arabic to Word made human.

The fruitfulness of this comparative inquiry returns Burrell to Rahner's concern for understanding Christianity among other religions. His periodization of Christian history paired 70, when Christians faced the decision not to circumcise pagan men desiring baptism, and 1970, when Christians face the need to learn to see their faith in the post-colonial context of religious diversity. Rahner judged *Nostra Aetate* as "the most significant document after Vatican II" because, unlike the others which had been long prepared for in theological discussion, it was an "ecclesial step" of the Council itself and thus especially has its theological depths yet to be plumbed. The document itself "properly finessed the delicate questions of truth," and Burrell in turn opens them only glancingly in his conclusion. He links the "gospel's criterion" of "by their fruits you shall know them" with John Paul II's recent repentance for Christian's recurrent failures over two millennia to live up to Christ's call in ways that would have "clearly and decisively" established the truth of Christianity. From this link he turns to the holy men and women of other religious communities, clearly transformed by their faith. Citing Aquinas's caution that in divine things our language signifies its subject imperfectly *at best*, Burrell invites us to conclude from that limitation an openness to learn more about ourselves from other traditions. While the "traces of the divine" are to be explored in the teaching of their theologians, the lives of their saints show those traces even more saliently. We can see in Burrell's essay a use of the christological confessions fully in keeping with the imperative to openness which, as previous essays have shown, characterizes their very normativity. As also noted by O'Collins and others, these confessions call us to fuller understanding by committing us to live transformed by the same openness to which they give voice in their very invitation to confess Jesus as Lord.

Rabbi Michael Signer's essay offers a Jewish response to the essays presented, which, we have seen, position christological discourse as both a self-sufficient normative discourse and at the same time a sublation of itself in its openness to the mystery it can fully describe only *as* a mystery. Signer's essay is the justification of his hope that the "presence of Jews and Christians in the world of the twenty-first century will be very different from the previous two millennia." First, he notes, partnership between ecclesial bodies and scholarship has created a number of new, interacting means of transforming old relationships. From the Church have come statements like *Nostra Aetate* and efforts like those of John Paul II toward reconciliation. Scholars have achieved the sort of intense contact between Jews and Christians that earlier generations (Abraham Geiger in the nineteenth century, for example) could only dream of. Indeed, John Meier has identified this cooperation as one of the distinguishing marks of the "third quest" for the historical Jesus. In the other direction, scholars are also seeing the need to have their work shape their communities of faith so that religious life is transformed at the level of the local and the daily. These gains have already allowed Christians and Jews to "come to understand each other in their own integrity—within the wholeness of their as-sembled communities and traditions." With negative images being addressed, the way is open for deeper gains in understanding.

Signer seeks to reverse the perspective that both Jews and Christians have had about the Jewish negation of Jesus. While still a "stumbling block," Christ "does not cause the downfall of either community" but is rather perhaps something like a boundary stone, a marker in identity. Thus, when Jews encounter Jesus' question, "Who do you say that I am?" Signer distinguishes two horizons of discussion possible in reply. In the "ontological horizon," the "deep private experience of a faith community," an outsider cannot enter the experience of transformation Christians speak of as accomplished in Christ. Yet, while remaining only as listeners, Jews are able, in a new atmosphere without fear of persecution or proselytism, to listen and learn in new ways.

The second horizon, the "temporal/eschatological" horizon of chris-tological discussion, allows for mutually helpful speech. Jews and Chris-tians share the "prophetic visions of divine judgment and mercy 'in the end of days' and the apocalyptic literature that promises justification for current suffering in the eschaton." Because Christians alone believe that Jesus Christ entered human history as the incarnation of God, the two horizons are fused for them, as they are not for Jews. Instead, on the temporal/eschatological horizon Jews assert that there "was"—not "is"—a man Jesus, fully human, but he was not "the Christ." In this understanding of the human Jesus, a member of the Jewish people, Jewish writers have been consistent from antiquity. This perspective not only negates Christian claims but affirms the continuing validity of God's revelation and commandments to the Jews. Thus, the rhetoric of these negations has sometimes been "angry, assertive, and almost scandalous." Signer proposes that these documents be seen as internal texts of identity, the arguments by which a vulnerable community defended itself—strategies analogous to those of Christian identity in, for example, Chrysostom's sermons. Signer illustrates this point with an extended description of two early medieval documents, influential at the level of popular literature for centuries. The *Toledot Yeshu* (a satiric parody of the life of Jesus) and the *Sefer Nestor HaKomer* (important in particular to later writers like Moses Mendelssohn).

These negations of Jesus as Christ, however, apply only to the Jewish community: "from antiquity through modernity Jewish theologians have been prepared to assert the independent validity of Christianity for Christians." On this subject, Signer's hopes for further dialogue, appealing to Franz Rosenzweig's assertions that Jews come to God as Jews and Christians as Christians. In the world we share, Jews have an interest, as observers and interlocutors, in what Christians are saying about Christ: Signer commends a number of current trends which on christological ground appreciate the Jewish loss in the Shoah, value mutual relations rather than hierarchical ones as imaging God, and see the face of Christ in the poor. He concludes: "It is precisely with Christians, through whom Christ acts, that Jews can enter into profound discoveries about the way that God acts in our lives and how our traditions make demands upon us to help in the establishment of divine sovereignty in the world. As Jews we have an interest in what you believe and how it transforms you."

If the authentic tradition of christological reflection is, even (and especially!) in its most specifically normative moments, at the very same time the declaration of a mystery which transcends exhaustive definition in words, it is perhaps appropriate that the final two essays in the collection draw on themes from the tradition of christological mysticism and spirituality. Elizabeth Dreyer, inspired by the long legacy of mystical attention to the images of Christ as lover and bridegroom, invites the imaginations of her hearers to enter into an intimacy and passionate intensity of relation with God. Finding the elusive character of sexuality, its "noninstrumental immediacy," to be both a challenge to approaching the subject and an indication of its potential richness, she seeks deliberately to avoid the deprecation of the physical and erotic which have often marked the treatments of nuptial language in the tradition.

Indeed, she identifies a number of arguments against the language of Jesus as lover: it has little place in the Bible (despite the importance of God as love in those writings). It strikes some readers as too individual and privatized, too hierarchical in its portrayal of the role of wife, too sentimental in a pragmatic world, or too subject to confusion with cheapened cultural language of the erotic. Yet, while conceding dangers in the tradition of nuptial images, Dreyer finds the tradition also capable of internal correction of many of those dangers, especially when it is brought into conversation with other perspectives. At the same time, to see Christ as Lover gives the Christian resources against other sorts of imbalance—against an over-intellectualized piety, for example, or a relation to God based too preponderantly on images of distance and power. Jesus as Lover and Bridegroom, she suggests, tells us something about God as one who is willing "to become vulnerable, to enter into the joyful transformation that intimate love makes possible, to experience the newness that comes with seeing oneself accepted and embraced." Even the cross of Christ receives deepened meaning when seen in the context of the loving relation which prompts the lover to give everything, to sacrifice even the self, for the beloved.

Dreyer argues, then, that the task of "mining the rich vein of the incarnation event" in ways responsive to contemporary issues and crises will in our time direct attention to aspects of the tradition which work toward giving "integrity to the material and the historical." Thus, the fact that the medieval mystical tradition was "overwhelmingly monastic and celibate" and so imaged Jesus from that specific context does not exhaust the potential suggestiveness of the nuptial image but rather invites contemporary Christians to explore the conviction "that all that is truly human exists as a sacrament of God's creative loving presence to the world." To take seriously that affirmation, she concludes, construes the Christian vocation as a "call to open oneself to God's embrace in Jesus and to be the continuing epiphany of God in all the concrete, ordinary events of our lives," rejoicing that "*all* forms of love are potential places for us to become the Word we speak and profess."

In the last essay of the collection, Lawrence Cunningham explores the question, "Who is Jesus Christ for us today?" through another, "How is the presence of the Christ instantiated in the contemporary world, especially in those parts of the world where Christ is either not known or understood as a kind of cultural artifact belonging to an age long gone?" He begins with Karl Rahner's statement that the Christian of the future would either be a mystic "who has experienced something," or would "cease to be anything at all"—since only significant religious experience would sustain the life of faith in the midst of a culture whose best values were indifferent or hostile to it. Cunningham himself begins with a confession of Jesus as "the Christ, the Ikon of God, and Savior." This profession is a commitment to the discovering and rediscovering of the "reality behind the christological titles as well as the person who bears them." He speaks especially of the *Christos Mystikos*, in the early Church's sense of "that which is hidden or beneath that which is experienced and grasped." In this "decidedly, empirically, and determinedly non-Christian world," then, Cunningham identifies three ways in which Christ remains both hidden and revealed: First, community worship—telling the story of Christ and enacting that story—is the "most dramatic thing" that Christians do to make present and reveal Christ. Second, gestures of care for the world's needy. Self-forgetting service to others, Cunningham says, is a way of knowing Christ. When Christians perform the scriptures—the word of Jesus in Matthew 25:31ff, for example—they are performing a kind of evangelism. Third, and most subtly, the hidden Christ is made manifest in ways suggested by Paul's speech on the Areopagus (Acts 17), a favorite scriptural passage of the present pope. When Paul affirmed that "God is not far from each of us," he inspired mission based on a positive approach to other forms of religiosity. To seek a hearing in a contemporary Areopagus, Cunningham suggests that first of all the Christian community should be on the side of every moral question which reflects the faithful view that human life is made in God's image and likeness, "thickened and deepened" by the mystery of the Incarnation. Such advocacy will build solidarity with others who are not Christian, and such solidarity is in itself an "incarnational strategy." There is also dialogue, not only formally in interreligious forums, but in the daily lives of people—living together in mutual assistance, working together for justice and peace, and nourished by the deep experiences which sustain the inner life. Whether these people need to become Christian raises serious questions, but it is at least certain that Christians will be wary of the idolatry of forcing our own distorted images of Christ onto the other person, in whom, we believe, Christ is already present and to be found.

The essays in this volume are bound together by the conviction that the faith of the Church has the normativity of a mystery, the very expression of which entails an openness to development and understanding. Development and understanding generate not relativity but a fuller statement and understanding of the original mystery, stated ever so definitively as before. Have we truly left behind docetism until we understand the relation of Jesus' humanity to the reality of the poor? Have we understood the intention of the councils in declaring the Incarnation if we do not understand that it is "one of the Trinity" who has suffered, in a human nature, in solidarity with the poor and the oppressed? Have we adequately comprehended the reticence of the conciliar confessions if we do not see in them an invitation to dialogue with those who do not share these confessions? We go beyond the bounds of Christian confession if we fail to confess that Jesus is the Word Incarnate, but have we understood what we are saying if we refuse the memories and narratives of history as a challenge to understand the radical solidarity with human beings that the Incarnation proclaims? On the other hand, it is, paradoxically, the frank confession of the faith of the Church, not its renunciation or dilution, which orients us to the openness inherent in the mystery we confess. There is no answer to the question "Who do you say that I am?" which can either evade the confession, in all the precision garnered by the ages, that "You are the Christ," or which can evade the risks and indeed the suffering in which, as Peter discovered, such confession immediately and necessarily implicates us.

CHAPTER ONE

Who Do You Say That I Am—Not?

The Power of Negative Thinking in the Decrees of the Ecumenical Councils

JAROSLAV PELIKAN

"Who do you say that I am?" A positive question like that would, on the face of it, seem to call for an affirmative answer. But it probably behooves me, as a historian of the development of doctrine and as the editor of the four volumes of *Creeds and Confessions of Faith in the Christian Tradition* (2003), to examine instead "the power of *negative* thinking" in the history of the Church's teaching about the person of Jesus Christ. A review of the creeds and conciliar confessions of the first several centuries discloses their persistent reliance on a combination of affirmative and negative formulas to answer this positive question, as well as their reliance on a combination of biblical and nonbiblical formulas to answer this biblical question.[1] As the Second Council of Constantinople would say in 553, "the notion of 'union' can be understood in many different ways [πολυτρόπως]":[2] it was the task of negation to help sort out those many ways.

1. Nicaea I (325)

γεννηθέντα οὐ ποιηθέντα, ὁμοούσιον τῷ πατρί

"begotten *not* made, consubstantial with the Father"[3]

The formula for which the First Council of Nicaea is justly famous (or infamous) is, of course, the ὁμοούσιον τῷ πατρί; but grammatically—

17

and, above all, confessionally—that formula stands in apposition to the formula γεννηθέντα οὐ ποιηθέντα. Although the ὁμοούσιον was, notoriously, a term of nonbiblical, even of heretical, provenance,[4] both of the terms being joined and yet kept apart by negation in γεννηθέντα οὐ ποιηθέντα were eminently biblical:[5] ποιέω was the first verb to appear in the Septuagint Bible (which in its canon, text, and translations was, of course, *the* "Old Testament" of the early Church), "In the beginning God ἐποίησεν heaven and earth";[6] and γεννάω was the first verb to appear in the New Testament, "Abraham ἐγέννησεν Isaac."[7] They could, moreover, be employed more or less synonymously, as they seem to be, for example, in the statement of the Epistle to the Hebrews that Jesus "was trustworthy τῷ ποιήσαντι αὐτόν [NJB, to the one who appointed him]."[8] Indeed, as applied to the relation between the Father and the Son, γεννάω also had to be seen as possibly synonymous with a third verb, whose use for that relation was, if anything, even more problematical than either of these, the verb κτίζω, the technical term for "create," eventually even for "create *ex nihilo*."[9] For in the eighth chapter of the Book of Proverbs—which in the fourth-century debates both before and after Nicaea over the answer to our question, "Who do you say that I am?" was, arguably, more important than was any passage even of the New Testament except the prologue to the Gospel of John[10]—personified Wisdom said that κύριος ἔκτισέν με ἀρχὴν ὁδῶν αὐτοῦ εἰς ἔργα αὐτοῦ . . . πρὸ δὲ πάντων βουνῶν γεννᾷ με.[11] These words, apparently equating the "begetting" of Wisdom with the "creating," became, as Athanasius was obliged to admit, a formidable mainstay of the Arian teaching that the Father had created/begotten the Son as the prime creature, through whom all the (other) creatures had been made—even though Athanasius insisted that, to the contrary, the passage "has a very religious and orthodox sense,"[12] and that γεννάω and κτίζω did not mean the same at all, even when applied to God's relation to human beings.[13]

With the negative formula γεννηθέντα οὐ ποιηθέντα the Council of Nicaea was answering the special form that the question of our theme took this first time that it was asked and answered by a conciliar confession: in Harnack's trenchant paraphrase, "Is the Divine that has appeared on earth and reunited men with God identical with the Supreme Divine, which governs the heaven and earth, or is it a demigod?"[14] Only by denying that the two terms, γεννηθέντα and ποιηθέντα, were synonyms here, regardless of what they may have been anywhere else even in Scripture, could the Council go on to make its own the trinitarian and christological confession, ὁμοούσιον τῷ πατρί. Its ultimate concern was not metaphysical or philosophical, but soteriological: salvation was not the work of any being lower than "the Supreme Divine." This soteriological (and negative) confession was articulated in the declaration, which was peculiar to the Septuagint text of Isaiah rather than to the Hebrew text and was quoted as a proof-text by one church father after another, both before and after Nicaea, eventually becoming the first Troparion of the "Royal Hours" for Holy Friday: "It was no messenger or angel, but [the Lord himself] saved them [οὐ πρέσβυς οὐδὲ ἄγγελος, ἀλλ' αὐτὸς κύριος ἔσωσεν αὐτούς]."[15] Thereby the First Council of Nicaea also prescribed the christological terms within which all subsequent creeds and conciliar confessions would have to operate: a divine nature that was γεννηθέντα, which was united (somehow) to a human nature that was ποιηθέντα. Unpacking the several negative and affirmative implications of that set of relations was to be, after the γεννηθέντα οὐ ποιηθέντα of the Council of Nicaea, the continuing assignment.

2. Constantinople I (381)
οὗ τῆς βασιλείας οὐκ ἔσται τέλος
"his kingdom will have *no* end"[16]

In the checkered history of the reciprocal process of Tradition by which exegesis has controlled dogma but at the same time has been controlled by dogma, the use of this quotation from the gospel narrative of the Annunciation of the archangel Gabriel to the Virgin Mary,[17] which concludes the christological articles of the decree of the First Council of Constantinople and therefore of the Niceno-Constantinopolitan Creed (usually known throughout history as "the Nicene Creed"), must occupy a special place. For by it a divine oracle that should, despite its being inside the covers of the *New* Testament, be classified as chronologically one of the last messianic prophecies to have been uttered before the birth of the Messiah was employed to make more precise, even in a sense to correct, the obvious implications of a saying of the apostle Paul, which had been much beloved of Origen: "After that will come the end, when [Christ] will hand over the kingdom to God the Father. . . . For [the Son] is to be king until [the Father] has made [the Son's] enemies [the Son's] footstool. . . . But when it is said everything is subjected, this obviously cannot include the One who subjected everything to [the Son]. When everything has been subjected to [the Son], then the Son himself will be subjected to the One who has subjected everything to him, so that God may be all in all."[18]

Historically, the insertion of this clause from the angel of the Annunciation into the Creed is bound up with the complex and controversial teaching of one of the most stalwart champions of the Council of Nicaea, Marcellus of Ancyra.[19] As summarized by Johannes Quasten, "In his attempt to prove the Arian heresy no more than a poorly veiled polytheism, he himself teaches a monotheism which knows only an economical trinity. . . . It is this tendency which leads him to the heretical doctrine that before the creation of the world the Logos was only in God and that at the end he will be only in God."[20] Because of its obvious affinities with the Sabellianism ("modalistic monarchianism") that is perhaps best known to us from Tertullian's attack on Praxeas (who had "put to flight the Paraclete and crucified the Father"),[21] this teaching of Marcellus created difficulties for the defenders of Nicaea—significantly, more so in the East than in the West, perhaps because of the differing theories of the Trinity that were already at work in the fourth century and that would break into the open in the controversy over the *Filioque*. The Creed of Nicaea had anathematized "those who say 'there once was when he was not [ἦν ποτε ὅτε οὐκ ἦν]'"; now, to be able to assert at one and the same time that there had been no beginning of the Logos-Son but that he had always been distinct from the Father, also before Creation and Incarnation, it seemed necessary to assert that there would likewise be no end of his kingdom and rule, which was, properly understood, precisely what, according to Luke, the angel had promised to the Virgin at the Annunciation.

3.   Ephesus (431)

οὐχ ὡς συνάφειαν . . . οὔτε μὴν κατὰ παράθεσιν . . .
οὔτε μὴν ὡς κατὰ μέθεξιν

"*not* with the sort of composition that a man might have with God . . .
nor one of juxtaposition . . . *nor* relative participation"[22]

The Third Ecumenical Council, the Council of Ephesus in 431, marks the transition from answering the question "Who do you say that I am?"

by means of the dogma of the Trinity (which is what the first two councils did) to answering it by means of the dogma of the person of Christ (which is what the next four—or five—councils did). But, as Père Congar comments, a bit wryly, "the history of the third Council was hardly such as to allow it to be considered as properly ecumenical"; and a comparison between Ephesus 431 and Ephesus 449 (the "Robber Synod") is still a productive exercise in the determination of what is meant by reception, defined by Congar as "the process by means of which a church [body] truly takes over as its own a resolution that it did not originate as to its self, and acknowledges the measure it promulgates as a rule applicable to its own life. . . . It includes a degree of consent, and possibly of judgment, in which the life of a body is expressed which brings into play its own, original spiritual resources."[23]

If theological language is ineluctably analogical,[24] it has been the dual responsibility of the Church's creeds and confessions of faith, especially in dealing with Christology, to seek analogies—and then to distrust them. Thus the *Quicunque* or Athanasian Creed draws upon the familiar but ultimately mysterious relation between the soul and the body as an analogy for the relation between the two natures in Christ: "Just as rational soul and flesh are a single man, so God and man are a single Christ."[25] But by the time that Western Latin creed was formulated (whenever that may have been), the Church had learned to its dismay in the Apollinarist controversy just how misleading the analogy in the christological equation "Jesus Christ = λόγος + σάρξ" could be.[26] The three technical terms in this Ephesian formula are:

συνάφεια [composition], a term that had been employed for the relation between the divine and the human in Christ "in early writers without hint of heterodoxy," but was applied to that relation by Theodore of Mopsuestia and Nestorius in a meaning that led to error, even though later orthodox theologians such as Pope Leo I still made occasional use of it;[27]

παράθεσις [juxtaposition], the most general of the three terms, which was applied even to such areas as accounting, literary composition, and rhetoric, and was therefore unable to convey with precision how divine and human were united through the Incarnation;[28]

μέθεξις [participation], a favorite term of Cyril's for the participation of the believer in Christ and in the Holy Spirit through

grace, with which, according to Cyril, Nestorius equated the participation of Christ the man in the Logos through grace.[29]

All three of these analogies, initially more or less harmless, were ruled
out at Ephesus, because, even by putting them together in such a way
that each would modify the others (the technique that was to be applied
in the alpha-privatives of the Creed of Chalcedon), they appeared incapable of specifying the distinction between "*the* Son of God" and "sons of
God," a qualitative rather than a merely quantitative difference between
the Incarnation of the Logos and what later came to be called the *unio
mystica*.

4.   Chalcedon (451)
ἀσυγχύτως, ἀτρέπτως, ἀδιαιρέτως, ἀχωρίστως
"*no* confusion, *no* change, *no* division, *no* separation"[30]

Both grammatically and theologically, these four alpha-privatives and their
corollary negations bear the major burden of the Creed of Chalcedon.[31]
The four negations by means of alpha-privatives are arranged in two pairs,
each of which is backed up by a further negation in addition: to reinforce
"no confusion [ἀσυγχύτως]" and "no change [ἀτρέπτως]," the Creed
of Chalcedon goes on to say that "at no point [οὐδαμοῦ] was the difference between the natures taken away through the union"; and to underline "no division [ἀδιαιρέτως]" and "no separation [ἀχωρίστως]," it
specifies that Christ "is not [οὐκ] parted or divided into two persons."
But the line that these Chalcedonian negations drew was more of a
circle than it was a straight line in the sand.[32] There were still those on
the inside and those on the outside, as the separation between the "Chalcedonian" and the "non-Chalcedonian" (or the "Eastern Orthodox" and the
"Oriental Orthodox") churches until the present day graphically and
tragically shows.[33] But when the council had spoken, it had, by the first
two alpha-privatives, left room within the Chalcedonian circle for the
traditionally "Antiochean" emphasis in looking at the person of Christ,
as the impeccable orthodoxy of John Chrysostom documents; it shared
with this emphasis a primary commitment to keep the integrity of the
human nature of Christ from being impaired or overwhelmed or annihi-

lated by the Incarnation, which (in seeking to make Christ more than human) would have made him less than completely human, and thus to safeguard the bond, the ὁμοουσία between our common humanity and the human nature of Christ. At the same time the second pair of alpha-privatives left room for the more "Alexandrian" emphasis of those who were bent on protecting, against the endemic tendency to exaggerate distinction into separation, the oneness of the incarnate Logos.

With its alpha-privatives the Creed of Chalcedon did both of these on the condition that all parties acknowledge the authority of the circle and be willing to pursue their distinctive concerns inside that Chalcedonian circle. Without putting an undue amount of the weight of the historical-theological argument on the quantification of vocables, it is instructive to note a difference between Classical and Patristic Greek: "Of the 1,568 pages in the Lampe *Lexicon of Patristic Greek*, 281 pages, or 18 percent, are given over to the letter alpha, while in the Liddell-Scott-Jones *Greek-English Lexicon*, the ratio, though still remarkably high considering the number of letters in the Greek alphabet, is significantly lower, 300 of 2,042, or 15 percent."[34] Although this method of affirmation-through-negation, while never absent, seems to have become less prominent in the Reformation confessions of faith than it had been in patristic texts, especially among the Greek fathers, this Chalcedonian set of negative formulas did become important there. Several Reformed confessions—including the *Fidei ratio* of Ulrich Zwingli of 1530, *The Westminster Confession of Faith* of 1647, and *The Waldensian Confession of Faith* of 1655—quoted verbatim, and in Greek, the four alpha-privatives of the Creed of Chalcedon;[35] and the Lutheran *Formula of Concord* quoted not only the four adverbs but the entire Creed of Chalcedon in its "Catalog of Testimonies."[36]

5.   Constantinople II (553)

οὔτε γὰρ προσθήκην προσώπου, ἤγουν ὑποστάσεως,
ἐπεδέξατο ἡ ἁγία τρίας

"no addition of person or subsistence to the Holy Trinity"[37]

The occasion for the Fifth Ecumenical Council was the controversy over the condemnation of the "Three Chapters" (Theodore of Mopsuestia, Theodoret of Cyrrhus, and Ibas of Edessa), which was heavily involved in politics, both imperial and ecclesiastical. This council is also usually re-membered for the condemnation of the teachings of Origen in the eleventh of its anathemas, but the textual and juridical status of that condemnation is ambiguous.[38] In the course of articulating its anathema against Theodore and of repeating the anathemas of Ephesus and Chalcedon against Nes-torius, the Second Council of Constantinople also addressed the impli-cations of these heresies for the doctrine of the Trinity; for it charged Nestorius and Theodore with "trying to introduce into the mystery of Christ two subsistences or two persons [δύο ὑποστάσεις, ἤτοι δύο πρόσωπα]." Because ὑπόστασις and πρόσωπον (whether used as syno-nyms or not) were the usual terms for the Three, with οὐσία as the technical term for the One, the Council went on from these anathemas to the assertion-by-negation, "There has been no addition of person or sub-sistence to the Holy Trinity even after one of its members, God the Word, became flesh." There seems to be no reason to suppose that anyone had in fact posited such a Quarternity or "addition to the Holy Trinity," and this may well be yet another instance of polemical *Konsequenzmacherei*; nevertheless, this assertion-by-negation did deal with an important and vexing question.

Chronologically but also logically and theologically, the dogma of the Trinity had preceded the dogma of the person of Christ. The ques-tion that forms our theme was answered first, therefore, by addressing both the relationship of the Son of God to God the Father (Nicaea I) and the relationship of the One to the Three (Constantinople I). Then at the third through the sixth council, the issue of divine and human *within* the person of Christ took over the agenda: nature [φύσις], will [θέλημα], activity [ἐνέργεια], etc. But 250 years after the First Council of Nicaea the relation between the two dogmas arises once more as an issue—as indeed it had been all along. One of the neglected problems had been the ease with which terms and formulas originally suited to the doctrine of the Trinity were being applied to the doctrine of the person of Christ. In some cases the transfer was successful, as with the development at Chalcedon by which the Trinitarian ὁμοούσιον was applied, evidently for the first time by a council, also to the relation between Christ's human nature and ours, rather than only, as at Nicaea I, to the relation between Christ's divine nature and the divinity of the Father. But when the ter-minological imprecision at Nicaea I, employing ὑπόστασις and οὐσία more or less as synonyms—"ἐξ ἑτέρας ὑποστάσεως ἢ οὐσίας"[39]—

was, thanks in significant measure to the Three Cappadocians, replaced by the more exact trinitarian distinction between the two, it became necessary also to construct a dogmatic firewall to protect ὑπόστασις as applied to the Second in the Trinity from ὑπόστασις (or πρόσωπον) as applied to the Human in Christology.

6. Constantinople III (680/681)
τὸ ἀνθρώπινον αὐτοῦ θέλημα θεωθὲν οὐκ ἀνηρέθη
"his human will was *not* destroyed by being made divine"[40]

As the Christology of Theodore of Pharan (also known as Theodore of Raïthu) documents,[41] the repeated condemnations of "Monophysitism" in the centuries after Chalcedon did not succeed in reversing the inherent tendency of Greek Christian spirituality to press both the unity of the person of Christ and the definition of salvation as θέωσις just as far—or, to put it more accurately, at least as far—as the limits of orthodoxy would allow. For both in Christ and in the believer, human nature was seen as having been radically transformed. It had been raised by the Incarnation to a divinized status, the status with which in turn it endowed the humanity of those who shared in his salvation, so as to make it possible for them, in the words of the towering New Testament text, to become "sharers in the divine nature [θείας κοινωνοὶ φύσεως],"[42] while nevertheless remaining fully human. Of the various dualities that the Chalcedonians of the sixth and seventh centuries defended against those whom they regarded as Mono-physites, Mono-theletes, and Mon-energists, the duality of wills (θελήματα) was in some ways the most difficult. The Pseudo-Dionysius had spoken of καινήν τινα τὴν θεανδρικὴν ἐνέργειαν, thereby fueling the Monenergist controversy.[43] But it was in a key passage of the gospels themselves that the divine-human Christ had prayed, with a special combination of affirmation and negation: "Let your will be done, not mine [μὴ τὸ θέλημά μου ἀλλὰ τὸ σὸν γινέσθω],"[44] the singular τὸ θέλημά μου apparently making "will" a function of the one person rather than of the two natures.

It would appear to have been the logic of such a conclusion that led the hapless Pope Honorius I to his fateful declaration of a single will, and thus this Council to its condemnation of him, with its far-reaching consequences for the debates of the nineteenth century on papal infallibility.[45]

But what the Sixth Ecumenical Council saw to be at stake here and what it strove to preserve by its negation was not merely the symmetry or consistency of "two wills" and "two activities" as a corollary of "two natures," but the integrity of the human will, whether of Christ in his Incarnation or of men and women in their deification. The negative axiom of Gregory of Nazianzus, "τὸ γὰρ ἀπρόσληπτον, ἀθεράπευτον, Whatever was not assumed [in the Incarnation] was not healed [in the deification],"[46] required both that "his human will was not destroyed by being made divine," as the council stated explicitly, and, as it was stating implicitly, that *our* "human will was not destroyed by being made divine." And once again, the narrative of the Annunciation, upon which the First Council of Constantinople had drawn for its affirmation-through-negation about the kingdom of Christ, was also the affirmative-negative paradigm here, because the free human will of the Theotokos was not destroyed, but saved and fulfilled, in the *Fiat mihi*[47] of her unconstrained response.

7. Nicaea II (787)

Εἴ τις Χριστὸν τὸν θεὸν ἡμῶν περιγραπτὸν
οὐχ ὁμολογεῖ κατὰ τὸ ἀνθρώπινον
"if anyone does *not* confess that Christ our God
can be represented in his humanity"[48]

In the controversies over images, the most overt negation was, of course, on the side of the icono*clasts;* it was a negation expressed not only in words but in deeds, by which all but a handful of the existing images (many of these being at St. Catherine's in the Sinai) were annihilated. The decrees of the Seventh Ecumenical Council in 787 affirming the legitimacy of the icons, and the reaffirmation of these decrees with the establishment of the Feast of Orthodoxy in 843, were in that sense positive rather than negative. But the negation expressed in the words quoted from the "Anathemas Concerning Holy Images" of 787, "If anyone does not confess that Christ our God can be represented in his humanity, let him be anathema," had to resort to negation because the *Horos* of the iconoclastic synod of 754 and the theological case against images, had, in effect, located the controversy in the apostolic succession of the preceding councils by raising the christological objection. Ironically, therefore, this argument from Christology, which was to become in many ways the most powerful weapon in the theological arsenal of the Orthodox defenders of images, seems to have been introduced by their iconoclast opponents.[49] Beginning with the famous disjunctive question of Eusebius to Constantia, sister of Emperor Constantine the Great, "Which icon of Christ do you mean? That which is true and unchangeable and which bears the characteristics of his [divine] nature, or that which he assumed for us, the figure, that is, that he took 'in the form of a slave' [Phil 2:7]?" they argued that (in Georges Florovsky's summary), "Christians do not need any artificial image of Christ, . . . [for] Christ's 'historical' image, the 'form' of his humiliation, has already been superseded by his Divine splendor, in which he now abides."[50]

In response, the iconodules formulated the "aesthetic implications of the Incarnation," which included the quoted anathema.[51] Grammatically it would make sense if, by inversion, this formula were recast to attach the negation to the passive participle rather than to the verb: οὐκ περιγραπτὸν ὁμολογεῖ, "If anyone confesses that Christ our God cannot be represented in his humanity," rather than περιγραπτὸν οὐχ ὁμολογεῖ as the decree stands. For the real issue was whether or not the human in Christ could be *circum*-scribed and therefore visually *de*-scribed and portrayed in an icon. The iconoclasts replied that it could not; but the defenders of the icons replied that it was impossible to separate the divine and the human natures, which were as Chalcedon said united with "no division [ἀδιαιρέτως]," and therefore that "if anyone does not confess that Christ our God can be represented in his humanity," that was tantamount to the division forbidden by the Creed of Chalcedon in 451. So it was that even this conflict over what Karl Schwarzlose called "the identity and the freedom" of the Eastern Orthodox Church[52] came down to yet another variation on the same theme: "Who do you say that I am—not?"

Five Theses on the Power of Negative Thinking

This brief review of the seven councils obliges us, perhaps also entitles us, to identify and to itemize in thetical form at least five functions of the negation in their dogmatic decrees concerning the person of Jesus Christ.

1. The obvious function was to refute and to correct heresy by teaching "not this but that." "Refutation [λύσις]," according to Aristotle's *Rhetoric*, could take place, "either by stating an opposite syllogism or by

bringing an objection [ἔνστασις]”;[53] and both of these have always been prominent in the creeds and concilar confessions of faith. But because, in Newman's aphorism, "No doctrine is defined till it is violated,"[54] refutation by means of negation has often been indispensable to any definition by means of affirmation.

2. Closely related to this polemical function was the exegetical one: to rule out, from among the several grammatically possible meanings of a biblical word or passage, those in which grammar had to be corrected by confession. Augustine in *De Trinitate* formulated a "canonical rule" (or set of rules) for interpreting scripture christologically. "We hold most firmly, concerning our Lord Jesus Christ, what may be called the canonical rule [*canonica regula*], . . . that the Son of God is both understood to be equal to the Father according to the form of God in which He is, and less than the Father according to the form of a slave which He took," although there were, he was obliged to add, "some things in the sacred text so put as to leave ambiguous to which [part of that] rule they are to be referred."[55]

3. Because of the dual meaning of ὀρθοδοξία as "holding to correct doctrine" (δόξα meaning "opinion") and as "rendering correct worship" (δόξα meaning "glory," hence the Slavic *Pravoslavie*), and the corresponding formula of "lex orandi lex credendi," negation had the task of identifying, in the language of private devotion and even in the public language of liturgy, what the believer or the Church could say, especially about Christ or his Mother, in poetry while kneeling but could not say in so many words in prose while teaching and confessing; for the language of love speaks in hyperbole. Perhaps the most celebrated instance of this was the exclamation of the *Exultet* for Holy Saturday; "O certe necessarium Adae peccatum, quod Christi morte deletum est! O felix culpa, quae talem ac tantum meruit habere redemptorem!"[56]

4. Conversely, it was primarily by their use of negative language that the councils connected what Athanasius called the διπλοῦν κήρυγμα [double proclamation][57] of Christology simultaneously to its two constituent doctrines, the doctrine of God as Trinity and the doctrine of man, and yet kept them distinct. In this sense negation served as an instrument for the dialectic that had long been the modality of the Church's language in response to the question of our theme, already in the "creedal" portions of the New Testament itself.[58]

5. Another function of negative language, and probably the most profound one, was to provide a "lexicon of transcendence."[59] Various prefixes also helped to serve that function, for example, ὑπέρ in Greek and *super* in Latin, rendered variously in English as "above" or "beyond." But in response not only to heresies such as that of Eunomius, who is said to have claimed that he understood the divine nature as well as God does, but to the perennial temptation of the human mind, including the orthodox theological mind, to claim to know more than is possible, the pious skepticism of apophatic language was the most effective weapon. And it still is.

NOTES

1. Conciliar decrees and their translations are quoted from Norman P. Tanner, ed., *Decrees of the Ecumenical Councils,* 2 vols. (Washington, D.C., 1990), hereafter cited as "Tanner." English translations of biblical passages are usually from the New Jerusalem Bible (1985). I shall be relying throughout on C.J. Hefele, *Histoire des concils d'après les documents originaux,* trans. H. Leclercq, 11 vols. (Paris, 1907–1952), hereafter cited as "Hefele-Leclercq."

2. "Anathemas against the 'Three Chapters'," number 4, Tanner 1:115.

3. "The Profession of Faith of the 318 Fathers," Tanner 1:5; Hefele-Leclercq 1–I:335–632.

4. G.L. Prestige, *God in Patristic Thought* (London, 1952), 197–218.

5. On their patristic use, see Geoffrey W.H. Lampe, ed., *A Patristic Greek Lexicon* (Oxford, 1961), 311, 1108; hereafter abbreviated as "Lampe."

6. Gn 1:1.

7. Mt 1:2.

8. Heb 3:2.

9. Gerhard May, *Creatio ex nihilo: The Doctrine of "Creation out of Nothing" in Early Christian Thought,* trans. A.S. Worrall (Edinburgh, 1994); cf. Lampe 782.

10. See, for example, the lengthy explication of the text in Athansius, *Discourses Against the Arians,* II.18–68.

11. Prv 8:22, 25.

12. Athanasius, *De decretis* iii.13–14.

13. Athanasius, *Discourses Against the Arians* II.59.

14. Adolf Harnack, *[Grundrisz der] Dogmengeschichte,* 4th ed. (Tübingen, 1905), 192.

15. Is 63:9 (LXX), translating the Greek literally as "the Lord himself" instead of the rendering "his presence" in the NJB. On the patristic use of the

passage, see Jaroslav Pelikan, *The Christian Tradition: A History of the Development of Doctrine*, 5 vols. (Chicago, 1971–1989), 1:177, 182, 190, 206, 214, 227. For its liturgical use, *Holy Friday Matins*, ed. John Erickson and David Anderson (New York, 1988), 111.

16. "The Exposition of the 150 Fathers," Tanner 1:24; Hefele-Leclercq 2–I:1–48.

17. Lk 1:33.

18. 1 Cor 15:24–28.

19. Among the most recent studies are: K. Seibt, *Die Theologie des Markell von Ankyra* (Berlin, 1994); G. Feige, *Die Lehre Markells von Ankyra in der Darstellung seiner Gegner* (Leipzig, 1991).

20. Johannes Quasten, *Patrology*, 4 vols. (Westminster, Md., 1951–1986), 3:199.

21. Tertullian, *Adversus Praxean* 1.5 (trans. Ernest Evans).

22. "Third Letter of Cyril to Nestorius," Tanner 1:52; Hefele-Leclercq 2–I:287–377.

23. Yves Congar, "Reception as an Ecclesiological Reality," in *Election and Consensus in the Church*, ed. Guiseppe Alberigo and Anton Weiler (New York, 1972), 45–46.

24. David Burrell, *Analogy and Philosophical Language* (New Haven, Conn., 1973).

25. *Quicunque* 37: J. N. D. Kelly, *The Athanasian Creed* (New York, 1964), 20.

26. Aloys Grillmeier, *Christ in Christian Tradition from the Apostolic Age to Chalcedon (451)*, trans. J. S. Bowden (New York, 1965), 220–33.

27. Lampe 1308–10.

28. Lampe 1016.

29. Lampe 837–38.

30. "Definition of the Faith," Tanner 1:86; Hefele-Leclercq 2–II:649–857.

31. Ignacio Ortiz de Urbina, "Das Glaubenssymbol von Chalkedon—sein Text, sein Werden, seine dogmatische Bedeutung," in *Das Konzil von Chalkedon: Geschichte und Gegenwart*, ed. Aloys Grillmeier and Heinrich Bacht, 3 vols. (Würzburg, 1951), 1:389–418.

32. This and the following sentences are adapted from "Comprehensiveness or Catholicity?" the Twenty-first Paul Wattson Lecture, delivered at the University of San Francisco, 28 January, 2000.

33. Joseph Lebon, "La christologie du monophysisme syrien," in Grillmeier and Bacht, *Chalkedon*, 1:425–580.

34. Jaroslav Pelikan, *Christianity and Classical Culture: The Metamorphosis of Natural Theology in the Christian Encounter with Hellenism*, Gifford Lectures at Aberdeen for 1992–1993 (New Haven, Conn., 1993), 40.

35. *Westminster Confession of Faith* 8.2; *Fidei ratio* 1; *Waldensian Confession of Faith* 13.

36. *Formula of Concord: Catalogus Testimoniorum.*

37. "Anathemas Against the 'Three Chapters'," number 5, Tanner 1:116; Hefele-Leclercq 3–II:1–156.

38. F. Diekamp, *Die origenistischen Streitigkeiten im sechsten Jahrhundert und das fünfte allgemeine Konzil* (Münster, 1899), 77–98.

39. "The Profession of Faith of the 318 Fathers," Tanner 1:5.

40. "Exposition of Faith," Tanner 1:128; Hefele–Leclercq 3–I:472–538.

41. Werner Elert, *Der Ausgang der altkirchlichen Christologie: Eine Untersuchung über Theodor von Pharan und seine Zeit als Einführung in die alte Dogmengeschichte*, ed. Wilhelm Maurer and Elisabeth Bergsträßer (Berlin, 1957), 185–259.

42. 2 Pt 1:4.

43. Dionysius the Areopagite, *Epistles* 4.

44. Lk 22:42.

45. Pelikan, *The Christian Tradition*, 2:150–53, 5:250–52.

46. Gregory of Nazianzus, *Epistles* 101. For a brief critical examination of this axiom, see Maurice F. Wiles, "The Unassumed Is the Unhealed," *Religious Studies* 4 (1968): 47–56.

47. Lk 1:38 (Vulg.).

48. "Anathemas Concerning Holy Images," number 1, Tanner 1:137; Hefele-Leclercq 3–II:741–98.

49. Jaroslav Pelikan, *Imago Dei: The Byzantine Apologia for Icons*, Andrew W. Mellon Lectures in the Fine Arts at the National Gallery of Art for 1987 (Princeton, N.J., 1990), 72–77.

50. Georges V. Florovsky, *Collected Works* (Belmont, Mass., 1972–), 2:108–109.

51. Pelikan, *Imago Dei*, 67–98.

52. Karl Schwarzlose, *Der Bilderstreit: Ein Kampf der griechischen Kirche um ihre Eigenart und um ihre Freiheit* (Gotha, 1890).

53. Aristotle, *Rhetoric* II.xxv.1 (trans. George A. Kennedy).

54. John Henry Newman, *An Essay on the Development of Christian Doctrine*, 6th ed. (1878; Notre Dame, Ind., 1989), 151.

55. Augustine, *De Trinitate* II.i.2.

56. Cf. A.O. Lovejoy, "Milton and the Paradox of the Fortunate Fall," *Essays in the History of Ideas* (Baltimore, 1948), 284–87.

57. Athanasius, *Contra Apollinarium* I.

58. Phil 2:5–11; 1 Tm 3:16.

59. Pelikan, *Christianity and Classical Culture*, 200–214.

CHAPTER TWO

Their Thoughts Are Not
as Our Thoughts

MORNA HOOKER

When more than 500 bishops gathered together in the Church of St. Euphemia at Chalcedon in October A.D. 451, a copy of the scriptures was placed in the center of the council as a symbol of the fact that their deliberations began from scripture, and that they believed themselves to be expounding scripture. The definition they eventually produced was an interpretation of the Nicene Creed, which was, in turn, understood to be an exposition of scripture.

It is, then, a little disconcerting to a New Testament scholar to find the careful definition of Chalcedon couched in language which is utterly foreign, not simply to the ideas and language with which we are familiar today, but to those we identify as belonging to the writers of the New Testament: how very different is this description of Christ's person from what the New Testament writers have to say about him! We might perhaps have expected the Fathers of the Church, being closer in time to the New Testament, to have been closer in understanding. Yet the gap between the approaches of the first and the fifth centuries appears to be as great as that between those of the fifth and the twenty-first. Nothing could be a clearer demonstration of the way in which scripture is always interpreted in the language and thought-forms of the age—in this particular case an age whose ideas are as far removed from those of our own time as they are from those of our New Testament writers.

33

The problem in this particular instance, of course, lies in the fact that the interpretation of the Christian story which was laid down at Chalcedon became normative for later understanding of the scriptures. Because of its crucial role in the formation of Christian doctrine, this particular interpretation (albeit in less complex terms) became the yardstick for future understanding of the person of Christ. Whereas the interpretations which emerged in other periods can be laid aside and abandoned, as belonging to the *Zeitgeist* which helped to create them, the Chalcedonian definition became part of the given, with the result that generations of Christians have read the New Testament through Chalcedonian spectacles, unaware of the fact that they were imposing the interpretations and doctrines of a later age onto a first-century text.

My concern is not to question the validity of later definitions and interpretations, but simply to remind ourselves that they were formulated to deal with particular theological problems at particular times. To understand these definitions fully, it is necessary to discover the questions they were intended to answer. The danger, however, is that a particular interpretation is fossilized and becomes regarded as the interpretation of the text for all time. When that happens, then—to use Paul's imagery—scripture is inscribed in letters on tablets of stone, rather than being written by the Holy Spirit in our hearts.[1] As an example of how this can happen, we may note the way in which generations of Protestants read St. Paul's teaching about the Law through Lutheran spectacles. What had been, for Martin Luther, an apposite interpretation of the contrast between faith and works became for many the accepted understanding of Paul's own situation. Most presentday scholars believe that Paul's particular situation and problems were rather different from those of Luther; ours are different again.

Every generation of Christians reads the biblical text through the eyes of faith, and in the light of its own understanding of reality. The interpretation of the biblical story given by the church fathers was also couched in contemporary language and was intended to deal with the problems of their own day. If the Holy Spirit speaks through scripture, then we should not be surprised if it is found to be relevant to the needs of Christians whatever their situation and is interpreted in different ways down the centuries. The question "Who is Jesus?" challenges us today, but the answer we give must be *our* answer. Past answers will not necessarily correspond with *our* theological problems, or help *us* to answer the question "Who do you say that I am?" They may even hinder us. Moreover, if we want to look at the answer—or answers—which the New Testament itself offers to this question, we must certainly put those other answers out of our minds.

So let us turn to our New Testament authors, and the answers they give to the question "Who do you say that I am?" Now I have to confess that I have problems with this particular question. This may surprise you, since it is certainly scriptural, possibly dominical. Nevertheless, if by it we wish to discover not simply who *we*, as Christians, believe Jesus to be, but—as any New Testament scholar must—what *they* (our New Testament authors) believed him to be, and possibly even what he believed about himself, then, for various reasons, this particular question is likely to lead us astray.

The first of my hesitations is due to what we may call the historical problem. The words are attributed to Jesus in the famous recognition scene at Caesarea Philippi; but did he in fact ever put the question himself? Many New Testament scholars deny the authenticity of the scene,[2] and it is certainly out of keeping with Jesus' behavior elsewhere in the synoptics. Although Jesus acts and speaks with tremendous authority, his teaching is about the Kingdom of God—about God's rule and demands—not about himself. The story may well represent the beliefs of the early Christian community, affirming their own faith in Jesus as more than a prophet. In itself, this view may not be as radical as it seems; for even if we accept it, it is nevertheless reasonable to suppose that Jesus must have pondered the question of his own call; moreover, the question as to whether or not Jesus was "the Messiah" must have arisen during his lifetime, since the tradition that he was executed on a charge of claiming to be "King of the Jews" seems to be historically secure. We may put it this way: even if Jesus himself did not ask this question in this direct form, the question was posed by what he did and said, and by the way in which he lived and died.[3]

Nevertheless, the *formulation* of this question marks the change in emphasis from the good news proclaimed *by* Jesus to the good news proclaimed *about* him. When our first evangelist, Mark, described the contents of his book as τὸ εὐαγγέλιον Ἰησοῦ Χριστοῦ, "the good news *of* Jesus Christ," he chose a phrase which holds together these two ideas. Grammarians argue as to whether the phrase is a subjective or an objective genitive, but there is no need to choose, for the former is the basis of the latter! Mark tells the story of the good news proclaimed and enacted *by* Jesus; but inevitably, by his telling of that story he tells the story of the good news *about* Jesus. Jesus confronted men and women with the demand that they respond to the gospel; but as we read Mark's "gospel," the story inevitably confronts *us* with the demand to respond to Jesus, and the all-important question is whether or not we become *his* disciples. For Jesus, the gospel was theocentric; for the evangelist, it is inevitably christocentric. The question, being itself christocentric, represents the concerns of the Christian community rather than those of Jesus. Already, *in the New Testament itself,* therefore, we see how the tradition is being read through the eyes of faith and interpreted in a particular way. The evangelists, also, were wearing spectacles.

My second problem with the question confronting us is that it requires a particular form of answer. It is a bit like those multi-choice questions where you are provided with various possible answers and required to put a tick in one of the boxes. For some questions, such as "What was the date of a certain event?" or "Who was the President/Prime Minister who did a certain thing?" this is appropriate, but for others it is not, and sometimes one wants to write an essay in response, rather than put a tick. Our particular question—"Who do you say that I am?"—seems to demand that we choose from a list of possible titles: "John the Baptist, Elijah, the Messiah, the Son of God." Now titles can be useful as summaries, which is why they tend to be used in confessions of faith, but they need explanation and elaboration—which is precisely what was attempted at Chalcedon. But titles are not the only way to express the truth, and using them was not the primary way chosen by our evangelists, for though they all use christological titles at key-points in their narratives, this was not their most important method of telling their readers who Jesus is. They, too, seem to have found it necessary to write an essay—or rather a story—rather than simply to affirm the truth of particular responses to the question. By telling us that story in particular ways, they make quite clear what reply they expect *us* to give. The titles are convenient shorthand summaries.

The evangelists are writing the stories and inviting *us* to tick the boxes: in offering us a succession of pictures, they have made it plain which of the possible options we should choose. With the question "Who do *you* say that I am?" the ball has been lobbed into our court, and it is we who are required to reply. But if we turn the question around and ask "But who do *you*, *Jesus*, say that you are?" we find that he refuses to use any titles of himself. Only the Johannine tradition consistently depicts Jesus as referring to himself as "the Son."[4] According to Mark's account, his response to Peter's confession of him as Messiah is lukewarm. The only "title" he uses of himself is the enigmatic non-titular phrase "the Son of man." The once-popular suggestion that this was a first-century "messianic" title has proved to be without foundation:[5] either it is, as some suggest, simply an idiomatic expression for "I" or, surely more likely, it refers to Israel's role and destiny as God's faithful and obedient people.[6] The term Jesus uses for himself expresses his vocation, his obedience, his mission, his confidence in his vindication by God, but it is not a term used by others to express their faith in him; in contrast, the credal titles—"Christ," "Son of God," "Lord," all express what *others* believe him to be. Once again, we find that the tradition of Jesus' own teaching is theocentric, while the faith of the Church is expressed in terms which appear to be essentially christocentric. Jesus' own term for himself, "the Son of man," reminds us of his dependence on and obedience to God; titles such as "Messiah," Son of God," and "Lord" affirm his authority. By using its own terms, rather than that used by Jesus himself, the Church inevitably changed the picture significantly.

Does that mean, then, that the early Christian community misinterpreted the evidence? Were the answers it gave to our question untrue? Does Christology rest on a mistake?[7] Or were the answers they gave simply making explicit what had been *implicit* in the life, teaching, death, and resurrection of Jesus? Is it true, as has been said, that Jesus proclaimed the Kingdom, and the Church proclaimed Jesus?

Let us attempt to answer this question by asking another, related question: why was it that the theocentric message of Jesus developed into the apparently christocentric gospel of the early Church? The answer to that question is obvious: it was Jesus, and what happened through Jesus, that represented what was *new* in the first Christians' experience. It was Jesus, and what happened through Jesus, that required explanation. But that explanation necessarily had to be given in terms of their previous beliefs: Jesus had to be slotted into their existing thought-patterns. If we are to understand what our New Testament writers are saying about Jesus, we have to see him within the context of what Jews already believed about God.

Perhaps, however, I was wrong to describe the gospels as christocentric rather than theocentric. It may be that they appear to be more christocentric than they are. It is, indeed, easy to be misled by the gospel story! In all four of our canonical gospels, the spotlight is on Jesus from beginning to end. Even when the storyteller focuses on another character, such as John the Baptist, this is only because John is seen as pointing forward to Jesus. We are constantly confronted with the authority of Jesus, continually made to ask ourselves "Who, then, is this?" But we shall misunderstand the gospels if we lose sight of the real intention of the evangelists, which is to show how—to use Paul's phrase—"*God* was at work in Christ." It is *God's* Rule that is bursting into the world in Jesus. The Gospel about Christ is the Gospel about how *God* has fulfilled his promises: Jesus had to be explained in relation to God. Christology, then, has to be seen *within* theology. In the well-known words of the fourth evangelist: "God so loved the world that he gave his only Son; God sent his Son into the world, not to condemn the world, but in order that the world might be saved through him."[8] In this, the evangelists and Paul are at one: for all his emphasis on the relationship between Christ and the believer, Paul insists that he, Paul, was set aside for "the Gospel of God,"[9] which tells the good news of how God sent his Son,[10] gave him up for our sakes,[11] and raised him from the dead.[12]

It is this fundamental belief that the God of Israel is at work in Jesus that underlies all our gospels and that shapes their stories. In Mark, for example, the theme is set out in the opening lines, where we are told that what takes place is the fulfillment of words written by Isaiah: with the coming of Jesus we have the promised coming of "the Lord."[13] *This* is what his story is about. For all the evangelists, as for the disciples, the "building-blocks" of their Christology were found in the Old Testament and in intertestamental writings, since the God who was "at work in Christ" was the God whom they knew from the scriptures. If we are to understand their language, we must see them in that context, for when they are heard *out* of context, they can sound very different. Take, for example, the key "christological" term in Mark, "Son of God." Influenced by later doctrinal definitions, we regard this term as "high Christology," and so it is—but Mark's understanding of the phrase was nevertheless very different from that of the later fathers of the church! "Son of God" denoted election and privilege, and was a term used of Israel,[14] of her king[15] and of the righteous within Israel.[16] But sonship also implies obedience to the Father's will. There is good evidence that Jesus spoke of God as "Abba, Father,"[17] and thought of himself as in some sense God's son.[18] If he is now termed God's *beloved* Son by the believing community, this is an indication not only of his unique status, but of the fact that he alone is seen as the truly righteous Israelite—the one who is truly obedient.

Jesus, Mark tells us, came into Galilee declaring that the time is fulfilled and the Kingdom or Rule of God is at hand.[19] What, then, is the connection between Jesus himself and the coming of the Kingdom? Certainly both his preaching and his actions proclaim the coming of God's Rule: they can, indeed, be said to embody it. There is, moreover, an interesting correlation in Mark's gospel between the three occasions, all occurring at crucial points in the narrative, when Jesus is declared to be the Son of God, in chapters 1, 9, and 15,[20] and Jesus' three declarations of the imminent arrival of God's Kingdom, in chapters 1, 9, and 14.[21] Mark, at least, saw a very close connection between the coming of God's Rule or Kingdom and Jesus' identity as Son of God. If we ask what Jesus' proclamation demands of men and women, then the answer must surely be that, since the term βασιλεία means "rule" or "kingship," it implies their obedience to God's will. If God's Kingdom is present in Jesus, that is because he is the obedient Son, through whom the Spirit is at work:[22] here are the seeds of later trinitarian doctrine. But we must not read that trinitarian doctrine back into Mark's words.

Mark's key christological term is, after all, thoroughly theocentric, as indeed are all his christological terms. To understand the christological titles, we have to read them in their Jewish context. It is not, after all, such a big step between the Gospel *of* Jesus Christ and the Gospel *about* Jesus Christ; between Jesus' proclamation of the arrival of the Kingdom of God and Mark's proclamation of Jesus as the Son of God.

Our New Testament authors did what we all do, using the "building-blocks" available to them to deal with the questions that confronted them: new beliefs had to be expressed in largely familiar language. In their case, this meant using contemporary expectations and Old Testament imagery to express christological beliefs. For the first Jewish Christians, however, there was a particular tension in combining their previous faith and hopes with their new convictions, since the question with which they had to deal was how to *relate* old and new. On the one hand, it was the same God in whom they had always believed who had now revealed himself in Christ; on the other, the new revelation went far beyond what they had once believed. The hopes they had held in their past lives were fulfilled—but fulfilled in a way that astonished them. Their past faith was not abandoned but transformed.

In different ways, it is this problem with which all our New Testament writers are struggling. Our New Testament authors used the "building-blocks" available to them in answering the problems confronting them. To a large extent, the answers they give to the question "Who is Jesus?" use Old Testament terms, images, stories, and ideas, but inevitably, they found that their new experience and faith challenged the old categories. The building-blocks didn't quite fit, and had to be adapted for the new structure. Or, to change the metaphor, the new wine was bursting the old wineskins, and the new patch tearing the old garment.[23]

The need to explain what was new inevitably meant that the new was stressed, and the old assumed. New Testament theology was bound to be to a large extent christocentric, simply because it was concerned with trying to comprehend the new. Particularly important here is the fact that a great deal of Christology was formulated in the context of disputes between the first Christians and their fellow Jews, all appealing to the Jewish scriptures to justify their beliefs. It has to be admitted that at times some of the Christians (notably St. Paul) did some very strange things with the scriptures. In arguments, one naturally stresses the particular points at issue and ignores those on which there is agreement, and in this argument, the basic assumptions on both sides of the argument were Jewish. Once that is forgotten, however, the debate sounds very different, and when the Christian community split from Judaism, a shift in comprehension occurred. "Jew" and "Christian" came to be seen in opposition, "old" was opposed to "new," and in time people even came to speak about "the God of the Old Testament" as though he had nothing to do with the God of the New! So great was the shift in understanding that in later centuries one might wonder whether Marcion had, after all, been victorious, and had succeeded in cutting off the Christian faith from its Jewish roots. As for Jesus himself, until recently many scholars have, in the words of Leander Keck, "separated him from his heritage and environment." The criterion of dissimilarity, still being used by some scholars, has inevitably helped to drive a wedge between Jesus and Judaism.[24] The wonder of the Christian revelation blinded many to its continuity with the past, and understanding of Christology was inevitably skewed.

It is because this continuity has been forgotten that the New Testament itself is today assumed by some to be anti-Semitic or anti-Jewish. Attacks on "the Jews" in the fourth gospel, for example, are sometimes taken to be attacks on Judaism itself, and when that is done, Johannine Christology is distorted and misunderstood.

In the fourth gospel, we have an example of how Christology developed, becoming more overtly christocentric; at the same time, we see how Christology nevertheless still belongs *within theology*. We see the importance of understanding what were the Jewish building-blocks used by the evangelist, and the danger of misunderstanding the confrontation with Judaism. John offers us a marked change from the synoptics in the way in which Jesus is presented. Here, what is still implicit in the synoptic presentation of Jesus is transformed into explicit declarations as to who he is. Jesus no longer asks his disciples questions about his identity, but confronts us with statements, the truth of which we are expected to accept. We are no longer on a tennis court, endeavoring to respond to balls sent in our direction, but in a boxing ring, receiving knock-out blows. The narrative begins with clear declarations as to who Jesus is—from John the Baptist, from the first disciples, and from Jesus himself, so that by the end of the first chapter we know that he is the Lamb of God, the Son of God, the Messiah, the King of Israel, and the Son of man—who is now understood as the one who joins heaven and earth and who is the source of revelation. Questions about identity—is he the expected prophet? Elijah? the Messiah?—are asked now about John the Baptist, not about Jesus, who is recognized immediately by Andrew as the Messiah, and by Peter as the one about whom Moses and the prophets wrote. John's version of the Caesarea Philippi incident, when it comes, is a straightforward declaration that Jesus is the Holy One of God, who has the words of eternal life.[25]

From the very beginning of the story, then, the identity of Jesus is out in the open. Jesus speaks openly of himself as the Son, and refers to God as his Father. He claims, moreover, that he and his Father are one,[26] since he does the works of his Father[27] and speaks his words.[28] To see Jesus, therefore, is to see the Father,[29] since before Abraham was, "I am."[30] No wonder that, at the end of the story, Thomas declares "my Lord and my God."[31]

You may well feel that my introductory warning against Chalcedonian spectacles was unnecessary. Is not what John says the theology, the language even, of the later creeds? Are not later beliefs being clearly expressed here, within the New Testament itself? I do not for a moment want to deny that there is continuity in ideas—but continuity is *not* the same as identity. We must read the book from John's perspective if we are to understand him. John's purpose in writing was very different from that of the church fathers, and what he says must be understood in relation to that purpose. But what *was* that purpose? It is always difficult to reconstruct the situation behind a document, but it seems clear that the Johannine community was involved in heated argument with fellow Jews.[32] Expelled from the synagogue because of their beliefs, they attack their opponents—now disparagingly called "the Jews"—and accuse them of failing to understand the scriptures and to see that Jesus is the fulfillment of Old Testament hopes and beliefs. In a series of "signs" and discourses, Jesus himself is shown as demonstrating that he continues and completes God's revelation of himself in the past. Just as the Law and the prophets pointed forward to Jesus, so, too, did Israel's worship, her sacrifices and her feasts. God's glory—i.e., what God is—has been revealed in Jesus, and Jesus is therefore the one through whom God is glorified.

Like everyone else, the fourth evangelist has read the story of Jesus through spectacles. Fortunately, he provides these for us, since they are attached to the book in the form of the Prologue. Although Johannine scholars may argue about the Prologue's origins, these are unimportant. What is significant is the light this passage throws on the rest of the book: we *need* the Prologue if we are to understand what is being said in the pages that follow.

The Prologue is about the Word. It begins with a clear reference to the opening words of Genesis 1:1, and draws out their significance. The Word is the creative Word of God, since word and action are one: what God said was done. So the Word is the source of light and of life. There is considerable disagreement about the precise background of this imagery. Is John thinking of the *memra* of the Aramaic targums? If so, was this simply a way of referring to God without using the divine name, or was it a reference to some kind of divine hypostasis? Is he perhaps drawing on Jewish beliefs about angels? And how significant is the fact that the first-century Jewish philosopher Philo seems to think of the *Logos* as a separate, divine person?[33] Yet even in Philo, the *Logos* represents God's self-revelation to humans[34]—that which can be apprehended and experienced of God—just as in the Old Testament, those who meet angels can be said to have met God himself.[35] What we *can* say with certainty is that the concept of the Word has a rich background in Jewish thought; the Word was understood to be God's Agent in creation, and had been identified with Wisdom in the books of Proverbs and Wisdom.[36] The Word of God came again and again to the prophets, revealing to them the will of God. The Word is also identified with the Law, the embodiment of God's will, revealed on Sinai to Moses.[37] Jewish tradition identified this Word also with Wisdom: Sirach describes how Wisdom (revealed later to be the Law that Moses commanded us) sought a resting-place among the nations, until she made her dwelling in Israel.[38] Compare the words of John: "The Word was in the world, and the world came into being through him, and the world did not know him. He came to his own, and his own did not receive him. But to all who received him, he gave the power to become children of God." In speaking about the Word, John is clearly talking about God's creativity and self-revelation: God speaks; the world is created; the Law is given; God's glory—his nature—is revealed.

It is *this* Word who is made flesh, v. 14, *this* Word who dwells among us (just as Wisdom is said to have done in Sirach 24), and we have seen his glory—the glory which is even greater than the glory of the Law and which, for the Word-made-flesh, depends on the fact that he is his Father's only Son. As has often been said, it is this statement alone— "The Word became flesh"—which should surprise us, since this alone is not familiar to us from Judaism. And immediately we return to recognizably Jewish territory, for the final verses in the Prologue are as closely linked to Exodus 33–34 as are the opening verses to Genesis 1. In Exodus 33, Moses requests God for a favor—that is, in Hebrew and Greek, for "grace"—and asks to see God's glory (v. 18), a request that is only partly granted, since no one can see God and live (v. 20). While Moses is hidden in a cleft of the rock. God passes before him and proclaims his name, spelling out his attributes: he is a God merciful and gracious, slow to anger and abounding in steadfast love and faithfulness. What Moses glimpsed has now come among us, claims the fourth evangelist, for though the Law, revealing God's will, was given through Moses, God's *ḥesed* and *emet*, his steadfast love and faithfulness, in other words "grace and truth," came to us through Christ.[39]

In so far as there is a contrast in v. 17 it is between Moses, who was the recipient of revelation, and Christ, who is the Revealer: the Law was given through Moses, but grace and truth—the embodiment of God's glory—came among us in the person of the Father's Son. This is in no way to denigrate the Law: rather it is to insist on the continuity of what God had done in the past and has now done in Christ.[40] It is true that the Word is now heard more clearly, because the Word has been made flesh, and has "made God known" in a way impossible for anyone who has not seen God face to face, but the Word revealed to Moses and the prophets continues to be important, for it is this *same* Word that now speaks and acts through the person of Jesus.

The problem that the fourth evangelist is facing here is one that confronted all our New Testament authors—that of relating their previous beliefs with their new experiences; of understanding the revelation of God that has come to them through Christ to their conviction that he has revealed himself to Israel in the past. The fact that John has to argue this position in conflict with those who denied the validity of the new experience has distorted our understanding of what is going on: because "the Jews" are condemned, we think of the past as superseded or abolished. In fact the new affirms the old, because the old points forward to the new. It is the same God who has acted in the past, who has now acted in Christ, and his actions are consistent. The revelation in Christ is superior to that of the past, not because it is different, but because it is clearer.

The Christology of the fourth gospel must be seen in the light of the Prologue, and the theme of the Prologue is God's self-revelation through his Word. Christology has to be seen in the context of theology, for the function of the Son, who is the Word-made-flesh, is to reveal the Father's glory. God acts through him, speaks through him, reveals himself through him; the Son makes God known, and the glory we see in him is the glory of God.

When we turn to the rest of the gospel, we find that these themes are taken up. As in all the gospels, the spotlight is on Jesus throughout—and indeed, in John, the story is expressly about how Jesus manifested his glory. Nevertheless, his glory is shown to be, in fact, the glory of God, and Jesus' purpose is to glorify God, since he has come into the world in order to reveal God. The gospel, though it focuses on the figure of Jesus, is about how *God* was at work in him, speaking and acting *through* him.

This purpose is summed up in two parallel statements in the gospel, in 3:16–17, the passage we have already quoted: "God gave his only Son" and "sent his Son into the world in order to save it." The idea that Jesus has been sent by the Father is repeated many times in subsequent chapters.[41] Jesus is above,[42] and comes from God.[43] The works he does are the works of God,[44] and the words he speaks are the words of God.[45] The Son can do nothing on his own, and his only aim is to do the will of him who sent him,[46] not his own. He seeks God's glory, not his own,[47] and what he does is to the glory of God;[48] the glory he has is *from* God.[49] He has seen the Father[50] and knows him,[51] and his task is to make the Father known.[52] That is why to believe in him is to believe in the one who sent him,[53] and why those who see him see the Father,[54] so that he can even declare "before Abraham was, I am."[55] That is why he and the Father are one,[56] and why he can say that to know him is to know the Father,[57] and to hate him is to hate the Father.[58] Yet the Father is greater than he;[59] the Son keeps the Father's commandments,[60] and lays down his life at God's command;[61] he carries out judgment on his behalf;[62] he has been given life in himself, and so is able to give it to others.[63] He does not speak on his own,[64] neither is his work his own,[65] since everything is from God.[66] Jesus is the true bread, come down from heaven, but that bread is given by God.[67] Through his death and resurrection, men and women will be able to worship God.[68] In everything he does, and supremely in his death, God is glorified: in other words, God's true nature is revealed.[69]

John spells out the way in which Jesus completes the revelation of the past in a series of signs, performed by Jesus, interwoven with discourses which explain the significance of the signs and elaborate certain symbols.[70] Both signs and symbols show how Jewish Law and Jewish worship are fulfilled in him. Yet for all the emphasis on fulfillment, there is more to come. God continues to speak: his self-revelation does not cease with Jesus' glorification in death. The Father will send another Paraclete, the Spirit, who will enable the disciples to do even greater works than Jesus,[71] and will enable them to understand things which are still hidden from them.[72]

The questions with which John wrestled are reflected in other New Testament writings. Some—e.g., Mark and Luke—explain the relationship between old and new primarily in terms of fulfillment, and use proof-texts to make their case. Others, notably Paul and the author of Hebrews, use ideas similar to those used by John. It is surely no accident that in 2 Corinthians 3:1–4:6 Paul uses imagery very similar to that of John 1:1–18, for he was concerned with the same problem of reconciling God's past revelation to Israel and what had now occurred in Christ. Paul describes the glory of God, glimpsed by Moses on Sinai but now revealed in Christ, and links this glory with the light which shone out at the beginning through God's creative word.[73] The same concerns lie behind the Epistle to the Hebrews, whose opening lines tell how God spoke in the past by the prophets, but now has spoken by a Son, through whom he made all things. Matthew wrote his gospel out of the conviction that it was Christians, not Jews, who truly understood the scriptures and truly kept God's commands, which were "given through Moses," but whose meaning was now fully revealed in the words of Jesus.[74] God's self-revelation to his people was consistent.

If we are to understand our New Testament authors' responses to the question "Who do you say that I am?" we must remember firstly that, for them, all christological questions were essentially theological questions. First of all, they needed to ask whether *God* was behind what was happening or not—that is, whether he was at work in Christ. If this seems a statement of the obvious, it is perhaps worth pondering the fact that there are plenty of books which concentrate simply on "New Testament Christology" without considering it necessary to set that topic within theology. Second, we must remember the importance of the Jewish context in which Christianity was born, and which supplied the building-blocks out of which Christology was built. Unfortunately, as so often happens, the original structures were plundered and the source of the bricks was forgotten. The result was not only an anti-Semitic reading of the New Testament, but a misunderstanding of its Christology, for the irony is that it was the very conflict with "orthodox" Judaism that helped to forge Christology and to formulate early Christian beliefs.

How do these conclusions relate to the issue of the way we respond to the question "Who am I?" today? The answer we give must be *our* answer, and it will inevitably be shaped in part by the concerns, insights, and weaknesses of the twenty-first century. Nevertheless, we shall do well to begin by trying to comprehend the answers given by the first generation of Christians, to whom the question was first posed.

NOTES

1. 2 Cor 3:3, 7–8.
2. Notably R. Bultmann, *The History of the Synoptic Tradition*, trans. John Marsh (Oxford: Blackwell, 1963), 257–59. Others, e.g., F. Hahn, *The Titles of*

Jesus in Christology: Their History in Early Christianity, trans. Harold Knight and George Ogg (London: Lutterworth, 1969), have suggested that behind the present story one can detect a tradition that Jesus *rejected* the title of "Messiah."

3. Cf. Mk 4:41, where the disciples are driven by events to ask the question for themselves.

4. The one occasion in the "Q" tradition where Jesus speaks of himself in this way is the so-called "Johannine thunderbolt" in Mt 11:25–27//Lk 10:21–22.

5. Among the proponents of this view were H. E. Tödt, *The Son of Man in the Synoptic Tradition*, trans. Dorothea M. Barton (London: SCM, 1963); Hahn, *Titles of Jesus in Christology*. It was forcibly attacked by others, e.g., R. Leivestad, "Exit the Apocalyptic Son of Man," *New Testament Studies* 18 (1972): 243–67.

6. M. D. Hooker, *The Son of Man in Mark* (London: SPCK; Montreal: McGill, 1967); "Is the Son of Man Problem Really Insoluble?" in *Text and Interpretation: Studies in the New Testament Presented to Matthew Black*, ed. Ernest Best and R. McL. Wilson (Cambridge: Cambridge University Press, 1979), 155–68.

7. The question echoes one posed by Maurice Wiles, albeit of a somewhat different problem: "Does Christology Rest on a Mistake?" *Religious Studies* 6 (1970): 69–76, reprinted in *Christ, Faith and History: Cambridge Studies in Christology*, ed. S. W. Sykes and J. P. Clayton (Cambridge: Cambridge University Press, 1972), and M. F. Wiles, *Working Papers in Doctrine* (London, 1976).

8. Jn 3:16–17.

9. Rom 1:1.

10. Rom 8:3; Gal 4:4.

11. Rom 8:32.

12. Rom 4:24.

13. Mk 1:3.

14. Ex 4:22; Jer 31:20; Hos 11:1; cf. Wis 18:13. In other passages, the filial relationship is implied, e.g., Hos 1:10 (LXX 2:1); Jer 3:4, 19; 31:9. The plural is also used: Dt 14:1; Is 43:6. It is found especially in passages which rebuke Israel for not behaving as children should: Dt 32:5f., 18f.; Is 1:2, 4; 30:1, 9; 63:8; Jer 31:4, 22; 4:22; Mal 2:10.

15. 2 Sm 7:14; Ps 2:7; cf. Ps 89:26f.

16. Wis 2:18; 5:5.

17. The term "Abba," attributed to Jesus in Mk 14:36, is echoed by Paul in Rom 8:15, Gal 4:6, and may reasonably be thought to go back to Jesus. Its use in prayer was, however, not as surprising as Jeremias claimed. See J. Jeremias, *Abba. Studien zur neutestamentlichen Theologie und Zeitgeschichte* (Göttingen, 1966), 15–67, English translation, *The Prayers of Jesus* (London, 1967), 11–65; G. Vermes, *Jesus and the World of Judaism* (London, 1983), 39–43; J. Barr, "Abba Isn't Daddy," *Journal of Theological Studies* NS 39 (1988): 28–47.

18. The vital question here, of course, is "in *what* sense?" Was it simply as a member of Israel, who—together with his fellow Jews—thought of God as "Father"? (E.g., G. Vermes, *The Religion of Jesus the Jew* [London, 1983], 152–83.)

Was it as someone who felt himself to be "in a special relationship with God"? (Cf. C. Rowland, *Christian Origins* [London, 1985], 178f.) Or was it in a unique sense, as God's Messiah? (Cf. N. T. Wright, *Jesus and the Victory of God* [London, 1996], 648–51, who sees this messianic sonship as a "focusing" of Israel's sonship.) Although the phrase "the son of God" was used of the Davidic king (and so could refer to the Messiah), the extent to which the phrase was used in Judaism with a specific messianic reference is still a matter of debate.

19. Mk 1:15.

20. At Mk 1:11 and 9:7, in words spoken from heaven, and at 15:39 in the mouth of Jesus' executioner. The phrase occurs also at 3:11 and 5:7, where it is attributed to unclean spirits, and (according to some mss.) at 1:1.

21. At Mk 1:15, they occur in Jesus' opening words; at 9:1, they are part of the turning-point in the story; and at 14:25, they are Jesus' final words at the Last Supper.

22. Mk 1:9–11; Mt 12:28.

23. Mt 9:16–17//Mk 2:21–22. Cf. Lk 5:36–38.

24. For criticism of this criterion, see M. D. Hooker, "Christology and Methodology," *New Testament Studies* 17 (1971): 480–87.

25. Jn 6:66–71.

26. Jn 10:30.

27. Jn 10:37.

28. Jn 12:49.

29. Jn 14:19

30. Jn 8:58.

31. Jn 20:28.

32. See, e.g., John Ashton, *Understanding the Fourth Gospel* (Oxford: Clarendon, 1991).

33. *De Confusione Linguarum*, 146; *De Plantatione*, 8–9.

34. *De Opificio Mundi*, 24–25; *Quod Deus sit immutabilis*, 138; *Legum Allegoriae*, III:207.

35. Gn 18; Ex 3:2–6; 14:19; 23:20–22.

36. Prv 8:22–31; Wis 7:22–27.

37. Ps 119:16–18.

38. Sir 24:1–29.

39. Cf. M. D. Hooker, "The Johannine Prologue and the Messianic Secret," *New Testament Studies* 21 (1974): 40–58.

40. On the theme of continuity between old and new, see further M. D. Hooker, *Continuity and Discontinuity: Early Christianity in its Jewish Setting* (London: Epworth, 1986).

41. The verbs ἀποστέλλω and πέμπω are both used many times in this sense in the gospel.

42. Jn 3:13, 31; 6:33, 38, 50; 8:23.

43. Jn 5:43; 16:28, 30; 17:8.

44. Jn 5:17–21; 7:16–18; 9:3–4; 10:25, 37–38; 11:4, 40–42; 12:4.
45. Jn 8:47.
46. Jn 5:19, 30.
47. Jn 7:18; 8:50, 54.
48. Jn 12:28.
49. Jn 12:41; 17:22.
50. Jn 6:46.
51. Jn 7:29; 8:55; 9:15; 17:25.
52. Jn 15:15.
53. Jn 12:44; 13:20—just as he now sends his disciples.
54. Jn 12:45; 14:9.
55. Jn 8:58.
56. Jn 10:30.
57. Jn 14:7.
58. Jn 15:23–24.
59. Jn 14:28.
60. Jn 15:10.
61. Jn 10:18; 14:31.
62. Jn 5:22, 27; 9:39.
63. Jn 5:26; 6:54–58; 11:25.
64. Jn 12:49–50; 14:10; 17:8, 14.
65. Jn 14:10; 17:4.
66. Jn 17:7.
67. Jn 6:32.
68. Jn 2:19–22; 4:21–24.
69. Jn 15:8; 17:4.
70. E.g., the bronze serpent, Jn 3:14; bread, 6:32–33; living water, 7:38–3; the good shepherd, 10:11.
71. Jn 14:12.
72. Jn 16:12–15.
73. The belief that Christ represents the permanent and perfect, Moses the temporary and incomplete, is reflected in Paul's arguments about the place of the Law, e.g., Rom 2:17–3:20; 7; 9–11; Gal 3–5.
74. See, in particular, Mt 5:17–48. On this theme see my essay, "Creative Conflict: The Torah and Christology," in *Christology, Controversy and Community: New Testament Essays in Honour of David Catchpole*, ed. David G. Horrell and Christopher M. Tuckett, Novum Testamentum Supplement 99 (Leiden: Brill, 2000), 117–36.

CHAPTER THREE

Jesus as Lord and Teacher

GERALD O'COLLINS, S.J.

Two titles or distinctive names by which the New Testament designates Jesus, "Lord" and "Teacher" are among the very early answers Christians gave to the question: "What/Who do you say that I am?"[1] This question recalls an episode that occurred near Caesarea Philippi, in the far north of ancient Palestine. Jesus asked his disciples: "Who do people say that I am?" They told him that many people attributed to him a prophetic identity. Then he confronted them with the blunt question: "But who do you say that I am?" Simon Peter spoke up for the others and said, "You are the Christ (the Messiah)" (Mk 8:27–29). When he wrote his gospel some years after Mark, Matthew extended Peter's confession: "You are the Christ, the Son of the living God" (Mt 16:16). Before I examine "Lord" and "Teacher," let us consider briefly the pair of titles which come from the Caesarea Philippi episode.

Messiah and Son of God

Peter's answer expressed the disciples' faith in the messianic character of Jesus. First-century Judaism, as we know, exhibited a wide variety of messianic concepts, in particular, royal and priestly messianic notions, but they largely converged on a belief that God was to act dramatically in history through an appointed and anointed intermediary who would "redeem Israel" (Lk 24:21) from forces that oppressed it. The disciples saw in Jesus more than a teacher, a prophet, or a wonder-worker. He was/is God's chosen intermediary, the Redeemer or Liberator himself.

Matthew's gospel has Peter give Jesus two titles: not only "the Christ" but also "the Son of (the living) God." When the New Testament calls Jesus "Son of God," the title does not necessarily and always imply divine identity, in the sense of completely sharing in God's nature. The Hebrew Scriptures can refer to angels (Jb 1:6), kings (Ps 2:7; 2 Sm 7:14), and the whole people of Israel (Ex 4:22) as "sons of God." St. Paul identifies Christians as God's "sons and daughters" (2 Cor 6:18). By the time of Jesus the "Son of God" seems also to have referred to the coming, royal Messiah, *the* descendant of the Son of David (see Lk 1:32, 35).

Clearly in John's gospel, Jesus' divine sonship is unique (Jn 1:18) and entails his being "equal to God" (Jn 5:18) as one who shares literally in the divinity and so enjoys full and personal divine authority (Jn 3:35–36; 17:10). Jesus expresses his status unequivocally: "the Father and I are one" (Jn 10:30). But in what sense did Matthew and other Christians who wrote before John (above all, Paul) understand Jesus to be the Son of God? Paul calls Jesus "Son of God" sparingly—only fifteen times in the letters that, beyond reasonable doubt, come directly from the apostle—but all the same, like John, Paul acknowledges Jesus to be the unique divine Son who pre-existed with the Father until "sent" and revealed with the Incarnation and the gift of the Holy Spirit (Gal 4:4–7). Matthew also perceives Jesus to be "God's Son" in a unique sense, as one who enjoys special intimacy with his heavenly Father (Mt 11:27). The parable of the Wicked Tenants (Mt 21:33–41) climaxes when the landowner sends his son and heir to collect what is due from the tenants of the vineyard. The owner represents God and the son God's only Son. Much earlier in the story Matthew has depicted Jesus as God's unique Son, revealed in his identity and mission on the occasion of his baptism (Mt 3:13–17).

In short, Matthew's version of the Caesarea Philippi episode has Peter responding to the question "Who do you say that I am?" with a pair of titles: "the Christ" and "the Son of God," the former being a "low" or earthly title that refers to Jesus' human mission as God's designated Redeemer and the latter a "high" title that conveys his true divinity.

A Pair of Titles

Every now and then, the New Testament provides other pairs of titles that refer to Jesus. For instance, in John 13:13 it is Jesus himself who says to the disciples at the Last Supper: "You call me Teacher/Master (*didaskalos*) and Lord (*Kyrios*), and so I am." This is the only time in any of the gospels where Jesus quite explicitly names himself as "Lord." But this self-description is introduced by "you call me," and so reports the way the disciples confess him. Here we once again meet a "high" title linked with what is apparently a "low" title. I want to reflect on "Lord" in Paul's letters and "Teacher/Master" in the gospels to spell out the significance of this pair of titles that also respond to the question "Who do you say that I am?" These christological titles or distinctive names point to Jesus' attributes, explain his identity, and indicate his redemptive work. They reply very naturally to anyone who puts such questions as: "Who is Jesus in himself? What is his origin and his destiny? What has he done, what is he doing, and what will he do for human beings and their world?"

I do not want to exaggerate the importance of christological titles, but one should not dart to the other extreme and underestimate their power and impact. They expressed and galvanized the way the earliest Christians confessed Jesus, followed him, and worshipped him. Ultimately, it is at our peril that we ignore their foundational and persistent relevance for Christian faith and theology.

The New Testament yields around 130 christological titles—a chorus of praise and confession directed toward the crucified and resurrected Jesus. Some appear only once: for instance, "the Lion from the tribe of Judah" (Rv 5:5) and "the bright Morning Star" (Rv 22:16). Other titles turn up more frequently: for example, "the Bridegroom" (16 times), "Savior" (16 times), and "the (Good) Shepherd" (8 times). I have to say "around" 130 titles, since a few examples on my list could be challenged: for instance, Christ as God's "Amen" (Rv 3:14). Is "Amen" a title? Furthermore, translations may conceal difficulties. Rendering 1 Corinthians 15:20 as Christ being "the first fruits of those who have fallen asleep" can be debated. Translating *aparche* in upper case, "the First Fruits," makes it easier to appreciate its titular force instead of explaining it (away?) as a non-titular description. Nevertheless, by indicating something of Jesus' status and function, these two cases ("Amen" and "the First Fruits") fit the normal account of a christological title. They too are distinctive names that denote attributes of Jesus, illuminate his being and mission, and respond to any who ask: "Who do you say that he was/is?" Another reason for being unable to nominate a precise number of christological titles in the New Testament comes from the difficulty about deciding whether a few of them should be treated as simply synonymous. For instance, after entitling the risen Jesus "the Last Adam" (1 Cor 15:45), Paul then calls him the "second man" (or "Second Man") and then the "man from heaven" (or "Man from heaven") (1 Cor 15:47–49). Are these distinct titles, or mere synonyms for "the Last Adam"?

Only eight titles occur more than twenty times in the New Testament. These eight are: "Christ" (540 times), "Lord" (used of Jesus around 485 times, with roughly half of these occurrences in the Pauline letters[2]), "Son of Man" (85 times), "Son" (83 times), "Teacher" (43 times in the gospels as *didaskalos*, 16 times in the gospels as *rabbi* [or *rabbouni*], with 10 of these occurrences in John, 6 times in Luke as *epistata*, and once as *kathegetes* [Mt 23:10]), "Son of God" (43 times), "King" (38 times), and "Lamb" (29 times as *arnion* and 4 times as *amnos*).[3]

Christ as Lord

Out of the "big eight," I want to examine "Lord" and "Teacher." Incorporated in the oldest confessions of Christian faith, "Lord" moved ahead in the aftermath of the First Council of Nicaea (A.D. 325) and, with "Christ" and "Son of God," enjoys its central place in the Nicene-Constantinopolitan Creed, the creed used by all Christians in the eucharist and by many at baptism. As recently as the common christological declaration, signed in November 1994 by Mar Dinkha IV (the Patriarch of the Assyrian Church of the East) and Pope John Paul II, the traditional titles of "Christ," "Lord," and "Son of God" occur several times.

At times, in the New Testament and beyond, the title *kyrios* could be merely a polite way of addressing a man and should be simply translated as "sir" (Jn 4:11; 5:7). It could also be applied to such male figures of authority as the head of a family (Mt 21:30), a ruler (Mt 27:63), the owner of a large estate (Mt 13:27), or an authoritative teacher (Lk 12:42; 18:6). But *Kyrios* was also a common name for God, being so used over six thousand times in the Greek translation (the Septuagint) of the Hebrew Scriptures to represent the Tetragrammaton or sacred name. In short, the title *kyrios* harbors an ambiguity that must be resolved by examining the particular contexts in which it occurs. Determining its specific meaning in the various contexts creates no more difficulty than we find today when construing the sense of its modern (partial) equivalents in French ("seigneur"), German ("Herr"), Italian ("signore") and Spanish ("señor"). When used in the European Parliament, these terms are no more than courteous forms of address between human beings; when used in the setting of public worship and private devotion, they open, continue, or close prayer to God. In John 20:28 ("My Lord and my God"), *Kyrios* obviously conveys a "high," divine sense as when the Septuagint renders "YHWH/Elohim" as "Lord God" (Ps 35:23). The same holds true in Revelation 4:11, when the elders fall before God's throne and sing of "our Lord and God." John's gospel opens with Jesus receiving from the first disciples the title of "Rabbi/Teacher," "Messiah," "the Son of God," and the "King of Israel" (Jn 1:38, 41, 50); it closes with Thomas addressing him in the language with which Israel addressed God.

Around 230 times and right from his first letter (1 Thessalonians), Paul gives Jesus the title of "Lord."[4] At times he does so in passages that seem to derive from a pre-Pauline tradition (e.g., Rom 10:9; 1 Cor 16:22; Phil 2:11). Such passages open a window for us onto christological faith in the first two decades of Christianity. An established credal formula, perhaps a baptismal confession, may lie behind Romans 10:9: "If you confess with your mouth that *Jesus is Lord* and believe in your heart that God has raised him from the dead, you will be saved." Here we see how early Christians confessed that the risen and exalted Jesus shares in the divine lordship. Paul presses on and applies to Jesus a LXX passage that calls God "Lord" (Jl 2:32): "Everyone who calls on the name of the Lord will be saved" (Rom 10:13). Here prayer that belongs to God is directed toward the exalted Jesus. He is likewise invoked in an old prayer that derives from Aramaic-speaking Christians: "Maranatha, Our Lord, come" (1 Cor 16:22). Believers begged Jesus, now acknowledged as a divine being, to return quickly from heaven. Gordon Fee comments: "This prayer is clear evidence that in very earliest days the Aramaic-speaking church referred to Jesus by the title that in the OT belongs to God alone."[5]

In a poetic, probably hymnic, passage that may well derive from a pre-Pauline tradition (Phil 2:6–11),[6] Paul presents the pre-existent Jesus as being "in the form of God" and "equal to God," taking "the form of a slave" by "being born like human beings" and "assuming human form." Here Pauline language approaches John's incarnation talk of "the Word becoming flesh" (Jn 1:14). Through—(or should we say?) despite—the self-emptying of the Incarnation and the humiliating death of crucifixion, Jesus' equality with God is revealed. He receives "*the Name* which is above every name," in that the divine name of "Lord" is transferred to the highly exalted Jesus, and all created beings (in the heavens, on the earth, and under the earth) acknowledge in worship Jesus' lordship. "Every knee shall bow" and "every tongue confess that Jesus Christ is Lord to the glory of God the Father" (Phil 2:10–11). These two verses echo Isaiah 45:18–24, a classic text that declares God's dominion over all nations and their so-called "gods." While proclaiming the divine identity of Jesus, Paul also maintains monotheistic faith through the concluding phrase, "to the glory of God the Father."[7]

For Paul himself, Christians are characterized by confessing Jesus as divine Lord, but always within a monotheistic faith. Here 1 Corinthians 8:5–6 enjoys its special importance. The apostle contrasts the many, so-called "gods" (the traditional deities) and "lords" (as the deities of mystery cults were usually called) of pagan religion with "our" one God: "For us there is one God, the Father, from whom are all things and for whom we exist, and one Lord, Jesus Christ, through whom are all things and through whom we exist." The apostle splits the Jewish confession of monotheism from Deuteronomy 6:4–5 by glossing "one God" with "Father" and "one Lord" with "Jesus Christ." Thus Paul puts Jesus as Lord right alongside God the Father and presents him also as (divine) agent of creation. The prepositions distinguish the Father and the Lord Jesus (implicitly recognized as Son) in their divine activity, with Christ as the mediator through whom God created all things and redeemed us. In this new, christological monotheism, Lord, *the* designation in the Old Testament for the one God, belongs to the Son. Without in any way denying monotheism, Paul clearly distinguishes between the two divine "persons" (to use the language of a later day).

Thus far I have looked at four Pauline passages which involve the title "Lord" and which the apostle does not repeat as such elsewhere. He has, however, a greeting to his correspondents that recurs in his letters: "Grace to you and peace from God our Father and *the Lord* Jesus Christ" (Rom 1:7; see also e.g. 1 Cor 1:3; 2 Cor 1:2; Gal 1:3; Phil 1:2; Phlm 3). This greeting or blessing may reflect early Christian liturgical usage. Or it may be the apostle's own creation, in which he draws on Hellenistic and, even more, Jewish models such as Numbers 6:25–26: "May the Lord . . . be gracious to you . . . and bring you peace." Whatever its antecedents and origins, in this Pauline greeting "the Lord" (who is implied to be the Son of [God] the Father) works with the Father to redeem humankind. In this common work of salvation, no distinction is drawn between the two divine persons, as if the Son/Lord were playing an essentially subordinate role.

Before leaving "Lord," a central christological title in Paul's letters, a word about its correlative, believers as the slaves of the Lord. The apostle knew "slave" to be an honorific title in this (religious) context. For his Jewish predecessors it meant belonging exclusively and unconditionally to the one true God. Paul's happiest boast was to be a "slave" of the Lord Jesus (Rom 1:1; Gal 1:10; Phil 1:1). The apostle's practice and some of Jesus' rebukes highlighted what confessing the "Lord" entailed. Matthew reported Jesus as reproaching those who call him "Lord, Lord," but fail to follow his teaching (Mt 7:21–23; see Lk 6:46). Assigning titles to Jesus was and remains a radically self-involving exercise. This holds true also of a christological title found only in the gospels, "Teacher."

Christ as Teacher

Jesus' ministry provided the historical foundation for the title of "Teacher." He taught in the synagogues, gave his judgment on disputed points in Jewish law, and gathered around himself a body of students or pupils (*mathetai*). His method of teaching differed markedly from the scribes, those highly trained religious and legal experts many of whom were Pharisees. He had not received any scribal education. His audience saw how Jesus' teaching diverged from that of the scribes (Mk 1:22,27; Mt 7:29). The people of his home village of Nazareth were astonished at his wise teaching (Mk 6:2–3). The scribes themselves challenged the basis of his authority to teach and act as he did (Mk 11:27–28). According to

John, some highlighted Jesus' lack of formal training (Jn 7:15). They refused to acknowledge in him one who was a trained and officially authorized interpreter of the law.

Jesus' teaching authority led to his being addressed with the title "Teacher" (*didaskalos* or *epistates* in Greek, behind which lay the Hebrew title of *rabbi* or its Aramaic equivalent *rabbouni*, "my Master"). This was a reverential address to a person of authority (Jn 3:21), and sometimes given to one who worked miracles (Mk 10:51).

At first glance, "Teacher" comes across as a "low," human title for Jesus. But we should not overlook the striking directness and authority of his teaching style. Jesus did not, for instance, appeal to previous "authorities" when he pronounced upon central matters of the Mosaic law (Mt 5:31–42). He spoke with his own authority, prefacing his teaching with "I say to you" and not with such prophetic rubrics as "thus says the Lord" or "an oracle of the Lord." He taught not merely as the final emissary of divine Wisdom but as divine Wisdom in person (Lk 7:31–35; 10:21–22; 11:49–51). Through such parables as that of the prodigal son (Lk 15:11–32) and the workers in the vineyard (Mt 20:1–15), he challenged the world of conventional wisdom. The voices of the prodigal's older brother and that of the worker who had toiled all day in the vineyard express the conventional wisdom of the world. Jesus' subversive wisdom contrasted the normal ordering of life on the basis of rewards and punishments with the astonishing graciousness of the prodigal's father and the vineyard's owner. Cosmic generosity characterized Jesus' authoritative vision of God.

We need to remember Jesus' decisive authority if we are to appreciate the correlative of the christological title of "Teacher" in "disciple" or *mathetes*. Disciples are those who "follow" or accompany (see Mk 15:40–41) Jesus on his mission and have made a radical break with their previous lifestyle to do so. For them he is more than an ordinary teacher or rabbi, and even more than a charismatic prophet. We are meant to think rather of someone like Elisha abruptly called by the prophet Elijah (1 Kgs 19: 19–21). That story served as a model for scenes in which Jesus rebukes those who wish to meet regular family obligations before joining him (Mt 8:21–22; Lk 9:59–60). Those who find in Jesus their "Teacher" are not simply pupils who can learn his doctrine and move away. They are called to abandon home and family, so as to devote themselves to the task of proclaiming the coming kingdom of God. In committing themselves to Jesus, they share his wandering life and follow him on his mission.

Conclusion

These two titles, "Lord" and "Teacher," combine with many others in responding to the question "Who do you say that I am?" Both responses are self-involving and obviously intertwined closely with worship and discipleship. Down through the ages christological titles have led the way in giving life and substance to Christian hymns. Take the hymn by an evangelical divine, John Newton (1745–1807), "How sweet the name of Jesus sounds." Its next-to-last verse names and pictures Jesus in ten respects, almost all of which are titles: "Jesus, my shepherd, brother, friend, / my prophet, priest and king, / my lord, my life, my way, my end, / accept the praise I bring."

In my essay I have largely limited myself to discussing two christological titles that belong among the "big eight" in the New Testament. Another essay could take up further biblical titles or scrutinize fresh titles and images that have emerged in modern times: for instance, Jesus the Jew, the (Charismatic) Healer, the Liberator, my/our Brother, my/our Friend, our Mother, the Cosmic Christ, and so forth. Such titles are solidly based in the New Testament, as well as being firmly anchored in the Hebrew Bible. It is important for the apostle Paul that Jesus was born a Jew (Rom 9:5; Gal 3:16). Jesus' ministry of healing bulks large in the gospels, and provides the frame for his remark about being the "physician" come for the sick and sinful (Mk 2:17). The liberating power exercised by Jesus in his earthly ministry and at work in his risen glory more than justifies the title of Liberator. The titles of "Jesus my Brother and Friend" enjoy their warrant not only from the scriptures but also from such witnesses to tradition as St. Richard of Chichester (d. 1253). Jesus' own homely picture of himself as a hen with her chickens (Lk 13:34) helps provide part of the backing for those who have styled Jesus "our Mother." The christological hymn in the first chapter of Colossians represents Jesus as creator and conserver of the universe (Col 1:15–17); it supports talk of the Cosmic Christ, a title which can also be maintained for other reasons. In surveying rapidly these modern titles for Jesus, I have pointed only briefly to their New Testament warrant. Those who know the Hebrew Bible will find even older roots for these images and titles.

The sheer number of titles, old and new, bears eloquent witness to the fact that no one title exhausts the mystery of Christ. They also illustrate how we put ourselves into our words, above all when we attribute titles to Jesus. An acceptance of discipleship shines through always, not least in the lovely prayer by Richard of Chichester who commits himself in the very act of assigning five titles to Jesus: "Thanks be to thee, my Lord Jesus Christ for all the benefits which thou has given me—for all the pains and insults thou hast borne for me. O most merciful Redeemer, Friend and Brother, may I know thee more clearly, love thee more dearly, and follow thee more nearly." St. Richard begins with two central titles from the Creed ("my Lord Jesus Christ"), and makes "Lord" and "Christ" more intimate and personal by saying "my Lord Jesus Christ." Then he makes the tone even more intimate and personal with three further titles: "O most merciful Redeemer, Friend and Brother." There is a touching and effective movement from "Redeemer" to "Friend" and "Brother." As much as anything I have ever read, Richard of Chichester's full prayer brings out the power, beauty, and importance of our titles for Jesus. By naming him in these and other ways, we are in a position to know him, follow him, and pray to him and with him. The christological titles have always been among the primary means for expressing and stimulating our knowledge of Jesus, our discipleship, and our worship of him.

NOTES

1. As a background to what follows, see my "Images of Jesus: Reappropriating Titular Christology," *Theology Digest* 44 (1997): 303–18.

2. One cannot be utterly precise, mainly because it occasionally remains unclear whether "Lord" refers to God (the Father) or to Christ.

3. This list corrects slightly that provided in my "Images of Jesus," 305.

4. See L. W. Hurtado, "Lord," in *Dictionary of Paul and His Letters*, ed. G. F. Hawthorne et al. (Downers Grove, Ill.: InterVarsity Press, 1993), 560–69.

5. Gordon Fee, *The First Epistle to the Corinthians* (Grand Rapids, Mich.: Eerdmans, 1987), 839.

6. See J. A. Fitzmyer, "The Aramaic Background to Philippians 2:6–11," *Catholic Biblical Quarterly* 50 (1988): 470–83.

7. See R. Bauckham, "Jesus, Worship of," in *Anchor Bible Dictionary*, ed. D. N. Freedman, vol. 3 (New York: Doubleday, 1992), 812–19; R. P. Martin, "Worship," in *Dictionary of Paul and His Letters*, ed. G. F. Hawthorne et al. (Downers Grove, Ill.: InterVarsity Press, 1993), 982–91.

CHAPTER FOUR

Messiahship and Incarnation

Particularity and Universality Are Reconciled

GEORGE LINDBECK

Righteousness and peace have kissed each other
—Ps 85:10

The text for this discussion is the first great christological confession, that of Peter at Caesarea Phillipi as reported in Matthew 16. For most Christians down through history, this confession says that Jesus is equally and unitedly the messiah of Israel and the incarnate Son of the living God. It is this understanding that will serve as the basis of our reflections.

The words "of Israel" and "incarnate," to be sure, are not in the text, and while "of Israel" could be implied, the notion that Jesus is the incarnate Son of God, the enfleshed Logos, as the Gospel of John puts it, was foreign to Matthew and presumably could not have been in Peter's mind on the hypothesis that he said these words. As for doubts that he said them, it will be recalled that John puts the closest approximation of Matthew's version of Peter's confession into the mouth of Martha, and she was neither an apostle, nor a man, nor particularly well regarded in the tradition as a whole in comparison to her more contemplative sister Mary. Our concern, however, is not with these historical-critical questions regarding original meaning, but with what has seemed to most

Christians down through the millennia the plain sense of this confession: messiahship and incarnation are to be integrally affirmed of Jesus.

The Church's official teachings, however, have not preserved this symmetry. In the great catholic creeds of Nicaea and Chalcedon, for example, incarnation has swallowed up messiahship, and "Christ" has become simply a proper name without any hint of its original messianic meaning. What were once two interwoven strands of christological discourse have separated, and one of them has largely disappeared from doctrinal formulations even if not from hymnody and liturgy. It is only recently that this omission has been widely perceived as a problem, but, as we shall see, current developments do not so much rectify as reverse the balance. The two strands remain unreconciled.

It is not so much with the content as with the formal aspect (or the "conceptual grammar," as I shall sometimes call it) of messiahship and incarnation that this essay is concerned. The first section outlines the structural interrelations of these concepts, and the succeeding sections trace the course of Christology from their perspective. Thus the second section deals with scriptural warrants, the third with the later neglect of messiahship and its separation from incarnationalism, the fourth with the dogmatic possibilities of reconciliation, and the fifth with current emphases on messianism. Even more than is usual in grammatical studies, this one is tentative throughout: its descriptions of the grammar of Christology badly need to be supplemented by other investigations, especially by testing against actual usage. If it stimulates others to do better what is here done poorly, it will have served its purpose.

I

The formalities with which I start need more explication than I shall give them, but they are fundamental for what follows, and will perhaps become more intelligible in later sections. My basic suggestion is that, formally considered, messiahship singularizes incarnation and incarnation universalizes messiahship.

Messiahship singularizes because there can be only one messianic person, coterie, or age. These are eschatological realities that by definition are singular. In their paradigmatic instances in the religions of the Book, Judaism, Christianity, and Islam, they conclude or climax a tempo-

rally finite universe that moves irreversibly from creation to consummation. Finality is unrepeatable. In the three Middle Eastern monotheisms,
the messiah or *mahdi*,[1] or whatever he is called, is *epaphax*, a singularity in
the modern cosmological sense of being as unprecedented and non-iterable
as is the scientists' Big Bang (which in this respect resembles the initial
act of creation as understood in the theological mainstreams of each of
these three traditions). Speaking now of Christianity, although doing
Christology from below, i.e., messianically, does not exclude the universality of the messiah's creative, redemptive, and revelational work, it also
does not necessarily imply it. Incarnation is needed in order to universa-
lize messiahship.

Incarnation by itself, in turn, lacks singularity as is perhaps most
vividly manifest in the proliferation of incarnate deities in Hinduism. If
the divine can be enfleshed, then there seems to be nothing to prevent
this from happening over and over again. Christologies which are exclusively from above, exclusively incarnational, have difficulty explaining
why the Logos, the Second Person of the Trinity, cannot become human
in times or places other than as a Jew in first-century Palestine. Late medieval scholastics, it may be recalled, even asked why God assumed
materiality in human form—why not also in sticks, stones, or animals?
These questions can perhaps be answered non-messianically with the help
of trinitarian doctrine, but in ways that are bound to seem unsatisfac-
tory in the light of scriptural testimony; the very name "Christ," we recall, is the translation of "Messiah." Thus the vertical incarnational move
into the world of space and time whether from above or from below lacks
self-evident concreteness and particularity apart from intersection with
the horizontal messianic dimension. Incarnation needs singularizing no
less than messiahship needs universalizing.

The relation between these two dimensions, it must be stressed, is
not that of a zero-sum game. When incarnation is emphasized at the expense of messiahship, it is not only singularity but also universality that
suffers. The singularity which comes in humanly knowable form only
through embodiment, through location in space and time, will of course
be weakened, but also lost is the universality of the incarnate one's significance for the temporal and historical dimension of the universe. In
the once-Christian West, the very idea of universally meaningful history
is inseparable from that of a messianically or eschatologically structured
universe, a temporally irreversible and teleologically directed continuum

with a center, climax, and goal. Converse gains and losses occur if the messianic is exalted at the expense of the incarnational. When the incarnational glue which reconciles the separated is de-emphasized, universality weakens, but so also does singularity. A messiah who is not universal, whose belonging to one people is not conjoined with saving significance for all, can be pluralized, and there is nothing more violent than the collision of particularistic messianisms. In short, singularity and universalism both flourish when messiahship and incarnation kiss each other, and they both fade when they break their embrace.

As we have already said, it is chiefly messiahship that has been lost from view, but the form that it impressed on Christology retains priority even in the creeds that make no mention of it. In the order of knowing (though not necessarily of being), the horizontal plane that is the locus of Jesus and of messiahship comes first. This is the realm of narrative, the home of what the philosopher, Louis Mink, has called the "configurational" comprehension by means of which particulars are identified by the stories told about them. In contrast to this, the paramount modes of comprehension and of discourse in the vertical dimension are "categoreal" and "theoretic."[2] Christologies influenced by platonism, for example, chiefly conceive incarnation categoreally (and sometimes also theoretically) on analogy to, though infinitely surpassing, the participation of material entities in universal, transcendent forms, and tend to demote configurational or narrative modes of comprehension to merely metaphorical or allegorical roles. In the Bible, in contrast, the horizontal has precedence. The messiah is endowed with utter singularity by the stories told about him and then, in a logically subsequent step, universal attributes and titles derivable from the vertical dimension are predicated of him and thereby also rendered singular. It is because of Jesus' messianically derived uniqueness that he alone among God's children is, as the creed puts it, "begotten, not made." Thus even the *homoousios*, the ultimate buttress of the affirmation that Jesus is uniquely God incarnate, conforms in conceptual grammar even if not in vocabulary to the credally unmentioned messianic depth structure of the faith.

As this example shows, however, theological and doctrinal construction does not require explicit knowledge of the underlying structures. Formal disciplines such as logic, mathematics, and grammar focus on relations in abstraction from the subject terms that they relate, and thus messiahship and incarnation function as variables or blank spaces that may be filled with very different content. If this is so, however—if it is possible, perhaps even normal, for Christologies that are grammatically similar to be materially different, and vice versa—what is the theological usefulness of an investigation such as the one on which we are embarked?

Describing theological grammar has its uses, as we shall see, but only in abnormal circumstances. Like the study of other types of grammar or logic, it is instrumental, part of the Organon in Aristotle's classification, and thus dispensable. We acquire the know-how of speaking grammatically far better in our early years when we are unaware of the grammatical rules that we are following than we do later on when we depend on grammar books in learning foreign tongues. Nor is this only a childhood phenomenon. Homer, the supreme master of grammar according to the Greek grammarians, knew no grammar. It seems that much the same situation exists in reference to faith and theology. There is no reliable correlation between knowing *how* to be grammatical, how to follow the truly fruitful interconnections of words and concepts in prayer, praise, preaching, and theological reflection, and knowing *what* that grammar is. Sometimes those ignorant of grammar are the most grammatical, and vice versa. In any case, as Wittgenstein has told us, grammarians of the philosophical (and, by extension, the theological) variety should leave language games untouched as long as they are working well. Grammar, just because the object of its study is not beliefs nor, even less, the realities that are believed, but rather the formal relations between terms, is theologically dispensable.[3]

Yet, to borrow again from Wittgenstein, when discourse is diseased, grammar can play a therapeutic role. Diagnosis, however, must precede prescriptions, and it is to a diagnostic use that I propose to put the diagram of messianic and incarnational interrelationships that I have sketched. This diagram will serve as a set of tentative suggestions for evaluating the twists and turns in what from its perspective are the two all-encompassing dimensions of Christian talk about Jesus Christ.[4]

II

The starting point is the Bible, but this for Christians is not a text to be evaluated, but the standard by which all our measuring rods are measured. To speak in Lutheran confessional terms, it is the judge of all teaching (not to mention conduct), including the grammar of the grammar of Christology we are exploring, and is not to be judged by anything other than itself.

The issue is not that of actually testing the proposal as to its scriptural acceptability; that would take volumes. The question is rather the hermeneutical one of the conditions under which this testing can or should take place, of how the Bible can serve as judge. Is it meaningful to interpret scripture holistically as if it were a single book containing a or the biblical understanding of messiahship and incarnation by means of which a schema such as I have outlined can be evaluated?

The consensus in the guild of biblical scholars is negative. The patterns of discourse in the different biblical writings are diverse, and any attempt to synthesize them in a unified description cannot be critically persuasive. John, and to a lesser extent Paul, constructed Christologies from above that later gave birth to full-blown incarnationalism, while Mark, and to a smaller extent, Luke and Matthew, did messianic Christologies from below. Never the twain shall meet, at least not by historical-critical means. When one adds the Old Testament to the grab bag of writings to be reconciled, the task becomes absurd rather than merely impossible.

Some members of the biblical guild might complain that this is an exaggeration. They would rightly insist that not all practitioners of modern historical methods are splitters, breaking the canon into unrelated fragments; some are lumpers who see connections the splitters miss. Nils Dahl, the New Testament scholar to whom I am most indebted, long my colleague at Yale and still living in retirement in Oslo, did a notable job of lumping in a 1952 essay, "The Crucified Messiah,"[5] that has grown in influence for half a century and is now assumed to be the standard view by even so notable a scholar as Martin Hengel.[6] He argues that Jesus' crucifixion as "King of the Jews" occasioned, not a break with a pre-existent view of messiahship, but the forging of the multiple first-century messianisms into a unified and specifically Christian New Testament understanding. (The technical notion of "vagueness" may be helpful at this point: vague concepts can be, so to speak, enriched rather than replaced by the new meanings they acquire when predicated of an unexpected but not previously excluded particular—and of this the crucified and resurrected Jesus would be a parade example).[7] Moreover, incarnation was not wholly alien even to the pre-Christian form of messiahship. If William

Horbury is right in his recent *Jewish Messianism and the Cult of Christ*,[8] the most persuasive study of the topic I have been able to find, the incarnationalism that grows out of the New Testament acclamations of Jesus as the Christ can be best understood as the intensification and fusing of messianic expectations and of royal cults, themselves quasi-incarnational, that began in the Old Testament and increased in the intertestimental period. Nor is it only in these cults that Israel celebrated God's embodied presence in his people. Rabbi Neusner has pointed to the proto-incarnationalism implied by the anthropomorphic concreteness of the Jewish worship of the One who is nevertheless so wholly transcendent that his proper name cannot be uttered,[9] and another rabbi, Michael Wyschogrod, goes so far as to say that the "divinity of Jesus" can be understood as a "more concentrated" form of the covenental "indwelling of God in the people Israel."[10] As research and reflection accumulate, it becomes possible for scholars who are so inclined to move toward a closer and more balanced integration of New Testament and pre–New Testament messiahship and incarnation than was before adjudged possible.

No matter how chastened historical-critical scholarship becomes, however, there are severe limits to the lumping that the discipline allows. Its focus on the single sense of texts in their original settings undermines the operational unity of the Bible even when, as in the case of canonically oriented scholars, it is the historical-critical meaning of the individual books in their total scriptural context that is the object of study. What is needed, it seems, is a broadening of the focus to include attention, not only to historical-critical reconstructions, but also to the specifically narrative and other literary senses, the multiple meanings and typological and allegorical interpretations that enabled premodern readers to construe the whole of scripture from Genesis to Revelation as a single work.[11] Only thus is it possible to escape from the splitting inherent in the view that texts have an inherent single sense, the original meaning, to which historical criticism has privileged access.

Prospects for this broadening of hermeneutical focus seem far better than in my youth. Continental postmodernism and, more soberly, anglophone philosophical developments ease the path for those interested in the critical retrieval of premodern interpretive practices. They have the best of both worlds, of both modernity and premodernity. Liberated from fixation on the myth of original meaning, they are free to engage, not only in theological interpretation, but in the study of previously neglected aspects of history, readers' response, and *Wirkungsgeschichte*, that give texts their living significance. As for their advantage over premodernity, that comes from their openness to correction by critical history. The importance of such corrective retrievals has been amply illustrated in recent decades by the demolition of church-dividing doctrinal disagreements (not least the christological ones separating Eastern and Western and Chalcedonian and non-Chalcedonian Christians). There is reason to hope that their constructive potential for making possible (though not guaranteeing) scriptural consensus will become more and more manifest.

That day, however, has not yet arrived: it is not yet possible to submit the proposed harmonization of the grammars of messiahship and incarnation to the public, the communally mediated, judgment of scriptural scholarship. There are bright spots, but scholars continue for the most part to be splitters who see no possibility and therefore no obligation to try to assess post-biblical christological developments by reference to the Bible taken as a whole—that is, read holistically in its canonical unity. As is often the case in contemporary theology, we must proceed without much help from biblical studies as to whether what we shall be doing is biblically authorized.

III

What first needs to be assessed is the shift from messianism to incarnationalism and the separation between the two strands of discourse. This combined shift and separation began, as we have already mentioned in passing, with St. Paul's mission to the gentiles; we thus have evidence for it in the very earliest New Testament writings. It continued in the theological developments of the first centuries. As befitted the apologetic needs of the church's gentile membership, emphasis on the universally immanent Logos, the true light that enlightens everyone who comes into the world according to the Prologue to the Gospel of John, tended to displace the particularistic messianic expectations of Israel as the primary *praeparatio evangelica*. It was thus that the relation of God's Word to God's Self, of the pre-existent Son to the Father, became the center of theological developments that reached their unsurpassed and perhaps unsurpassable dogmatic climax in the affirmation at Nicaea of the consubstantiality of the Son with the Father and, at Chalcedon, of the personal unity of the fully divine and fully human in Jesus Christ. Messianism was not excluded —it could not be except by rejecting the Old Testament and bowdlerizing the New as Marcion did—but it was neglected. In the long run, even the credal references to Jesus' future coming as judge of the quick and dead and to his kingdom as having no end tended to be transposed from a messianic into an incarnational key—points to which I shall later return. It could not be otherwise in view of the non-apocalyptic and de-eschatologized world pictures which have prevailed not only in ancient but in modern times. (For modernity, think of Schleiermacher, for example.) Only recently, as we have already mentioned, has incarnational hegemony been challenged in the theological mainstream to any great extent.

There have, however, been countercurrents that we need to keep in mind in order to avoid misunderstanding the official dominance of incarnationalism. They have been strong enough outside of the theological establishments to give a distinctively messianic stamp to Western culture as a whole. This messianic shaping of culture has in some respects become more rather than less manifest in our increasingly post-Christian and secularized age. Marxism is the most evident and unsettling example. Bertrand Russell, atheist though he was, contended, not altogether humorously, that Marx adapted the biblical messianism to socialism in much the same way Augustine adapted it to Christendom. The dialectical materialism that governs the historical process corresponds to God, Marx to the messiah, the proletariat to the elect, the communist party to the church, and the revolution to the judgment day that hurls capitalists into the hell of dispossession and ushers the elect into a millennial age of secular bliss.[12] Marxism had universalistic pretensions on the horizontal plane of purely this-worldly history (that is, to the exclusion of existential depths or transcendental heights), but other modern movements of a less universalist kind, especially nationalistic ones, have also had a messianic shape. Poles, Swedes, Dutch, French, British Israelites, and, not least, Americans have thought of their nations as elect peoples with world-embracing missions. The beliefs involved are for the most part not even implicitly Christian and are often explicitly anti-Christian, yet they are grammatically analogous in their conceptual encoding to the messianic strands in biblical religion. Christian genes have been implanted in alien organisms with results that have sometimes been benign (so-called

"Western values" are often Christian in origin), but at their worst are even more disastrous, so it can be argued, than the opposite phenomenon, alien genes within Christianity.

The most frequently noted problem with de-messianizing the faith, as we shall see in the next section, is that it deprives the redemption for which Christians hope of its temporally futuristic and this-worldly social aspect, and reduces it to individualistic other-worldliness. Another and no less troubling consequence, however, is what happens to the messianic hopes that manage to survive. They percolate beneath the surface and then burst forth in untoward forms. Whenever messianism becomes apocalyptic, as it tends to do in times of turmoil, it cannot help but evoke expectations of Christ's imminent return. Classic Christology with its heavily incarnational emphasis is normally not overtly rejected by movements centered on such expectations, but it is marginalized. The cry, "Maranatha, come Lord Jesus" replaces even Peter's and Martha's twofold confession of messiahship and incarnate sonship as the operative core of Christ-centered devotion. This can lead on occasion to revitalization and mass missionary outreach, as is evident in the best of contemporary pentecostalism and evangelicalism, but the weakening of universalistic emphases and the growth of tribalistic parochialism is also possible. Outbreaks of violence are not unknown, though quietistic (and sometimes heroically pacifistic) withdrawals from society have been more common. One generalization seems to hold, however: messianisms have tended throughout church history to be as one-sided as the incarnational hegemonies that they oppose and, as could be expected of protest movements, much more divisive. So it was in second-century chiliasm, and so it is in much twenty-first–century premillennialism, not to mention the many outbursts of apocalyptic fervor in the nearly two thousand years in between. Messianism spawned in opposition to incarnationalism is dangerous.

These messianic eruptions are difficult to understand if one thinks of Christology deductively rather than discursively. In deductive models, the foundations are located, oxymoronically, at the top. Faith seeking understanding is imagined as starting with creeds and dogmas. These are then construed as premises or summaries from which the whole body of Christian teaching can be theologically derived and then transmitted to clergy and catechists who, in turn, instruct the laity. If this were the way Christian discourse operated, the messianic undercurrents and outbursts that we have been recalling would be unthinkable.

It makes more sense to think of community-forming Christologies as embedded in the religious discourse of the believing masses rather than in the theological formulations of the upper classes. They are sedimented in the scriptures the faithful recite in their liturgies, hear in their sermons, sing in their hymns, pray in their devotions, read in their Bibles, and, not least, enact in their conduct, in what once was called the "conversation" of the saints. The influence of reflectively formulated creeds, dogmas, and theology on the ebb and flow of this basic christological discourse may often be decisive, but sometimes the Christ-talk of the faithful pours forth in doctrinally unconstrained directions. Dogmatic developments, we recall, more generally follow than precede the *consensus fidelium:* the worship of Christ as God came long before the *homoousios*, and the cult of icons before the Seventh Ecumenical Council. It follows that dogmas are for the most part defensive rather than prescriptive: they originate in conflicts, and the Church seeks by defining them to exclude error rather than to stipulate the one and only right way to speak the truth.[13]

For those who think in this fashion of communally important Christologies as acquiring substance from below and being at most regulated from above, there is no mystery about outbursts of messianic enthusiasm in churches where messiahship has been neglected. Messianic discourse may become vacuously metaphorical; or, more positively expressed, its materially and temporally referential plain sense may be replaced by spiritual meanings. The eschatological new heaven and earth may be relocated outside of space and time in unchanging and eternal transcendence, while the Second Coming that inaugurates the fullness of the Kingdom is reduced to what every individual experiences when he or she encounters Jesus at death. Yet the bare bones of the messianic words remain present in the hymns (not least the Christmas hymns which celebrate incarnation) and in liturgy, not to mention scripture, and these words retain the possibility of being re-clothed in their plain sense and of flowering (or, less benignly, exploding) into messianic life.

How, then, should we assess this situation? It does not take the formal analysis with which we began to see that it is unhealthy. The analysis, however, makes possible a more differentiated description. The one-sidedly incarnational discourse that has dominated mainstream Christianity emphasizes the universality of Jesus at the expense of his singularity and, as far as redemption is concerned, stresses spiritualizing inwardness more than visible transformation. It abstracts the Savior and those he saves from the particularities of their historical and communal situations: salvation is conceived in terms that are both universalistic and individualistic, as a spiritual reality that is basically the same for all individuals everywhere. The universality of the Church as an institution (or, in subjectivizing incarnationalisms, as an invisible communion) is emphasized, but not its this-worldliness. In contrast to this, the one-sidedly messianic discourse that lurks beneath the mainstream surface and turbulently erupts from time to time lacks universality rather than singularity. The individual is lost in the communal, the universal in the tribal, and the spiritual in the material. Jesus Christ and the community that is his body is seen as an inner-worldly transforming or revolutionary force, if not in this age, then in the age to come. So far so good: it is almost universally agreed these days that the Church has been too other-worldly in the past. The downside, however, is that the messianism of those who are oppressed often, though not always, takes a violent turn, sometimes in this time between the times, and almost always in imagining the revenge of the saints in the last days. That is one reason that Revelation, a messianic book if there ever was one, has been problematic for the established churches. The conclusion seems irresistible that the conjoining of the two strands of christological discourse is required so that they can capitalize on each other's strengths, remedy each other's weaknesses, and correct each other's faults. The question is whether that reconciliation is possible.

IV

First I shall propose that there are no dogmatic barriers to reconciliation, and then, in the next and final section, comment on the current theological possibilities. Reconciliation on the fundamental and most important level, that of liturgy, sermons, hymns, extra-liturgical devotions, and the conversation of the saints, will be left to others and to other occasions.

The dogmatic objections to reconciliation can be over-ridden, but some more easily than others. Insofar as a dogmatic development is the product of situationally specific pastoral concerns, it need not be authoritative in relevantly different situations even while retaining its force in similar ones. Does not this apply to the great shift from messiahship to incarnation? Its beginnings were motivated by Paul's pastoral concern to bring the gospel to the gentiles, and we can plausibly speculate that he would have favored more emphasis on messiahship at later stages of the developments on which we have commented. He was, after all, adept in adapting the presentation of the gospel to the context, in becoming "all things to all men, that I might by all means save some," as he himself put it (1 Cor 9:22). Situationally formulated doctrinal decisions may be irrevocable, but their relevance is contextual.

Creeds and dogmas, however, may also have trans-situational relevance, and the central decisions of the councils of Nicaea I and Constantinople I in the fourth century and of Chalcedon in the fifth are prime candidates for this category. They are pivotal to the understanding of Jesus Christ, and by the universal consent of both Christians and non-Christians, there is no Christianity without him. Those decisions were intended to preserve Christian agreement on the basic christological confession of faith by settling unity-threatening controversies on issues that had not before been formulated but that have repeatedly and transculturally recurred ever since. They succeeded admirably. The mainstream of christological discourse that coalesced around these decisions now includes, not only the historic Eastern Orthodox, Roman Catholic, and Reformation traditions but also the hundreds of millions of conservative evangelicals and pentecostals who are multiplying especially in Africa, Asia, and Latin America. Many of these Christians profess no creed but the Bible, and yet their reading of scripture is guided, without their knowing it, by Nicaea's decision on the *homoousios* and Chalcedon's on the hypostatic union. The evidence that these professedly creedless Christians are so guided is that they are not in the least inclined to deny the affirmations when they hear them that the Son is one being with the Father and that Jesus Christ is both fully God and fully human. Whatever may be true of other dogmas, the relevance of these creeds seems thoroughly catholic, thoroughly transcultural.

Does this abiding and expansive relevance also apply to the omission of messiahship by these creeds? The Logos theologians of the early church did not, needless to say, deny what the New Testament says about Jesus as messiah, but it plays little or no part in their understanding of the person or work of Christ. They use it chiefly in arguing from prophecy for Christ's divinity and as evidence of Jewish culpability in rejecting him. Thus the absence of messiahship from the creeds can easily be construed as authoritatively implying that it is a dispensable attribution when it comes to understanding who Jesus is and what he does: the word "Christ" may legitimately be regarded as simply a proper name, and it is sufficient for the Church to limit its confession, as it appears to do when it recites the creed, to only half of that of Peter and Martha, viz., that Jesus is the incarnate son of the living God. If so, the reconciliation of the two strands of christological discourse is dogmatically impossible. Despite the need to bring them together that seems apparent from Christian history, the creed forbids that they be interwoven as coequals in ways consistent with the analysis with which this investigation started.

The issue stated in conceptual terms is whether the dispute-deciding affirmations of the creeds are separable or inseparable from the messianically inhospitable Logos-centered Christology from above that frames these affirmations. If they are separable, one can take their christological dogmatic decisions (which concerned incarnation not messiahship) as authoritative but not the messiah-omitting theological framework within which they were made. The affirmations can be combined with some other conceptual framework, with a different theological Christology, in which Jesus as also messiah is important and indispensable.

There are those, however, who contend that the dogmatic affirmations and the theological framework must be accepted or rejected together. In our day, it is chiefly critics of the classic creeds such as John Hick and Maurice Wiles and other contributors to, for example, *The Myth of God Incarnate*[14] who insist most strongly on the inseparability of affirmations and framework; they argue that because the particular Christology that frames the decisions is unacceptable ("unbelievable" is the word preferred), the decisions themselves must be rejected. Their complaint is essentially that of Loofs over a hundred years ago: the identification of the Son with the Logos detaches the Son from the historical person of Jesus Christ and turns Christology into mythology.[15] It is not concern for Jesus as messiah that motivates these rejectionists, but rather opposition to incarnation; I cite them because, if they are right, messianic Christologies are incompatible with creedal incarnationalism.

From the perspective of this essay, the presumed inseparability of the credal decisions from the particular Christology that frames them depends on the untenable deductive model of doctrine that I earlier outlined, a model that treats creeds and dogmas as premises or summaries of all that is to be believed. If, however, it is credal decisions on specific issues that are magisterially authoritative and not the conceptual frameworks, then silence on messiahship does not exclude but leaves room for messianically balanced or even unbalanced Christologies: messianic extremism is as credally permissible as the incarnational variety providing commitment to the fullness of the deity as well as humanity in Jesus Christ is maintained; and that is why neither chiliasm nor premillennialism have been officially anathematized. Unlike the picture of a closed dogmatic system that critics like to equate with credal orthodoxy, the historic doctrines of the Church, though vitally important, are rare and scattered points of orientation in a vast and open landscape full of dangers they do not warn against and of wonders of which they give no hint. There are, on this view, no dogmatic barriers to reconciling messiahship and incarnation.[16]

V

Yet efforts to unite the two strands of christological discourse are lacking. The problem, however, is no longer the neglect of the messianic strand. With the doubtful exception of the Joachimite outbreak in the Middle Ages,[17] messianism is now more widespread in the theological mainstream than at any time since the early church. Instead of integration into classic incarnational Christology from above, however, modern messianic Christology from below opposes it. Why this is the case needs explanation.

The collapse of incarnational hegemony that began at the time of the Reformation helped make the current messianic upsurge possible, but was not directly a cause. Undermining started in the sixteenth century with the rationalistic and scripturally literalistic attacks of the Socinians and other antitrinitarians against the catholic creeds. Defenders of the creeds, already estranged from classic hermeneutics by late-medieval developments, counterattacked with much the same proto-Enlightenment, univocist logic that their opponents utilized. They were not wholly unsuccessful: incarnationalism from above retained its dominance within the christological mainstream until well into the eighteenth century.

Its collapse became definitive, however, when historical-criticism, beginning in the seventeenth century with the likes of Spinoza and Simon, replaced proof-texting for and against Christologies from above by the question of whether it is possible to begin below with the Jesus of history and reach upward to the transcendent Christ of faith. If one does this, the central issue is no longer what the Bible or the early church affirm about the one Jesus Christ who was born, crucified, and buried and is now seated at the right hand of God, but rather what Jesus thought of himself in his days on earth. His consciousness of his messiahship or lack thereof became christologically crucial and long remained so.[18]

Yet although this development undermined incarnational hegemony, it was messianic only in a pickwickian sense. The messianic consciousness on which this modern discussion focused had little to do with the public role in human and cosmic history that scripture and tradition assigned to the messiah. Christologies constructed on the basis of Jesus' messianic consciousness owed more, it seems, to the philosophical turn to the subject from Descartes to Heidegger than to the search for the historical Jesus. They attributed Jesus' saving significance to what Schleiermacher called his God-consciousness, his inward awareness of the divine. This was so pure and powerful that it could serve as an inspiring stimulus and model of the experience of the divine available inwardly to everyone. That what Jesus was originally, everyone ultimately would be dependently, was guaranteed by the inevitability of human progress, the modern version of providential guidance. This inward authenticity that is the future of humanity was understood as expressible in outward language and behavior, but it is not dependent on nor assessable by anything external. In terms of our original diagram, the modern turn to the subject evoked an experience of divine-human union emerging vertically from the depths that is better analyzed in the vertical dimension as an individualistic incarnationalism from below and from within than as an outburst on the outer, horizontal, social level of hope for a messianic age or figure. An incarnational consciousness disguised under the name "messianic" replaced the ancient incarnationalism from above.[19]

This incarnationalism from below and within, however, is now also in decline for a variety of reasons. For one thing, although modern Christian inwardness is not a cause of anti-semitism, it is vulnerable to that disease. It is deeply anticommunal and antinomian and thus Judaism can become for it the epitome of an oppressive religion of external works-righteousness (to use Reformation categories that in their original intention were neither anticommunal nor antinomian). Furthermore, the question of Jesus' messianic consciousness has now largely disappeared from the biblical and theological agenda partly because, at least in anglophone

scholarship, agency is increasingly seen as a better category than consciousness for understanding personal identity, but also because of the
historical difficulty of establishing anything about anybody's consciousness and, most of all, as was mentioned earlier, because messiahship in
first-century Judaism is a concept too vague and multifaceted to have
much meaning apart from its specific applications. (In other words, it is
pointless to ask what messiahship signifies if predicated of Jesus apart
from his crucifixion and resurrection.)[20] Thus, as modern Christologies
of inwardness join Christologies from above on the discard heap of history, the way has opened in mainstream theology for the first time since
Joachamitism for plausibly horizontal (that is, public, social, and temporally futurist) messianisms. These also, however, as we shall see, are typically modern in their aversion to incarnationalism and their indifference
to reconciliation with it.

This messianism is dominated by what has come to be technically
called "the category of the messianic." In a German study of this category
in contemporary systematic theology, Ulrich H.J. Koertner[21] defines it
by reference to Gershom Scholem's well-known essay "The Messianic
Idea in Judaism." Scholem affirms that Judaism steadfastly maintains a
concept of messianic redemption as "occurring publicly and communally
on the stage of history; it is most decidedly located in the visible world,
without which visibility it cannot be conceived" [my translation].[22] When
described in these terms, it is not only possible for a theology to be messianic without a messiah, but it also need not be eschatological, much less
apocalyptic (although such characterizations are not to be excluded
despite Moltmann's predelictions to the contrary in reference to apocalypticism). Moreover, salvation as understood in most Christian theological movements in the last half century has affinities to what Scholem
describes. Theologies of hope, revolution, liberation whether Latin American, black, or feminist, together with political theology and the emerging ecological concerns also point to the public, this-worldly character
of God's saving work, and the beginnings of the same emphases go back
to the social gospel of liberal Protestantism in the nineteenth century.
The category of the messianic does not so much add content to these other
trends as give them a different and, after Auschwitz, an arguably more
believable shape. In contrast to the past, neither Christian nor worldly
optimism is possible; and although activist Christians continue to think
of themselves as called upon to be "cooperators" (sometimes even

"co-creators") with God in the struggles for righteousness (summed up by the World Council of Churches in the acronym JPIC, standing for "Justice, Peace and the Integrity of Creation"), they now more fully acknowledge the ghastly sins and failures of Christianity and of secular progressivisms. Yet even in their hopelessness, their seeming pointlessness, struggles for righteousness can be harbingers, foretastes, and anticipations of the messianic age.

Yet praiseworthy though the realism implied by the category of the messianic may be, this realism is deficient from the perspective of "The Idea of the Messianic" in two respects. First, for rabbinic Judaism (though not for zealots) human beings do not "cooperate with God" in bringing in the messianic Kingdom; that is entirely God's work however much he may use human activity to further his purposes. Second, and in relation to this, there is a radical discontinuity between salvation in this present world and the messianic fullness of salvation in the world to come. To lack these emphases is to be unrealistic even when, as in the category of the messianic, righteousness and redemption are rightly conceived as primarily communal and public rather than individual and inward. There is no evidence either empirical or biblical that human struggles for righteousness contribute to the coming of the Kingdom; to suppose that they do is to attribute to them an occult property. Moreover, this occultness diminishes the visibility of the Kingdom itself when these struggles in our unredeemed world are said to be the beginnings or first fruits of redemption. It is as if the resurrection begins in rather than reverses the crucifixion. The category of the messianic, it seems, is only marginally better than other forms of Christian realism: it also lacks the "irrevocable commitment to the concrete" that Scholem attributes to Judaism.

Whether emphasizing Jesus' messiahship helps overcome this deficiency depends on how Jesus is conceived. The "pale Galilean" of one-sidedly incarnational inwardness obviously intensifies rather than cures Christian abstractness, but the same is true of Jesus the social reformer or revolutionary without incarnational height and depth. What is needed is a fully canonical Jesus, one that draws from both Testaments and depicts him in the round both horizontally and vertically.

Some familiar emphases in Dietrich Bonhoeffer's *Letters and Papers from Prison*,[23] are helpful in this connection. While his concern was not specifically with messiahship, the neglect of the public and communal dimension of salvation definitely was. The problem that troubled him, it will be recalled, was "religiousness," by which he chiefly meant something very much like the spiritualizing inwardness of the one-sided incarnationalisms generated from below by the modern turn to the subject (although it also embraced, for example, the "works righteousness" condemned by the Reformers). The solution he urged on Christians is to turn to the Old Testament; the New Testament by itself is misleading. When read apart from its Old Testament background, it can easily be twisted into a source and defense of the very religiousness that is the danger. This return to the Old Testament, furthermore, must be holistic, not fragmentary. It does not consist of simply picking favorite portions, as did the Social Gospel with its focus on the prophets' protests against injustice, or as do some black and some Latin American liberation theologies in their justifiable but at times too exclusive emphasis on the exodus story. Rather, Christians should saturate themselves in the piety of the Old Testament as a unified whole, and for this purpose, the Psalms, Bonhoeffer believed, are of central importance.[24] When it comes to the understanding of what God wants human beings to be, the Old Testament is fundamental and the New Testament is commentary; while crucial for interpretive purposes, it is not sufficient in itself. Although it is now an indispensable guide to the reading of what for the first Christians was their only Bible, it is incapable of being rightly construed as an independent body of writings.

Speaking of the Christian reappropriation of the Old Testament in Jerusalem's proximity (as this lecture originally did) adds urgency to the need to say something about how this can be done without expropriating it. Can Christians claim the Old Testament as their own without denying the legitimacy of Jewish interpretations of the common text, read as the Tanach, even when they contradict Christian interpretations of the same text, read as the Old Testament? It would seem that the only way this can be done, the only way to appropriate without expropriating, is to let the contradictions remain unsolved while awaiting their resolution at the coming of the messiah. There is a precedent for this in the talmudic practice of setting irreconcilable rabbinic opinions side by side on the same page without a hint of harmonization. This is a difficult art, but it is required of Christians in the present situation by a double and seemingly impossible imperative: first, the now official teaching of major Christian bodies, including the Roman Catholic Church, is that God has not revoked his covenant with Israel (ergo, Christians are forbidden to steal the Bible from the Jews as they long attempted to do); second, Christians need to turn to the Old Testament more intensely than they have ever done in order better to understand salvation, and inseparable from that, their Savior, Jesus Christ (ergo, the biblical text they share with the Jews is also their own).[25]

Because Savior and salvation are inseparable, the transformation of the Christian understanding of salvation that Bonhoeffer proposes would also deeply affect the interpretation of messiahship. Old Testament promises are related to New Testament fulfillment, not as shadow to reality, as has been traditionally supposed, but as substance or materiality to form. The materiality of the content imparted by Israel's scriptures to the eviscerated notions of redemption drawn from the New Testament when read in isolation from the Old can help restore the messianic concreteness and universality of Christian hope. Christians will be in a position to understand the intersections of the horizontal and vertical dimensions better than ever before and to learn what it means to confess Jesus as the messiah of Israel (and of all peoples) no less than the incarnate Son of God.

This is the hope that concludes this essay. Unfolding it would plunge us into the most controversial issues now roiling this center and cauldron of the world that is Jerusalem. As far as I can see, however, a Christian turn to the Old Testament for the sake of messianic fullness in the understanding of salvation and the Savior, while as susceptible to ideological manipulation as any other theological move in this sinful world, is not by itself to the political advantage of any of the conflicting parties. What we must hope and pray is that the reconciliation of messiahship and incarnation in Christian understanding will contribute to justice and peace kissing each other throughout the world and most especially in the land that Christians have long called holy.

NOTES

1. Viz., the last *imam*. Werblowsky cites Islam as an example of a "'morphologically' (or typologically, viz., phenomenologically) non-messianic religion" and attributes the strength of messianism in its post-Quaranic traditions to the fact that it "received its original impulse from two messianic religions."

He rightly remarks that there seems "no getting away from the fact that although 'messianic' type movements or ideologies have occurred throughout the world, they seem to be especially characteristic of the Jewish and Christian traditions, and of acculturative situations in which these traditions play a direct or indirect role" (R. J. Z. Werblowsky, "Jewish Messianism in Comparative Perspective," in *Messiah and Christos*, ed. I. Gruenwald [Tübingen: Mohr, 1992], 7–8, 2–3). For a fuller discussion of Islamic messianism that includes reference to Jesus' "second coming" as understood by Moslems, see H. Busse, "Messianismus und Eschatologie im Islam," *Jahrbuch für Biblische Theologie* 8 (1993): 273–90. The theme of this entire volume is "Der Messias."

2. Louis O. Mink, *Historical Understanding* (Ithaca and London: Cornell University Press, 1987), 38, 50, 184.

3. The ontological reason it is dispensable, as Aristotle might put it, is that its objects of study, relations, have no reality of their own while the terms which they relate do have such reality independent of any particular relation. Motherhood cannot even be conceived except as a relation between a mother and child, while the mother and child are each many things, many realities, beside their relation to each other. The terms of the relation can be studied in their entirety by everything from physics to theology, including the very real and extremely varied effects motherhood has on mothers and children, without ever adverting to its purely relational attributes, such as its non-transitiveness, with which disciplines such as logic and grammar are concerned. That, to repeat, is why the second-order study (not the first-order practice) of theological grammar is dispensable: theology as the reflective study of the beliefs and realities that faith holds dear can, in most circumstances, get along very well without it.

4. This diagram, it must be stressed, should not be thought of as a model to be imitated: Christologies are not to be measured by whether they equally and unitedly emphasize messiahship and incarnation, but by whether they follow the rules relevant to the particular aspects, problems, and contexts that they address. The one-sidedly incarnational Christology of the creeds, to anticipate later discussions, may exemplify right usage in reference to only part of the grammar of Christology, but this is not in itself a defect. Good theology speaks to particular audiences in particular situations for particular purposes; its aim is not to exhibit the entirety of the grammatical resources of Christology (that, in any case, are known only by God).

5. Nils Dahl, "The Crucified Messiah," reprinted in a collection of his essays entitled *The Crucified Messiah* (Minneapolis, Minn.: Augsburg, 1974), 10–36.

6. Martin Hengel, "Jesus, der Messias Israels," in *Messiah and Christos*, ed. I. Gruenwald (Tübingen: Mohr, 1992), 167.

7. The authors I have cited in effect agree, it seems to me, that the first-century idea of the messianic is "vague" in the technical sense I have in mind (though, needless to say, they do not use the term): it is neither confused nor ambiguous, and it cannot be clarified or made more determinate (except by

citing examples) without losing its general and powerfully evocative applicability. Wittgenstein's "family resemblance" generalizations are similar, but Charles Peirce more fully developed the notion of vagueness I have in mind. It applies, it should be mentioned, not only to messiahship but also to incarnation: both concepts are vague and cannot be defined (e.g., by species and difference) without losing their usefulness. Thus, without the category of vagueness, this essay could not be written, although I realized this only after I had finished. In my own thinking on these issues, I have drawn from (and, I fear, misused) Peter Ochs, *Peirce, Pragmatism, and the Logic of Scripture* (Cambridge: Cambridge University Press, 1998), esp. chap. 7.

8. William Harbury, *Messianism and the Cult of Christ* (London: SCM Press, 1998).

9. Jacob Neusner, *The Incarnation of God: The Character of Divinity in Formative Judaism* (Philadelphia, Pa.: Fortress, 1988).

10. Michael Wyschogrod, "Christology: The Immovable Object," *Religion and Intellectual Life* 3 (1986): 80.

11. For what remains the best historical study of the blindness of modern biblical scholarship to the literary aspects of scripture, see Hans Frei, *The Eclipse of Biblical Narrative* (New Haven, Conn.: Yale University Press, 1974).

12. Bertrand Russell, *History of Western Philosophy* (1946; reprint, London: George Allen, 1971), 361.

13. The understanding of dogma expressed in these remarks is developed at length in my *The Nature of Doctrine* (Philadelphia, Pa.: Westminster, 1984).

14. *The Myth of God Incarnate*, ed. John Hick (Philadelphia, Pa.: Westminster, 1977).

15. F. Loofs, "Christologie: Kirchenlehre," in *Realencyklopädie für Protestantische Theologie und Kirche*, ed. Johann Jakob Herzog, 3rd ed., vol. 4 (Leipzig: J.H. Hinrichs, 1898) 16–56, at p. 35.

16. It should be noted that the distinction I am trading on in this discussion between decisions, on the one hand, and the framing of issues, on the other, is not the least innovative. It is a variation on the distinction between the substance and form of doctrine pontifically enunciated, though not originated, by John XXIII at Vatican II, and it is a commonplace among theologians engaged in ecumenical dialogues. To deny it is, in effect, to absolutize the half-truth that "the medium is the message" and to be unable to account for the possibility of saying the same thing in different ways.

17. The exception is doubtful because the reign of God awaited by the Joachimites, although formally messianic in the sense being temporally future on the horizontal plane of "this-worldly" history, was concretely pictured as the age of the Spirit rather than of the Son, the messiah.

18. According to Wolfhart Pannenberg, the name "Christology from below" was first proposed by a disciple of Ritschl, F.H.R. Frank, in 1888, but the theological program the name implies was already laid out by Semler in 1777 when

he "replaced the doctrinal section on Christ's person by a chapter on his history that identified his messiahship as the true theme of the doctrine concerning him." See *Systematic Theology* I (Grand Rapids, Mich.: Eerdmans, 1994), 279f.

19. To suggest, as I have done, that consciousness Christology is more accurately spoken of as inverted incarnationalism than as messianic is not to accuse its proponents of bad faith or of heresy. The Christology that Schillebeeckx, for example, builds on the "abba experience" that is his version of Jesus' messianic consciousness has sufficient formal similarities to the Chalcedonian doctrine of the union of the two natures to make his claim to credal orthodoxy arguable. Moreover, the appeal of such incarnationalisms from below to modern sensibilities is great; it is plausible to suppose that millions of people remained Christian because of them during their heyday. That heyday, however, seems to have passed; the search for authentic inwardness has diffused into less and less explicitly Christian spiritualities and, as we shall now see, those whose concerns are more public and social than private and individualistic naturally prefer objectivizing understandings of biblical messianism to the subjectivizing ones characteristic of inverted incarnationalism.

20. Cf. notes 5–8 *supra* for references to supporting literature.

21. Ulrich H. J. Koertner, "Theologia messianica: Zur Kategorie des Messianischen in der gegenwärtigen dogmatischen Diskussion," *Jahrbuch für Biblische Theologie* 8 (1993): 347–70. Although the perspective of Koertner's study differs from that of the present essay, it is the most comprehensive discussion I know of the trend of thought with which it deals. None of the authors that it treats are interested in integrating their work with credal incarnationalism. Moltmann is closest to being an exception, but it is doubtful that he really is. He is completing a five-volume work of what he calls messianic theology, and the third volume, published a decade or so ago, is ex professo a messianic Christology. It keeps the door to accommodation with the incarnational tradition slightly ajar in that Moltmann thinks of himself as basically orthodox in his trinitarian and christological affirmations; yet his messianism in effect replaces incarnationalism. He wishes, for example, to reinterpret the tradition in terms of what has come to be called "Spirit Christology," but whether this as he develops it does justice to either the messianic or incarnational strand in scripture and tradition seems to me doubtful, though I am open to correction by others who know his position better than I do.

As for the other major Christology which professes to be messianic, that of Paul van Buren, Jesus is messiah only of the gentiles and not also of the Jews: the universalism that is integral to the incarnational claim has been abandoned. A third professedly messianic theology, that of Friedrich-Wilhelm Marquardt, I know only through the secondary literature, but it appears that for him there is no messianic age or figure, not even Jesus Christ, but only a "messianism of temporality." Time becomes messianically eventful ("ein messianisches Zeitgeschehens") in the history of God's dealings with Israel and with the nations.

While Jesus is crucial to God's involvement with the nations at least up to this point in history, he is messiah of neither Israel nor of the gentiles but is best spoken of simply as "the Jew." While Moltmann's position can be thought of, though perhaps implausibly, as not rejecting incarnational discourse and thus leaving more room for it than he himself explores, these other two messianic Christologies unambiguously exclude incarnation and its universalizing power; they end up limiting the attribution of messiahship to Jesus in one instance, and denying it in the other. In the latter case, that of Marquardt, the result is the oddity of a professedly Christian messianism without a messiah.

22. Gershom Scholem, "The Messianic Idea in Judaism," 347. The English translation of the essay from which this quotation is taken is in *The Messianic Idea in Judaism and Other Essays in Jewish Spirituality* (London, 1971).

23. This book exists in many editions. While my use of Bonhoeffer is different, I owe the idea of appealing to him at this point in the argument to R. Kendall Soulen, *The God of Israel and Christian Theology* (Minneapolis, Minn.: Fortress, 1996).

24. Dietrich Bonhoeffer, *Das Gebetbuch der Bibel* (MBK-Verlag, 1966).

25. *Christianity in Jewish Terms* contains two responses to the Jewish contributors to that volume in which I deal at length with this topic (ed. Tikva Frymer-Kensky, David Novak, Peter Ochs, David Sandmel, Michael A. Signer [Boulder, Colo.: Westview Press, 2000], 106–113; 357–66).

CHAPTER FIVE

Lectio Divina and Arguing over Jesus

An Ascetic for Christological Rebukes

JAMES J. BUCKLEY

A Story of Mutual Rebuke

Jesus' question "Who do you say that I am?" is answered with Peter's famous confession of Jesus as the Christ (Mt 16:16; Mk 8:29; Lk 9:20). This particular Jesus is Israel's story brought to its christic or messianic end—its ultimate, comprehensive *telos* and *eschaton*. If we have followed Peter's answer from what has gone before, his confession might raise questions such as "If Jesus is indeed Messiah of God, what is the relationship between Jesus and the God of Israel? What are the relationships as well between these Jewish disciples and the rest of Israel, along with all humanity?" But Jesus' response bypasses such questions. Instead, Jesus rebuked—"sternly ordered" (Mt 16:20; Mk 8:30; Lk 9:21)—the disciples to speak to no one about this, or him.[1] Jesus' reason for this classically perplexing rebuke is not an appeal to Israel's past but to Israel's future—to his own future passion and death and resurrection (Mt 16:21; Mk 8:31; Lk 9:22). The One confessed always exceeds the one confessing. But Peter's subsequent rebuke of Jesus in Matthew and Mark wants none of this future for Jesus (Mt 16:22; Mk 8:32). In turn, Jesus' rebuke of Peter in the same two synoptic gospels ups the stakes, for what is at issue is not only Jesus' future but the disciples'. That is, after rebuking Peter in turn,

Jesus speaks ascetical words to the disciples and/or the crowds: "if any would come after me, let him deny himself and take up his cross and follow me. For whoever saves his life will lose it, and whoever loses his life for my sake will find it" (Mt 16:25; Mk 34–35; Lk 9:23–24). Once again, Jesus seeks response, this time in deed as well as word. And we know the story of Peter's later denial and rebuke of Jesus—as well as Peter's later ministry in the pentecostal community.

It is this pattern of mutual rebuke that I wish to raise up for our consideration. What began as a seemingly harmless catechetical question and answer session ends much more ominously. I doubt that most of us church-people are positioned much differently than Peter is at this point in the story, stumbling our way toward death and resurrection. We rightly say our faith in one breath, and in the next deny it—often in the name of guarding it, as if protecting Jesus from his own death and resurrection. Jesus here teaches, however, that what we are really guarding or protecting is ourselves. This self-protective denial calls for rebuke. But what is the relationship between Jesus and the disciples, between Head and members, in the midst of such rebuke? Whether the milder mandate not to speak or the identification of Peter with Satan in Matthew and Mark, how is it that Jesus' rebuke disciplines without dispersing the disciples?

Answering such questions would involve developing "an *ascetic* understanding of Christ and the church," i.e., an understanding of the relationship between Jesus and the disciples where Christ disciplines the very body which remains his.[2] That a *rebuking* or disciplining of the disciples is required is obvious from this and any number of other gospel incidents. That the rebuked body *remains* Christ's is something that might be clear in Jesus' praise of Peter in Matthew, although it emerges most clearly only later in the story, when Jesus becomes the one rebuked on the cross and vindicated in the resurrection. In any case, this essay is, if only indirectly, a contribution to such an *ascetic* understanding of the relations between Christ and the disciples.

I say "indirectly" because my central interest in most of this essay is less in Jesus' rebukes of us than our rebukes of each other over the identity of the One who here rebukes Peter. Confession of Jesus Christ in what we might call "late modern" theology seems more than matched by rebukes, even as we also avoid such christological rebuke for fear of what such asceticism might do to the body of Christ. The rebukes on which I shall focus are such theological disputes—in particular, a set of arguments ingredient in debates between Karl Rahner, Hans Urs von Balthasar, and some of their critics. These rebukes have sometimes been relatively mild, like Jesus' initial rebuke of Peter after his true confession. But they have sometimes also been vehement, Balthasar's reproach of Rahner at least once approaching Jesus' anathema of Peter.[3] Their critics have exhibited a similar range of rebukes. The relatively mild rebukes of Rahner by Metz and liberation theology are countered by the more massive criticisms of Rahner by Milbank and "radical orthodoxy"—even as the latter offer more sympathetic criticisms of Balthasar.[4] I will not claim to offer "the" interpretation of this complex tradition of mutual rebuke. I will be interested in it as an example of late modern christological controversy. I am going to propose a way that we can locate these rebukes in the context of the larger Christian community—to suggest how disciples of Christ can rebuke each other within the same communion of saints. Such is how this synoptic incident of mutual rebuke helps us diagnose our rebukes of each other in such contemporary christological controversies.

Disciples and Crowds

To explain what I mean by such an ascetic of controversy and rebuke among ourselves, I begin with an important distinction related to the larger context of the synoptic incident. Christians have, for most of their history, professed (as Bruce Marshall has put it) that the particular Jesus whose life and death and resurrection are narrated in the gospels has universal and unsurpassable significance for the whole world.[5] Late modern Christology, I shall soon suggest, is, like one of Thomas Kuhn's unfinished puzzles,[6] constituted by a set of questions arising out of this claim—questions about Jesus' particularity, universality, and unsurpassability. However, our own time has challenged that claim and its attendant questions—challenged the puzzle in ways that sometimes abandon it, sometimes retain the frame of the puzzle but put the pieces in the oddest places. The challenges come from moderns like Immanuel Kant who hope for a more universal and perhaps even unsurpassable *humanitas* than God incarnate in a first-century Jew can provide. But they also come from postmoderns like Nietzsche who despair, with pride or indifference, in the face of humanity's certain death. And there are also the partly traditional, partly newly formulated challenges of Muslims, now augmented by those of Hinduism, Buddhism, and what some still call "other religions." Surely here there are controversies and rebukes that create their own set of issues.

We can hardly ignore such rebukes, or make our Christology invulnerable to them. But they are not the focus of the question from Jesus that forms the agenda here and now. Recall that, prior to asking his question of the disciples, Jesus had asked "Who do *the crowds* (or the *people*) say that I am?" (Mt 16:13; Mk 8:27; Lk 9:18). The reported answers of the crowd all fell short of Peter's later profession of Jesus as Israel's messianic *telos*. But, when told these answers, Jesus did not refute or rebuke them or the crowds. Instead, he used them as the occasion to challenge the disciples with our central question, "Who do *you* say that I am?" I emphasize that the disciples could hardly forget or ignore these crowds, any more than Jesus does. Recall that Mark's and probably Luke's Jesus (although not Matthew's) tells the disciples *and* the crowd to take up their cross and follow him (Mk 8:34; Lk 9:23). Neither can we disciples respond to Jesus' question to us as disciples without bearing in mind and heart the crowds of friends and relatives, members of other religions and of none at all who would not hear themselves addressed as disciples in this question. But neither can the disciples use the crowds as an excuse to ignore their own betrayals and denials and other rebukes. We need to let judgment begin with the household of God (1 Pt 4:17). The rebukes of our own crowds will periodically emerge in what follows. But my eye will be on patterns of rebukes among the disciples.

Lectio divina, questio divina

I have been making points and raising questions *about* a passage from the gospels. The points thus far made—that this is a story of christological rebuke as much as christological confession, ascetically directed more to the disciples than the crowds—presume a certain reading (a *lectio*) of a gospel scene, a reading that moves backward to previous scenes and forward to subsequent scenes in the larger biblical narrative. The first step in the ascetic I propose is to consider the nature of the theological reading that generated the question of an ascetic for christological rebuke in the first place.

"Theological reading" is how I shall temporarily translate what has traditionally been called *lectio divina*. By *lectio divina* I shall mean the traditional recommendation, as reiterated at Vatican II, that "prayer should accompany the reading of holy scripture, so that it becomes a dialogue between God and the human reader; for 'when we pray, we talk to him: when we read the divine word, we listen to him'."[7] But this is a necessary rather than sufficient description of *lectio divina*. That is, De Lubac, McGinn, and others have told a story of the increasing disengagement of *lectio divina* from *quaestio divina* in the Middle Ages—a disengagement to the detriment of both, for "theological reading" without "theological questions" became "uncritical" reading, and "theological questions" without "theological reading" became unformed by the in-Spired Word.[8] The recent recovery of *lectio divina* is surely in part a response to the way scholastic (or, moderns might say, academic) arguments—historical, philosophical, theological—have eclipsed the colloquium between God and persons at the center of *lectio divina*. But this literature only too often does not ask how we can retrieve *lectio divina* without reenacting the very problems with *lectio divina* that emerged in the Middle Ages. What shall we say to those who rebuke *lectio divina* as uncritical reading, or those engaged in *lectio divina* who think that theological questions are scholastic or academic?

This essay bears on that question, although only relative to the specific set of christological issues mentioned earlier. There are mutually illuminating analogies, I shall propose, between what I earlier called the late modern christological puzzle and certain features of *lectio divina*. Developing "an ascetic for christological rebuke" is pursuing these analogies. What I shall propose is that, while *lectio divina* provides the setting for disciplining the mutual rebukes of the late modern christological puzzle, the christological puzzle raises the theological questions that *lectio divina* needs if it is not to become a kind of hermeneutical pietism that presumes we already have the answers for the most important questions for disciples of Christ (e.g., "Who do you say that I am?").

Jesus Christ, I have said, is a particular person of universal and unsurpassable significance for the world. Analogously, I shall now propose, *lectio divina* is the reading of particular texts comprehensively, and prayerfully. It is by considering arguments over this Jesus in the context of *lectio divina* thus construed that we have the beginnings of an ascetical context for christological rebukes.

If space permitted, I would begin with the analogy between the particularity of Jesus and the particularity of the scriptural (canonical) texts.
There is a clear divide—and therefore abundant room for mild as well as
severe rebuke—between those who employ something like what Rahner
calls "a method of differentiation" for reading scriptural texts (where
texts are divided into their stages of composition, with varying authority
given to distinct stages)⁹ and Balthasar's insistence that scripture is part
of a "theodramatic" whole whereby the Word journeys among us, "proceeding once for all along the path from the earthly Jesus to the exalted
Christ—and yet, in the Holy Spirit, it is new at every moment for everyone who hears it."¹⁰ However, the rebukes that might be issued on this
score are analogous to differences within the New Testament itself—
for example, Luke's differentiation of the strata that go into his story
(Lk 1:1–4) and John's beginning with *the* Word who became flesh and
lived among us rather than Luke's differentiated strata (Jn 1). There is
no doubt that there is space for mutual rebuke on this issue, but there are
two other issues on which the rebukes are even more serious and which
provide a better focus for christological ascesis.

Jesus' Catholicity and Occasion-Comprehensive Scriptural Performance

Part of the Christian consensus that I mentioned earlier is that the Jesus
narrated in the gospels is a particular person of universal (or catholic or
comprehensive) importance for all the world, particularly the poor and
afflicted. Analogously, I shall here propose, *lectio divina* is not simply a kind
of reading we do on specific occasions but is what I shall call "occasion-
comprehensive performance," including reading by the illiterate. Let me
explain.

Jesus' universal significance is for the powerful as well as the powerless, for he scatters the powerful and raises up the lowly (Lk 1:52). But
the claim that the *particular* Jesus is of *universal* significance makes for an
often noted set of rebukes between Balthasar and Rahner.¹¹ Rahner argues that the comprehensive or universal significance of Jesus means that
there must be general patterns of experience that found, ground, or at
least correlate with the particular person of Jesus—for Rahner, our transcendental *Ausschau* or "lookout" for someone like Jesus.¹² This is the sort

of claim that troubles Balthasar. Once we seek some such general pattern of experience to ground or found the significance of the particularity of Jesus Christ, we have abstracted from the moment of Christian witness and made it possible to prescind from the particular Jesus who asks the question "Who do you say that I am?" The general pattern in which we might seek to "ground" Christology, I should now add, does not have to be transcendental as it is for Rahner. It might be more social or political, more liturgical or mystical. In all these cases, for Balthasar, the particular Jesus of the gospel drama thoroughly reshapes all such general patterns that found or correlate with the crucified and risen Christ, who is our place-taker in life and death. Rahner's counter-rebuke is: how, then, can we bring the particular Jesus to bear on our lives, comprehensively?

What can be said about this argument, this set of rebukes? I suggest that a certain understanding of *lectio divina* can set a context for disciplining this question—*lectio divina* as what I have called, borrowing a notion developed by William A. Christian, Sr., for other ends, "occasion-comprehensive" performance.[13] Here is what I mean. *Lectio divina* is not just explicating texts but (as Nicholas Lash has put it) "performing" them, using them for myriad ends.[14] That is, we use or perform scriptures not only on specific occasions (e.g., during the liturgy, in private devotions, in theological arguments, and so forth) but also comprehensively, throughout our lives. In this sense, *lectio divina* is not only "occasion-specific" but also "occasion-comprehensive" performance of scripture. Scriptural performance is not only done one by one but also together, much as "Who do you say that I am?" was addressed to the disciples in their irreducible individuality *and* solidarity. We could expand the ends of performance even further. We read theologically to pray in private and proclaim the scriptures at worship, to exalt the lowly and bring down the mighty. *Lectio divina* will be done differently by and with the educated and uneducated, adults and children, Christian and Jew and Greek, rich and poor. It is scripture thus used "in the life of the church" that is held in no less reverence (as Vatican II puts it) than the Lord's own eucharistic body,[15] the fully embodied *Sitz im Leben* of scriptures. Engaging in such performances takes different passions and virtues in irreducibly different readers and users of scriptures.

However, at this point, there are rebukes to *lectio divina* analogous to the christological rebukes Balthasar and Rahner have of each other. Just as there are controversies and rebukes over the texts of *lectio divina* (e.g., shall we read them as differentiated and/or dramatic wholes?), so also there are disputes over whether and how these texts are best performed comprehensively—not only performed in the eucharistic liturgy but also performed in our affectional lives as haughty or disconsolate persons, our political lives as powerful and powerless, our economic lives as rich and poor, our academic lives as historians and philosophers and literary critics, and so forth. Out of this welter of controversies and occasions for mutual rebuke, let me mention just two examples—one challenging a specific occasion of such performance, the other challenging the whole notion of "comprehensive" scriptural performance.

The first rebuke is this. *Lectio divina*, I have said, is theological reading of scriptural texts not simply on one occasion but at all times, comprehensively. Now someone like Karl Rahner would grant that scripture is one of the ways God's revelation is mediated in history, even a preeminent way (*norma non normata*). But it is only one of those ways.[16] Insofar as *lectio divina* is taken to include the occasion-comprehensive performance of scripture, Rahner might argue, it is or seems to absorb our natural lives, to be or become alien to our ordinary experience. In Rahner's technical terms, this sort of *lectio divina* seems to give categorial revelation a wrong kind of preeminence over transcendental revelation—analogous to the worries Rahner also has about "a too narrowly Christological approach" to theology generally.[17] But the criticism does not have to be put in these terms. Taking a page from theologies of the poor and afflicted, we could give Rahner's criticism a different twist. *Lectio divina* (we could say) is still "reading," a practice engaged in by educated Christians usually far from the illiteracy that is the fate of most of the world (including most Christians). Among Christians alone, most disciples of Christ are not readers (theological or otherwise), and never have been. *Lectio divina* can never, this counterargument goes, be performed comprehensively—except by the few, the relatively well educated, and the relatively rich. Whether we worry over scripture's "categoreality" or *lectio divina*'s seemingly "elitist" preoccupations, this counterargument implies that *lectio divina* is and at most only should be occasion-specific, not occasion-comprehensive.

This is an understandable rebuke that I need to address. *Lectio divina* is, I have so far presumed but not emphasized, a communal enterprise—a set of practices that particular members of the community engage in, in different ways. Precisely because *lectio divina* is practiced comprehensively, it is not necessary for an individual or even most members of a local church to know how to read to engage in this practice. Indeed, people who *do* know how to read may *not* be able to perform scripture comprehensively, particularly if they are readers reading for self-satisfying or self-devouring ends. As Paul Griffiths puts it, in contrast to such "consumerist" readers, "[r]eligious readers, paradoxically, need not know how to read."[18] Surely some members of the community must know how to read (e.g., how to pick up scriptures and read them out loud to a community), but not everyone does. "Lector" is an order or ministry of the Church—but only one of the *minor* orders, or ministries.

I do think the Church should encourage universal literacy in particular cultures, even at the risk of creating more consumerist readers. The abuse of reading does not destroy its use. But my point here is not to argue for such universal literacy. In fact, the goal of such comprehensive literacy is not to be confused with the theological literacy that is not simply reading scriptures but performing them comprehensively, consuming them sweet and bitter like Ezekiel (Ez 3:1–3) or John (Rv 10:10). Here I touch upon, only to leave unsettled, some crucial issues with regard to the occasion-comprehensive performance of scripture—issues Catholics know as one aspect of relating nature and grace. That is, how does *lectio divina* exceed and perfect without destroying *lectio humana*, especially the humanity of those who are poor or in any way afflicted—and here I mean those who cannot read? This raises important pastoral questions about how to teach the story of Jesus to Jew and Greek, male and female, slave and free—questions about the theological pragmatics of the Church's missionary activity, in its various intermingled stages, as we seek theological literacy in our local churches and the Church universal. But my point has been more abstract. The pastoral practice of *lectio divina* is occasion-comprehensive performance in theologically specific ways—ways that, for all their common ground with reading as a human practice, have their own comprehensively specific shape.

A second sort of rebuke to my claim that *lectio divina* involves the occasion-comprehensive performance of scripture is that it embodies an unacceptable "scriptural pragmatism," reducing texts and their Holy Inspirer to their uses by human communities. There are different versions of this rebuke. But consider how Balthasar might put it. Balthasar's *Theodrama* is a study of the divine drama starting from "the model of the theater" rather than "secular, social activity."[19] In the Romantic aesthetic tradition Balthasar sometimes cites, dramas are distinguished from the "epic" of Enlightened history as well as personal expressions of "poetic or lyric" faith.[20] One contrast between epic/lyric and drama is that the former are comprehensive or universal—either socially (epic) or personally (lyric), politically or mystically—whereas the theater's drama particularizes such universal performance without (so Balthasar claims) sacrificing its comprehensiveness. But (Balthasar's rebuke might go) what I have called occasion-comprehensive performance combines the mistakes of both liberation theology's epic comprehensiveness and transcendental theology's lyric comprehensiveness—the common mistake being that scriptures are reduced to their mystical or political uses, uses by transcendental-categorial subjects of liberal democracies and/or by the poor and afflicted of those same democracies or even more oppressive circumstances. In still other words, occasion-comprehensive performance of scripture (this rebuke might go) neglects the occasion-specific performance essential to *lectio divina* (and traditional ascetics): the prayer that would have some translate the Latin *lectio divina* as "prayerful reading."

With the mention of prayer we are finally getting to the deepest theological ingredients of the description of *lectio divina* with which I began. A brief response to the charge of scriptural pragmatism (as I have called it) is a convenient transition to a second analogy between Christology and *lectio divina*. There is, I hope Balthasar could grant, no reason Christians cannot use pragmatic gold, suitably distinguished from its dross, like Israel plundering jewelry and clothing from the Egyptians (Ex 3:22; 12:36). But the question is how to do this. Peter Ochs has proposed that a "Scriptural pragmatism" (with a capital "S") embracing Jewish and Christian readers is not only or primarily a subspecies of a more general "scriptural pragmatism."[21] Indeed, if Ochs is right, one of the theological weaknesses of American pragmatists—in the days when at least some of them would call themselves theists—is that they did not seem to recognize that occasion-comprehensive performance (including their own) is always enacted by specific communities—Jewish or Christian or pragmatist or other. Thus, the theist Peirce does not seem to notice that his "God" is (just?) a word that comes from a linguistically shaped tradition neither Jewish nor Christian but "theist."[22] For those who insist that how we name God (or how "God" is a proper name) is the crucial determinant of how we engage in *lectio divina*, there can be no reduction of *lectio divina* to its performance, no matter how occasion-comprehensive. In fact, I will insist on this when I momentarily turn to the third and final moment of *lectio divina*.

The rejoinder to this rebuke, in still other words, is that *lectio divina* can indeed be most appropriately translated "prayerful reading," before and to God. But, if so, we must at the same time recall the biblical mandate to "pray always," comprehensively (Lk 18:1; 21:36; 1 Thes 5:17; Eph 6:18)—not simply in the theater or in personal and liturgical prayer but through-out our personal and political lives. As Origen famously put it, "the only way we can accept the command to 'pray constantly' as referring to a real possibility is by saying that the entire life of the saint taken as a whole is a single great prayer. What is customarily called prayer is, then, a part of this."[23] Analogously, the only way we can accept the mandate to engage in prayerful reading as referring to a real possibility is by saying that the en-tire life of the Church taken as a whole is occasion-comprehensive scrip-tural performance, of which our personal practices of *lectio divina* are an irreducibly important part. This comprehensive practice of prayer and reading, prayerful reading, is essential to any ascetic.

Where does this notion of *lectio divina* leave us in relation to the mutual rebukes of Balthasar and Rahner I most recently mentioned—not the opposition or seeming opposition between differentiated and dramatically wholistic readings but between theodramatic, transcenden-tal, and even political ways of being occasion-comprehensive? If we can presume this sort of occasion-comprehensive *lectio divina*, we can also pre-sume that Balthasar, Rahner, and their liberationist or radically orthodox critics all agree that Jesus is self-constituted as Head and body, vine and branches inseparable, neither fully "saturated" without the other—but the Head ruling the body like a slave (washing our feet), the body enjoying communion as a gift-exchange. In any case, this means that the compre-hensiveness of our scriptural performance is creaturely participation in the universal or comprehensive scope of the person and work of Jesus. From this point of view, the key advantage to Balthasar's theodrama is a clear recognition of this christological prevenience. In terms of our original gos-pel scene, his theodrama is an abiding reminder that it is Jesus, not the disciples or the crowds, who asks "Who do you say that I am?"—that the members' rebukes of each other must be done in light of the Head. But the key rebuke to Balthasar on this score is whether this christologi-cal comprehensiveness embraces the sort of personal and political compre-hensiveness sought by transcendental and political theologies. This, I take it, has been the rebuke of more comprehensive theologies, whether liberal or more radically orthodox (see note 4).

On the other hand, the key advantage to more comprehensive theologies is their aspiration for such personal and/or political comprehensiveness. But the key challenge to them is whether their demand for such occasion-comprehensive performance eclipses this christological prevenience—whether they are necessarily a sort of mediating theology, presuming that some specific occasion or occasions more generally provides the mediating foundation for christological applicability and intelligibility.[24] My own bias is that there is much truth to the rebukes on each side, although I prefer Balthasar's set of problems on this one issue to Rahner's. The One confessed, as I have said from the beginning, always exceeds the one confessing. But, again, I am not trying to settle the rebukes here. I am proposing that occasion-comprehensive scriptural performance provide a context for disciples of Christ to ascetically discipline their debates, to rebuke each other as disciples, and therefore in communion and solidarity rather than in mere polemic, much less as crowds.

Jesus' Messianic Unsurpassability and Prayerful Reading of Scripture

There is a another side to the modern christological puzzle, and another feature of *lectio divina* that sets a context for modern christological rebukes. Recall Peter's Matthean confession of Jesus as "Messiah, Son of the living God." The confession compels us to ask how this particular gospel-person Jesus of such comprehensive, messianic significance is related to "the living God." It is this connection between Jesus and the living God of Israel that I am trying to capture in the notion— borrowed from Rahner but deployed more systematically by George Lindbeck and Paul Griffiths—of "unsurpassability."[25] This is not just *any* unsurpassability (say, the unsurpassability of a trigrammaton, God) but the messianic unsurpassability of the God of Israel.[26] What do I mean by "unsurpassability"?

The living God of Israel is of comprehensive significance for each as well as every creature, for each and every event. But God's identity is not exhausted in this comprehensive significance. As we just saw in connection with occasion-comprehensive performance of scripture, God is always other than any such performance. Now Christians have marked God's otherness, God's unsurpassable primacy and uniqueness, in various ways— Gregory of Nyssa's "infinite enclosed by no boundary," Anselm's one "than whom a greater cannot be conceived," Aquinas's "truest and best and noblest of things," Rahner's holy mystery, Charles Taylor's God as incomparable good, and in other ways.[27] My point here is not to analyze these different predicates, much less propose a super-predicate to embrace them all (perhaps a "greatest being" ontotheology). The point is that questions of God's unsurpassability and unrestricted importance cannot be reduced to some other issue or question. This is why addressing the issue of God's unsurpassability must be a distinct part of any ascetic for christological rebukes.

Where, then, are the rebukes on this score? There are the rebukes of our crowds—those for whom the God of Jesus Christ is not the true God, or those for whom there is no true God, or those for whom there is no unsurpassable, incomparable good at all. In many such rebukes there is a presumption of what Kathryn Tanner has called a "competitive understanding of the relationship between God and world (in which the more we emphasize Jesus' humanity the less we emphasize his divinity, and vice versa)."[28] But let us presume there is no such competitive relationship—let us presume with Balthasar and Rahner and their Christian critics, that there is no competitive relationship between God's comprehensive word and work and God's unsurpassable life and light, between God's immanence and transcendence. (I am not trying to dismiss such dissents but only to suggest that these rebukes are not center stage before Jesus' question "Who do you say that I am?" and Peter's response, the confession of Jesus' messianic unsurpassability.) There is no rivalry between God's *comprehensive* significance and God's *unsurpassable* importance, any more than there is an intrinsic rivalry between what I called above the particularity of the scriptural text and its occasion-comprehensive performance.

The mutual rebukes at this moment or stage have less to do with the indissoluble connections between the living God's comprehensive scope and unsurpassable life than with how to articulate the connections with the issue with which we began, the particularity of Jesus Christ. One way to suggest the rebukes that arise is to consider a passing remark Rahner once made about his own Christology, in the context of criticizing Balthasar's (according to Rahner) veritably "gnostic" theology of God's death. "Perhaps," Rahner said, "it is possible to be an orthodox Nestorian or an orthodox Monophysite. If this were the case, then I would prefer to be an orthodox Nestorian," the implication being that Balthasar would be the orthodox Monophysite.[29] Setting aside a number of important historical issues, I will presume that "orthodox" here means roughly "Chalcedonian" and that Rahner here trades on our increasing appreciation of the room Chalcedon leaves for some kinds of so-called "Monophysite" emphasis on the Chalcedonian *hypostasis* and so-called "Nestorian" emphasis on the Chalcedonian *physes*.[30] Rahner's orthodox Nestorian would worry that the wrong sort of identification of Jesus and the ever-greater God would jeopardize both God's unsurpassability and Jesus' full humanity—or, as Rahner puts it, would advocate "a real identification" (*Realidentifikation*) rather than "a unity of really different realities" (*Einheit von real verschiedenen . . . Wirklichkeiten*).[31] Balthasar's orthodox Monophysite would worry that giving such preeminence to the two natures will jeopardize the unsurpassable hypostatic unity between Jesus and the living God, the Jesus who is dramatically found "alone" on the mount of transfiguration, or who dramatically appears risen after the crucifixion precisely when we would expect to see God.

The issues raised at this point—the mutual rebukes by orthodox Monophysites and orthodox Nestorians—are the issues raised by what I would call (for lack of a better word) christological metaphysics (i.e., an account of the being of each and every thing in the light of Jesus Christ's unsurpassable "primacy in all things" [Col 1:18]). But, rather than take off immediately into those metaphysical airs, I need to return to the ground of *lectio divina*. Can a final consideration of *lectio divina* set a context for ascetically disciplining such rebukes? Besides arguments over scriptural texts and the performance of such texts, there is a feature of *lectio divina*— the feature that makes it most specifically "theological" (*divina*). *Lectio divina* includes reading writings for sundry ends *coram Deo*, in the presence of God, giving thanks for scriptures as Word of God—to echo part of the liturgical assembly's response to the readings—because they are God's gift to us. To use the traditional description of *lectio divina* mentioned above, this is the time when God converses with us. *Lectio divina* is not only reading certain writings or reading them for certain practical ends. Such writings are not written for intratextual (in)coherence alone— nor for (in)coherence between text and human performance alone. They are written and used as well and primarily as the body through whom God imparts self in Word and Spirit, as in-Spired Word and Body of Christ.[32]

Like the previous analogies between Christology and *lectio divina*, this one raises questions. A good way to highlight these questions is to recall the traditional recommendation, quoted earlier from Vatican II's *Dogmatic Constitution on Divine Revelation*, that "prayer should accompany the reading of holy scripture, so that it becomes a dialogue between God and the human reader; for 'when we pray, we talk to him: when we read the divine word, we listen to him'." What is most peculiar about the internal quotation from Ambrose is not the implied mandate that scriptures be read, nor that prayer accompany that reading in all circumstances (occasion-comprehensively) but that it is *God* who does the speaking to which we listen as we pray and talk and read and otherwise use and perform these texts. And what is *most* peculiar about Ambrose's aphorism is the reverential veiling (as I will call it) of exactly what *God* is doing in *our lectio divina*. That is, I just said that God "does the speaking." This was a not unreasonable inference from a common presumption that what we typically listen for is someone else speaking. But Ambrose himself does not here *say* that God "speaks." He also does not say that God reads, while we listen. But, if we pray and talk (as Ambrose's *lectio divina* requires we do), must not God listen? But then how shall we listen for God's listening? Here surely belongs the famous story, so important to the ascetic of praying, of Elijah hearing God in the paradoxical "sound of sheer silence" (1 Kgs 19:12 NRSV). But how do we know when to pray by speaking and when to pray in silence—not the silence of those who have nothing to say (or who only say a postmodern nothing) but the silence of a breathing that rests in God, listening for God's word as pre-legomena to our own?

Could this be included in the sort of silence Jesus enjoins on the disciples after Peter's confession? In any case, *lectio divina* is a strange sort of colloquium or dialogue. There is something like Kierkegaard's indirect communication going on in Ambrose's aphorism. That is, the reverential veiling of what God is doing in our *lectio divina* is, I propose, a trace or icon of the unsurpassability of the God who speaks to us. *Lectio divina* is not simply reading a text, or performing scriptures comprehensively. *Lectio divina* is also a listening, a parable of the faith that comes by hearing (Rom 10:17), the *auditus fidei* that sets the context for the *intellectus fidei*. We cannot engage in a theological reading of these texts except prayerfully, except in colloquium with God—and this means, of course, our active voice, our pleas, our theological questions, the *intellectus fidei*, occasion-comprehensive performance. But the God with whom we dialogue is the God who speaks with us and to us first, as the God with whom we commune is the One who loves us first—as Jesus is the One who first poses the question of his identity to us.

The aphorism from Ambrose is embedded in a larger treatise (*De officiis ministrorum*) framed by paradoxes of the asymmetry and simultaneity of teaching and learning, speaking and being silent. There is much to ponder there in this regard. But how does this feature of *lectio divina* contribute to the debate between what I earlier called orthodox Nestorians and orthodox Monophysites? Nothing more (or less) complex is involved at this point than the insistence that the christological rebukes be more deeply embedded in rebukes over the triune God than I have so far insisted. *Lectio divina* as thus far described sets a context for this debate insofar as the *divina* is triune—and, thus, insofar as our colloquium with God participates in the unsurpassable trinitarian colloquium.

Here I reach another of those points where I am going to have to be satisfied with proposing a context for disciplining christological rebukes rather than completely settling them. That is, the disagreement between orthodox Nestorians and orthodox Monophysites reemerges at this point, now changed into an argument over the relationship between what Rahner and Balthasar call the immanent (or absolute) and economic trinity. Rahner's well-known axiom identifies the two; Balthasar dissents, concerned that world process will become a necessary stage in God's effort to "realize himself" and asserts that "the economic form of the Trinity is suspended and absorbed into the immanent" at Jesus' resurrection.[33] But the same Rahner who characterized himself as an orthodox Nestorian worried about confusing the two natures can also insist that the humanity of the Logos is "the self-disclosure of the Logos itself, so that when God, expressing himself, exteriorizes himself, that very thing appears which we call the humanity of the Logos."[34] The same Balthasar who calls the work on which I have focused a "theodrama" in which God is playwright and actor and director drawing us and the world into the drama of the living God can also insist that God "is *above* the play in that he is not trapped in it but *in* it insofar as he is fully involved in it."[35]

What is the relationship between Rahner's claims that the differentiation of natures is basic to their unity *and* that the humanity of Jesus is

Realsymbol of the unsurpassable Logos? What is the relationship between Balthasar's claims that there really is "theodrama" *and* that the unsurpassable God is "above the play"? I am going to leave these puzzles internal to their theologies unresolved for purposes of this essay, recognizing that much more could be said by way of rebuke on both sides. Part of what is at stake at this point is how to characterize God's *trinitarian* unsurpassability, when the Spirit's work in Church and world is incomplete. But, despite the space I have spent on Balthasar and Rahner, my goal was not to completely analyze their theologies or settle the debate between them. It was rather to propose a context for their debates, a context for disciplining rebukes among the disciples of Christ, an ascetic for christological rebukes. They are particularly good examples of a larger problem—the larger issue here being how our christological rebukes need to be situated in the context of prayerful reading, even as that very reading may be challenged and rebuked by the unsurpassable triune God in and to whom we pray. What I have proposed is that by considering their dispute in the context of *lectio divina*—not simply the reading of a text, or the occasion-comprehensive performance of a text but the hearing of (listening to) the unsurpassable Word of God uttered by the Father in the Spirit—enables us to rebuke each other "ascetically," to subject each other to discipline as members of the same body.

Conclusion

I have left behind the specific text with which I began but not (I hope) the specific person who asked the question "Who do you say that I am?" I have proposed that late modern christological rebukes among disciples of Christ over Jesus' particularity, comprehensive significance, and unsurpassability can be ascetically disciplined by our arguments over reading scriptural texts in their particularity, in their comprehensive significance for our lives as we "pray always," in the unsurpassable in-Spired Word they speak to us as we listen in our reading. And vice versa: our uses of (including arguments over) scriptural texts are disciplined by attention to Jesus Christ in his particularity that is of universal and unsurpassable significance.

At every step of the way, the relationship between our christological arguments and our *lectio divina* has been a kind of parable of the complex

relationship of lordship and service between Jesus and the Church. Jesus
Christ calls the disciples to a confession always exceeded by the One confessed, always ahead of the one confessing, in life and death and resurrection. Whether the rebukes are the relatively mild command to silence or the
more damning identification of Peter and Satan is almost eclipsed by this
christological prevenience. But this is not an "exceeding" where the One
confessed judges the one confessing from afar. The ascetical *disciplining* is
a disciplining of *his own* body. By the end of the story we learn that the
point of Jesus' asceticism is to draw us more comprehensively (mystically and politically) into God's unsurpassable communion that exceeds
even as it perfects our *lectio divina*, our scholastic questions, our occasion-
specific as well as occasion-comprehensive responses. It is to draw our
death and resurrection into his that we might find our lives by losing
them for his sake. Our rebukes of each other should do the same. A more
complete account of how to do so would be a more complete ascetics for
christological rebukes than I have provided here.

If this has been a parable of the relationship between Jesus and the
Church, then among the unaddressed issues has been the relationship between these disciples and the crowds, between Peter's confession of messianic unsurpassability and the concrete pentecostal chore of forming and
reforming a communion of Jews and Gentiles. Here the question "Who
do you say that I am?" becomes inseparable from the question "Who do
you say that 'you' are, that we are?" (including the rebukes ingredient
therein), and this question inseparable from a more full-blown trinitarian
theology. But those questions must remain for another day.

NOTES

1. Jesus here uses the same word [ἐπετίμησεν or ἐπιτιμᾶν] that Mark
will use for Peter's upcoming rebuke of Jesus (Mk 8:32) and that Jesus will use
again in rebuking Peter (Mk 8:33).

2. Robert W. Jenson, *Unbaptized God: The Basic Flaw in Ecumenical Theology*
(Minneapolis, Minn.: Fortress Press, 1992), 100; cf. 51, 128.

3. The polemical high point was in 1966, translated as Hans Urs von
Balthasar, *The Moment of Christian Witness*, trans. Richard Beckley and Adrian
Walker, 3rd ed. (San Francisco: Ignatius Press, 1994). Rahner notes that neither
has accused the other to Rome of being a heretic (Paul Imhof and Hubert

Biallowons, eds., *Karl Rahner in Dialogue*, trans. Harvey D. Egan [abridged] [New York: Crossroad, 1986], 29). But the fact that this would have to be noted is a sign of the seriousness of the dispute.

4. Rahner has been criticized for a turn to the private subject that cannot account for the more public features of nature and politics and history (Kelsey, Metz)—and Balthasar has also been criticized for a theology less than vigorously political (Milbank, Bauerschmidt). But it has also been proposed that Rahner can be *internally* adjusted to provide the background for liberation theology (Tracy and Milbank, with opposite evaluations of that adjustment), and that Balthasar can be *internally* adjusted to the requirements of a more political theology neither liberal nor neo-conservative (Schindler), perhaps even "radically orthodox" (Milbank). See Johannes Metz, "A Transcendental and Idealistic or a Narrative and Practical Christianity?" in *Faith in History and Society: Toward a Practical Fundamental Theology*, trans. David Smith (New York: Seabury Press, 1980), 154–68 (to cite only one of Metz' sympathetic criticisms of Rahner); David Kelsey, "Human Being," in *Christian Theology: An Introduction to Its Traditions and Tasks*, ed. Peter C. Hodgson and Robert H. King (Philadelphia, Pa.: Fortress Press, 1982), chap. 6; David Tracy, "The Uneasy Alliance Reconceived: Catholic Theological Method, Modernity, and Postmodernity," *Theological Studies* 50 (1989): 548–70 (where Rahner and liberation theologies are aligned with Tracy's own correlational theology, Balthasar with postmodern and *ad hoc* apologetics); John Milbank, *Theology and Social Theory: Beyond Secular Reason* (Oxford: Basil Blackwell, 1990), chap. 8 (where Rahner and liberation theologies are criticized for naturalizing the supernatural, Balthasar and de Lubac for failing to develop a social or political theology [209, 220, 225, 234, 246]); John Milbank, Catherine Pickstock, and Graham Ward, eds., *Radical Orthodoxy: A New Theology* (London and New York: Routledge, 1999), especially the editors' introduction; David L. Schindler, *Heart of the World, Center of the Church* (Grand Rapids, Mich.: Eerdmans; Edinburgh: T & T Clark, 1996); Frederick Christian Bauerschmidt, "Theo-Drama and Political Theology," *Communio* 25 (1998): 532–52 (with responses by Peter Casarella and J. Brian Benestad).

5. Bruce Marshall, *Christology in Conflict: The Identity of a Saviour in Rahner and Barth* (Oxford: Basil Blackwell, 1987), chap. 1. In the background of this view of late modern Christology is Hans W. Frei, *Types of Christian Theology*, ed. George Hunsinger and William C. Placher (New Haven, Conn. and London: Yale University Press, 1992).

6. Thomas S. Kuhn, *The Structure of Scientific Revolutions*, 2nd ed. (Chicago: University of Chicago, 1970), chap. 4.

7. Vatican II, *Dogmatic Constitution on Divine Revelation*, paragraph 25, where footnote 6 refers the internal quotation to Ambrosius, *De officiis ministrorum*, I, 20, 88; PL 16, 50 (Norman Tanner, ed., *Decrees of the Ecumenical Councils* (New York: Sheed & Ward; Washington, D.C.: Georgetown University Press, 1990), 2:980.

8. Henri de Lubac, S.J., *Medieval Exegesis*, vol. 1 of *The Four Senses of Scripture*, trans. Mark Sebanc (Grand Rapids, Mich.: William B. Eerdmans; Edinburgh: T & T Clark, 1998), esp. 40–74. On the "disengagement of the *questio* from the *lectio*" that had "both positive and negative results," see Bernard McGinn, *The Growth of Mysticism*, vol. 2 of *The Presence of God: A History of Western Christian Mysticism* (New York: Crossroad, 1994), 370, 386.

9. See Rahner's "Theology in the New Testament," in *Theological Investigations*, trans. Karl-H. Kruger, vol. 5 (Baltimore, Md.: Helicon Press, 1966), 23–41; *Foundations of Christian Faith: An Introduction to the Idea of Christianity*, trans. William V. Dych (New York: Seabury Press, 1978), e.g., 246; 282–93; originally published as *Grundkurs des Glaubens: Einführung in den Begriff des Christentums* (Freiburg: Herder, 1976).

10. Hans Urs von Balthasar, *The Dramatis Personae: Man in God*, vol. 2 of *Theo-Drama: Theological Dramatic Theory*, trans. Graham Harrison (San Francisco: Ignatius Press, 1990), 103–104.

11. I take some such opposition between Balthasar and Rahner to be a relatively standard way of casting these issues. Besides Marshall (note 5), see especially Rowan William, "Balthasar and Rahner," in *The Analogy of Beauty: The Theology of Hans Urs von Balthasar*, ed. John Riches (Edinburgh: T & T Clark, 1986), 11–34; Bruce Marshall, "Christology," in *The Blackwell Encyclopedia of Modern Christian Thought*, ed. Alister E. McGrath (Oxford: Blackwell, 1993), 80–93; International Theological Commission, "Select Questions on the Theology of God the Redeemer," *Communio* 24, no. 1 (spring 1997): 160–214 (the critical appreciation of Rahner on 192–94 is contrasted with retrieval of "a narrative or dramatic theology of redemption" [without mention of Balthasar] on 194–96).

12. Rahner, *Foundations of Christian Faith*, 206–212, 293–302, 311–21.

13. See William A. Christian, Sr., *The Doctrines of Religious Communities: A Philosophical Study* (New Haven, Conn. and London: Yale University Press, 1987), chap. 8 and 9 (esp. 188 and 225–26).

14. Nicholas Lash, "Performing the Scripture," *Theology on the Way to Emmaus* (London: SCM Press, 1986), 37–46.

15. *Dogmatic Constitution on Divine Revelation*, c. 6 in *Decrees of the Ecumenical Councils*, paragraph 21, 2:979.

16. See, for example, Rahner, *Foundations of Christian Faith*, 370 on "preeminence," and on a Catholic *sola scriptura*, see 361–65.

17. Rahner, *Foundations of Christian Faith*, 13.

18. Paul J. Griffiths, *Religious Reading: The Place of Reading in the Practice of Religion* (New York: Oxford, 1999), 40.

19. Hans Urs von Balthasar, *Prolegomena*, vol. 1 of *Theo-Drama: Theological Dramatic Theory*, trans. Graham Harrison (San Francisco: Ignatius Press, 1988), 11–12.

20. For a succinct history of this triad from the Greeks to Hegel, see Gérard Genette, *The Architext: An Introduction*, trans. Jane E. Lewin (Berkeley:

University of California Press, 1992). For a critique of Aristotle and Genette for missing the peculiarities of drama, see Aldo Tassi, "Philosophy and Theater," *International Philosophical Quarterly* 38 (1998): 43–54.

21. Peter Ochs, *Peirce, Pragmatism and the Logic of Scripture* (Cambridge: Cambridge University Press, 1998), esp. chap. 8.

22. Ochs, *Peirce*, 284–85. I say "just?" to leave open the possibility of some version of the claim that God (as Vatican I puts it) *can be* known "by the natural light of reason" without here claiming that God *is* thus known.

23. Origen, *On Prayer* 12, 2 in *Origen*, trans. Rowan A. Greer (New York: Paulist Press, 1979), 104.

24. See my "Revisionists and Liberals," in *The Modern Theologians*, ed. David F. Ford, 2nd ed. (Oxford: Blackwell, 1997), chap. 17, for the complexities of such mediating theologies. A question for Milbank is whether, in trying to fully saturate nature and politics and church with a christological poetics, he does not repeat the modern, mediating project of decentering Jesus in his particularity. This especially applies to his "The Name of Jesus," in *The Word Made Strange* (Oxford: Blackwell, 1997), chap. 6. See Frederick Christian Bauerschmidt, "The Word Made Speculative? John Milbank's Christological Poetics," *Modern Theology* 15 (1999): 417–32; R.R. Reno, "The Radical Orthodoxy Project," *First Things* 100 (February 2000): 37–44.

25. Rahner frequently uses the notion of unsurpassability (which usually translates *unüberbeitbar*, but sometimes *unüberholbar*) (e.g., *Foundations of Christian Faith*, 174, 279; *Grundkurs des Glaubens*, 176, 274). George Lindbeck and Paul Griffiths discuss unsurpassability as a predicate of things other than God like "religions," a quality they may be granted (on my use) by participation in Christ's unsurpassability; see Lindbeck's *The Nature of Doctrine: Religion and Theology in a Postliberal Age* (Philadelphia, Pa.: Westminster Press, 1984), 47–52 and Griffiths, *Religious Reading*, 9–10. Applied to the Christian religion, unsurpassability is what Lindbeck calls "christological maximalism" (*Nature of Doctrine*, 94).

26. Lest it be confusing what I am up to at this point, I should note that I believe Aquinas is entirely correct in his grammatical remarks that "God is a human being [*homo*]" and "A human being is God" are true (*Summa Theologiae* 3a. 16, 1 and 2). The question here is: who is God, and how do we identify God?

27. Gregory of Nyssa, *The Life of Moses*, trans. Abraham J. Malherbe and Everett Ferguson (New York: Paulist Press, 1978), par. 236, p. 115; Anselm, *Proslogion*, trans. M.J. Charlesworth (Oxford: Oxford University Press, 1965), throughout; Thomas Aquinas's *Summa Theologiae* Ia, 2, 3; Rahner, *Foundations of Christian Faith*, 65; Charles Taylor, *Sources of the Self: The Making of the Modern Identity* (Cambridge, Mass.: Harvard University Press, 1989), 19 and throughout.

28. Kathryn Tanner, *Christology Lectures* (Edinburgh: T & T Clark, forthcoming), lecture one, ms. p. 6. For a detailed study of these issues, see Tanner's *God and Creation in Christian Theology: Tyranny or Empowerment* (Oxford: Blackwell,

1988), along with the arguments by Tanner in *The God Who Acts: Philosophical and Theological Explorations*, ed. Thomas F. Tracy (University Park, Pa.: Pennsylvania State University Press, 1994).

29. Imhof and Biallowons, *Karl Rahner in Dialogue*, 127.

30. See, for example, J. Neuner, S.J., and J. Dupuis, S.J., *The Christian Faith in the Documents of the Catholic Church*, ed. Jacques Dupuis, 6th rev. ed. (New York: Alba House, 1996), par. 671a, p. 246 (Paul VI and Pope Shenouda III of Egypt) and par. 683, pp. 253–54 (John Paul II and Mar Dinkha IV, Patriarch of the Assyrian Church of the East).

31. Rahner, *Foundations of Christian Faith*, 290; *Grundkurs des Glaubens*, 284. Rahner has long worried that the tradition veers in a Monophysite or mythological (or, we might now say, theodramatic) direction; see "Current Problems in Christology" in *Theological Investigations*, trans. Cornelius Ernst (New York: Seabury Press, 1961, 1974), 149–200.

32. On scripture as Body of Christ as well as Word of God, see my "The Hermeneutical Deadlock between Revelationalists, Textualists, and Functionalists," *Modern Theology* 6 (1990): 325–39. On the theological issues raised by God's inspiration and the Church's uses of scripture, see David Yeago, "Scripture," in *Knowing the Triune God: The Work of the Spirit in the Practices of the Church*, ed. James J. Buckley and David Yeago (Grand Rapids, Mich.: Eerdmans, forthcoming), chap. 3.

33. Rahner, "Remarks on the Dogmatic Treatise 'De Trinitate'" in *Theological Investigations*, trans. Kevin Smyth (Baltimore: Helicon Press, 1966), 4: 77–102 (especially 87–102); *Foundations of the Christian Faith*, 136–137; Balthasar, *Dramatis Personae: The Person in Christ*, vol. 3 of *Theo-Drama: Theological Dramatic Theory*, trans. Graham Harrison (San Francisco: Ignatius Press, 1994), 505–37 (esp. 508 n.3, where Balthasar irenically notes that Rahner does not "completely" identify the two, and 522).

34. Rahner, "The Theology of the Symbol" in *Theological Investigations*, 4: 239; cf. "Remarks on the Dogmatic Treatise 'De Trinitate'" in *Theological Investigations*, 4: 92 (note 21); "On the Theology of the Incarnation" in *Theological Investigations*, 4: 116.

35. Balthasar, *The Dramatis Personae: The Person in Christ*, 514, 532–35. A complete analysis would have to take account of "the trinitarian drama" in "the final act" in *The Last Act*, vol. 4 of *Theo-drama: Theological Dramatic Theory*, trans. Graham Harrison (San Francisco: Ignatius Press, 1998), 247–488.

CHAPTER SIX

The Kingdom of God and
the Theologal Dimension of the Poor

The Jesuanic Principle

JON SOBRINO, S.J.

A number of years ago liberation theology put the poor at the center of faith, of the Church, and of theology. Gustavo Gutiérrez would talk about the "irruption (la irrupción) of the poor" in the continent of Latin America and stress their condition as a believing, suffering people: "the poor are those who die before their time." This can be truly affirmed to this very day: around forty to fifty million human beings die annually from hunger or diseases related to hunger.

Ignacio Ellacuría insisted passionately on the character of the poor as victims, and thus he called them 'crucified peoples'. In words that I have cited over and over again he said that even though the form of their crucifixion varies, "*the* sign of the times is *always* the crucified people," those who are stripped of life. And he would add "this crucified people is the historical continuation of the suffering servant of Yahweh."[1] By calling the poor 'crucified peoples' he was radicalizing their oppression and suffering, and their salvific character as well.[2]

He gave to them a theological character. For Ellacuría the crucified people (more than any other reality) is "that which characterizes an epoch"—what I have called a sign of the times in the historical-pastoral sense (see *Gaudium et Spes*, §4). More radically, and more frequently ignored, the crucified people is "the presence of God or of God's plans"—what I have called a sign of the times in the historical-theologal[3] sense (see *Gaudium et Spes*, §II). The poor, then, are theological loci and theologal realities, sacraments of God, a hermeneutical principle for understanding God. It would be difficult to press more strongly the importance of the poor for theology and for the faith. They enjoy a hermeneutical privilege (Edward Schillebeeckx).

Ellacuría affirmed that the crucified people is *always* the sign of the times. What I want to do in this essay is to reflect on this "always." One can discuss how well he formulated these bold claims, but what seems to me beyond discussion is the Christian *prejudice* or *pre-judgment* in favor of this *always*, verified daily—unfortunately—in historical reality. This demands that theology *always* give a central place to the poor, to the victims, to the crucified people.[4]

In my view, it is this insight that turned the theology of liberation, with all its limitations and even errors, into a "classic." Yet some years ago a tendency set in to ignore this insight and to take this central position away from the poor. J.B. Metz pointed it out lucidly, speaking of the general cultural atmosphere: "an everyday postmodernism of the heart is spreading far and wide which thrusts the poverty and misery of the so-called Third World into a greater and more anonymous distance."[5] Pedro Casadáliga repeatedly complains that "some people think that now it is time to change our ways of thinking," and wonders "what is left of the option for the poor?"[6]

While it is true that ideologies and even theologies have abandoned the centrality of the poor, the principal fact remains:

> Never has the world been so unequal and so poor. Never has there been so much of humanity deprived of human existence. We have gone from being poor to being outcasts, to being completely superfluous . . . . That there are 1.3 billion persons who get by on less than one dollar a day is more than an iniquity, seeing that around 1 percent of the world's income would be enough to eradicate global poverty.[7]

It is enough to cite the following fact from a recent report (1999) of the UN Department of Public Information (UNDPI) on the reality of poverty: the 200 richest persons on the planet own more than the 582 million inhabitants of the forty-three most underdeveloped nations of the world. This aberration is a catastrophe for the human species (if poverty is taken in an absolute sense) and for the human family (if the poverty of some is taken in relation to the abundance of others). Today's world keeps on producing poor, but ignores them more and more, and covers them up ever more brazenly, affirming that terrible denunciation that the evil one enslaves (Jn 8.34), is a murderer (8.44a-b), and a liar (8.44c-d), and in that order.

This is the context of these reflections—their veritable *Sitz im Leben*, which is also a *Sitz im Tode*, if I may put it thus.[8] My goal is to reverse the tendency described above, to get back to the pathos of Medellín, to put the poor at the center of theology. This is what I am going to argue for theologically. But whatever the fortunes of the conceptual argument, I intend to maintain—perhaps without defense—its conclusion: return to the poor their central place in theology, for faith, and for the Church.

This task is not an easy one, because the poor are disturbing realities for the theologian and for theology. Existentially, they problematize life and the theological endeavor (in my view) like no other historical reality. Theoretically, they call into question and transform every theological content, beginning with the deepest of them: the mystery of God. It has been said of the cross, and rightly so, that it christianizes theology, but first it interrogates it, and this in the most radical way. The same must be said of the poor. We have already said that they are sacraments of God, but they also raise the most radical questions about God. They keep the theodicy question ever current. As González Faus recalls, "according to a Christian tradition, quite real, but carefully forgotten, the greatest argument against the existence of God is the existence of the poor."[9] In our time J. B. Metz—confronted by the Auschwitz of the past, and those of the present—insists that it is absolutely fundamental, and not optional, to keep the theodicy question alive, not to be content with easy answers.[10]

This question has not typically come up in Latin America, given the massive ambient religiosity. Yet some twenty years ago Pedro Casadáliga wrote, "For some time—ever since I came into habitual contact with the indigenous populations—I have felt the disappearance of entire peoples to be an absurd mystery of historical iniquity that turns my faith into despondency. . . . Lord, why have you abandoned them?"[11] And Ignacio Ellacuría, again twenty years ago or so, wrote in more systematic language: "The problem of the poor is the problem of God. . . . The poor are God's failure. . . . The impotence of God in history is something that has to be accepted in the Christian confession of the omnipotence of God."[12]

Finally, the poor, who are not accustomed to doubt God, sometimes formulate the theodicy question too. In a combat zone in El Salvador, the campesinos asked in a time of repression: "How many times have we not said that God acts in our history. . . . But, Father, if he does act, when will this be over? And how many years of war and how many thousands of murders? What is going on with God?"[13]

The goal of this essay is to put theology on the side of the poor, and to put the poor on the side of a Christian theology. I have nonetheless begun with the way that the poor problematize *Theos*, which presents the greatest challenge to theo-logy. I do this to avoid a "cheap theology" that covers up reality and thereby makes it easier for the poor to disappear. Beginning with *theo*dicy seems important to me since this is—among other things— a potent way of taking reality seriously. For someone for whom God no longer means anything, let him or her think about *anthropo*dicy. Be the referent God or human beings, when reality protests it cannot be ignored or trivialized—and the poor are such a protest. When taken seriously, the reality of the poor is what best keeps theology from being enbourgeoisied or, in a more radical way, from collapsing into docetism—that is to say, choosing its own sphere of reality, swimming around in it like a fish in water, while ignoring the deeper reality: the reality of the poor and the victims. This challenge keeps theology from falling into cynicism, as Hugo Assman pointed out twenty-five years ago.[14]

Making the poor central in theology, then, is the goal of this essay. Toward this end, in the first part I will analyze what I take to be the fundamental theoretical-theological reason for forgetting about the poor: the gradual disappearance of the Kingdom of God from Christology. In the second part I will analyze the theologal centrality of the poor, according to the Jesuanic[15] principle: "God loves and defends the poor for the simple fact that they are poor." The poor are thus elevated to the rank of a theologal reality, which provides the strongest guarantee that they will be central to faith and to theology. Without this guarantee their relevance is reduced to the sphere of spirituality, of ethics, or of the social teachings of the Church. Finally, by means of some examples I will analyze the meaning and importance of the centrality of the poor for theology.

Strictly speaking, I am not going to say anything that I have not already said,[16] at times even in the same words. The relative novelty lies in entering more deeply into the perspective of the poor, in the influence this perspective has on the approach to certain theological themes, and above all, in the goal: saying it "again" in a social and theological situation that ignores the poor even more than before. In other words, however these lines and their argument fare, their purpose is to return the poor to the center of theology, the center of the Church, and, in all of this, to the center of human conscience.

1.   The Forgetfulness of the Kingdom of God in Christology

Forgetting the poor has gone hand in hand with forgetting the Kingdom of God. The latter is something that occurred gradually in Christology. Christology, in effect, developed from two starting points: the experience of Jesus' *resurrection* and the recollection of his *historical life*. Now, as far as his life goes, according to the synoptic gospels, Jesus' existence unfolded in an essential twofold relation: to a God who is *Abba* and to the *Kingdom* of God. However already in an incipient way in the New Testament, and certainly subsequent to it, *Christology* — the resurrection now a given — was developed in a fairly exclusive way from the starting point of the relationship that Jesus had with God — *Abba*. The result was that within a period of ten to twenty years (according to Martin Hengel[17]) Christology had taken up the orientation that it has followed to this very day: *Jesus is the Son of God*. Jesus' relation to the Kingdom of God, equally constitutive during his lifetime, gradually disappeared from christological thought, or, more precisely, was reinterpreted in such a way that with the passage of time its original content was ignored, as well as its centrality and its capacity to articulate the reality of salvation. By the time of the fourth-century conciliar debates it is clear that the Kingdom of God plays no role whatsoever in Christology.

In other words, faith in Christ rendered itself theoretical by relating itself to the *person of God* (which is better expressed in the titles of Son, Lord, Word — those titles that were most frequently used in the christological councils) and not — in addition — to the *Kingdom of God*. Jesus' most intimate reality came to be seen in terms of *filiation*, sacrament of the Father, historical presence of God in this world, and this (which is good news, to be sure) to the greatest degree possible in history. But the consequence of this was that even though he is also called Christ (Messiah), the title ceased to express the fact that "Messiah" was the referent of the hope and the salvation of the poor—that which points toward the Kingdom of God. It was being turned into a proper name, in practice, moreover, a merely denotative name. In this sense I have written that the Messiah was quickly "de-Messianized."[18] Christology will go on to delve more deeply into the relation of Jesus to the Father, the reality of the Son, while progressively weakening the relation of Jesus to the Kingdom to the point of ignoring it.

1.1   *The Fate of the Kingdom of God in the New Testament*

Whether this process had already begun—and to what degree—in the New Testament is a matter of debate, but I think that two things are indisputable: in Jesus' life, as it is presented by the synoptic gospels, the Kingdom of God is central; it is the good news that he announces. On the other hand, the Kingdom ceases to be central in the other strata of the New Testament. This does not mean, of course, that good news is no longer announced and that this good news does not have—in addition—a horizontal dimension. Because of this I will speak (using systematic language) of "equivalents" to the Kingdom, forms of the good news that do not adequately replace the Kingdom of God, but that certainly can be congruent with it. Allow me to list briefly some particulars in order to exemplify both of these things.

The first *formulas of faith* in Acts and in the Pauline letters focus—in a novel way with respect to Judaism—on Jesus. The Father and the Spirit are mentioned subsequently, but the Kingdom is not mentioned at all, that *eu-angelion* that was central to Jesus and that he proclaimed so that it could be accepted as such, in conversion and in *faith*. Likewise, the baptismal rite will be preceded by a catechesis about Jesus, his reality as exalted Lord, and about the good news of salvation, but the latter is no longer formulated as the Kingdom of God (with the exception of Acts 8:12), but rather as the salvation that has been brought about in Christ Jesus.

Nonetheless, the notion of *eu-angelion* continues to be central to the whole of the New Testament. In the Pauline message there clearly is an *eu-angelion*—the death and resurrection of Jesus, good news for the human being in justification by faith (the vertical dimension, let us say); for the human being in society in the life of the community (horizontal reality); for the human being within humanity and even in the cosmos, in the recapitulation of all things in Christ, in the final deification, when God will be all in all. Concrete dimensions of the Kingdom and of Jesuanic logic are also present: the gratuity of salvation; the privilege of the weak represented by Gentiles, women, and slaves;[19] the shared table. Of course the central reality in Paul did not disappear: the cross, which, historically speaking, may very well have meant living without the support of the law, "out in the open,"[20] and in theologal terms consisted in the reality that discloses God: through weakness God is reconciling the world to himself and is manifesting the gospel of grace.

In Acts the equivalent to the Kingdom of God could be expressed by the effects of the action of the Spirit, when human beings are transformed and shape their lives—very much in accord with Jesus—into mutual love, into the building up of community. In John the *eu-angelion* is the Son and eternal life. For all intents and purposes the Kingdom is not mentioned,[21] although by situating the Son within the framework of the historical Jesus this tendency is blunted to some degree, and by giving absolute primacy to love a totalizing and comprehensively salvific reality is offered: God in us and we in God.

So then, what is central to all of the New Testament is the fact that God's plan is found not only in the appearance of Jesus, the Son, which is a genuine *eu-angelion*, to be sure, but also in the "horizontalization," as it were, of this good news, in such a way that in relation to the Son or because of the Son this good news, which he is, overflows out toward human beings. This is why I talk about "equivalents" of the Kingdom of God, since in every stratum of the New Testament central elements of the Kingdom are captured, with varying nuances: a good news that saves the human being, first and foremost the weak; the gratuity of this salvation; its collective, social dimension; its dialectical dimension insofar as it appears in the presence of and in conflict with the forces of evil, both personal (hubris, desire, concupiscence, ambition) and "structural" (the sin of the world, principalities and powers, evil, death).

The point of these reflections is to raise the issue of the fate of the Kingdom of God—its presence or absence, its priority (in the synoptic gospels) or secondary status (in other texts)—in a sufficiently dialectical way so that it is not reduced to a matter of "Kingdom of God or not Kingdom of God." I do not think that the New Testament permits this sort of simplification—neither does the historicity of life and of the human condition. But it must be added that what I have here called "equivalents" are not by that token necessarily identical with the Kingdom of God. Given the historicity of the development of the Jesus movement, this would really have to be asserted in a rather *a priori* manner. The equivalents have their own dynamisms, which, even without intending it or being aware of it, can lead to the Kingdom, as Jesus proclaimed it, losing its centrality and along with that, some of its fundamental elements. In this sense I think that dynamisms unfold in the New Testament that, while carrying important values, some of which were expressed more profoundly than in the synoptic gospels (justification by faith in Paul, the capacity of love to enfold the divine and the human in John), also end up overshadowing Jesuanic values, above all those that center on the Kingdom of God. Specifically—and this is what is at issue—the centrality and privilege of the poor in God's eyes.

This overshadowing happened not long after the New Testament, and frequently without the counterweight of the magnificent theologies and the Kingdom-equivalents in Paul and John. There were cultural reasons (entry into the Graeco-Roman world, which was a culture without a utopian, hopeful, horizon), as well as social ones (the insignificance of the first communities in an empire that thought itself to be reformable but everlasting). But the fundamental reasons seem to be of the historical-theological order: Jesus' resurrection and the imminent expectation of the parousia. Both of these made it difficult to formulate the Christian utopia as the Kingdom of God.

As far as the resurrection goes, the apocalyptic traditions were not looking for the resurrection of an individual, but of a collectivity. Given this, Jesus' resurrection was understood proleptically, as the resurrection of the firstborn, an anticipation of the universal resurrection.[22] This comprehensive good news (at least for the just, although more precisely, for the victims) could very easily be taken as a new equivalent to the Kingdom.[23]

As far as the expectation of the parousia, in Luke—who no longer thinks the parousia imminent—the Church's time takes over the place of the utopia of the Kingdom, although to bring this off Luke has to idealize the Church. Paul's approach is different. He emphasizes the present moment as the "absolutely-not" of eschatology, because of which it is necessary to live in the time of the cross, without triumphalism or idealizations (recall his critique of the community at Corinth). And this means living in the "not-yet." Paul will nuance this stance, but for his whole life the expectation of the end continues to be like a live wire.[24] Even when he writes the letter to the Romans, "he continues to see the eschatological hope against the horizon of his own generation, but (now) with a temporally imprecise limit and without any specifics about the possible witnesses to the end."[25]

This firm conviction that God's judgment will happen soon can explain in part his focus on justification as good news, as well as the fact that the historical utopia is not formulated as the Kingdom of God, but as the building up of the community, which will have to be a leaven and an alternative to the present world (see the magnificent description of the Christian community that he gives in his first letter, 1 Thes 5:12–22). As Becker says, for Paul "the Church is not the People of God on earth, in the midst of a history that is opening up to a future without limits. Therefore, the Church is not supposed to shape a world in a political and cultural sense. It senses itself already liberated from this perverse present world (Gal 1:4) and longs with the Spirit of God for the end times (Rom 8:23). It lives in a relative distance from the world (1 Cor 7:29–31) because the end of history is approaching. It rejoices in the imminent coming of its Lord (Phil 4:4f.)."[26]

In sum, on the one hand, "the form of this world is passing away" (1 Cor 7:31), which does not facilitate social and historical behaviors like Jesus'.[27] On the other, the expectation of the end did not lead Paul to ethical and social inactivity, as he encouraged the creation of communities that would function as leaven and as an alternative while waiting for the final recapitulation.[28] The emphases, nonetheless, end up being different from those that the Kingdom of God, in all its concreteness, demands.

1.2 The Retrieval of the Kingdom of God

Whatever the specific development of this process in the New Testament and the subsequent centuries, when we get to the first councils the forgetfulness of the Kingdom of God is complete. On the theoretical level, the Kingdom no longer appears in the dogmatic definitions about Jesus Christ. Although it might seem so to us today, by the logic of the councils themselves this forgetfulness would not necessarily have had to happen. In effect, the councils found access to what is invisible in God by starting from what is visible in Jesus, as a consequence of which, as Juan Luis

Segundo writes, "God has to be [would have to be, I would say] understood following the key of Jesus' existence, which is nothing other than the historical project of the *Kingdom of God*, in all the concreteness he gave it."[29]

On a practical level the Church was coming to understand itself as the Kingdom, as what is ultimate on earth, with the power that this confers. As Eusebius of Caesaria recounts it in his *Life of Constantine*, the feast after Nicaea—the divinity of Christ just having been defined—is not the sign of the Kingdom of God; just the opposite, it is a sign of oppressive and worldly power. Situated at a peak moment of self-understanding from the perspective of power, "through an extraordinary but almost fatal reversal of the situation, Christianity, which on the eve was still a prohibited religion on the morrow began to be a state religion."[30] The Church would take a path that would not only in large measure ignore the Kingdom, but that in many ways would turn the Church into the anti-Kingdom. To express this deterioration in something fundamental: the Church went from being persecuted to being a persecutor.

In conclusion, "the Kingdom of God, which is central to the synoptic gospels is no longer the center for the rest of the New Testament. Just as it is no longer the center for the teaching of the Fathers of the Church nor in the theology of subsequent centuries."[31]

This tendency was reversed in theology—miraculously, one might say—almost two millennia after Jesus, with the discoveries of Albert Schweizer, Johannes Weiss, and so on. In the life of the Church the change began to make itself felt timidly around the time of Vatican II, and openly only with Medellín. In systematic Christology the Kingdom of God has to a great extent been restored. Thus, in Europe: J. I. González Faus, J. M. Castilo, J. Moltmann, although others have retrieved it in a way that is vague and, in my opinion, inadequate. Liberation theology has taken it up in a serious way (L. Boff, J. L. Segundo), and Ignacio Ellacuría elevated it to theology's central object: "The same thing that Jesus came to proclaim and realize, that is, the Kingdom of God, is what ought to be constituted as the unifying object of the whole of Christian theology, as well as of Christian ethics and pastoral action: the greatest possible realization of the Kingdom of God in history is what the true followers of Jesus ought to pursue."[32]

2.   The Jesuanic Principle

Now let us ask: Although all of this is true, why keep on insisting on the Kingdom of God? Are not the "equivalents" enough for faith and for theology? Is it not enough to formulate the Christian utopia as magnificently as Paul, John, and others, have done? Is it not enough to show what specifically belongs to it: the affirmation that God is salvation and good news, benevolent to human beings, and all of this by grace? Is it not sufficient to proclaim God's plan for God's creation: deification, recapitulation, redemption . . . ? Do not the well-known words of Karl Rahner show what is essential to this new God: "God has forever ceased to be symmetrical: possibly salvation, possibly condemnation. God is salvation"?

These are not just rhetorical questions. On the one hand, they show that in Christian faith there can and—given the unsoundable depths of its mystery—ought to be many diverse ways of formulating this God and God's salvation. But, on the other, they show that the formulations are not all interchangeable, and that not all of them capture the same features of the good news of God.[33]

No doubt the theologies of Paul and of John are indispensable, brilliant, and enriching, in relation to the synoptic gospels. But it is necessary to get back to the Kingdom of God because it proclaims what is fundamental about Jesus in a way that is not so clearly and directly present in other New Testament formulations. It is necessary to get back to what is specific to the Kingdom so that it does not end up being interchangeable with other good news and values—and thus distorted. This is, in my opinion, the great weakness of some theologies that talk about the Kingdom, but without making what is specific to it the center. Consider this passage of Walter Kasper in his well-known book about Jesus Christ:

> We can summarize this as follows: The salvation of the Kingdom of God means the coming to power in and through human beings of the self-communicating love of God. Love reveals itself as the meaning of life. The world and man find fulfilment only in love. . . . The news of the coming of the Kingdom of God is therefore a promise about everything that is done in the world out of love. It says that, against all appearances, what is done out of love will endure for ever; that it is the only thing which lasts forever.[34]

What this beautiful text says about love is true, but it does not adequately reproduce what the Kingdom of God is according to Jesus. This has grave consequences, since a specific understanding of God, as well as—what I would stress here—the restoration of the poor and the weak, and their elevation to theologal rank, all depend on the proper retrieval of the Kingdom of God. Talking about the Kingdom of God is not, then, only a matter of reclaiming "the historical Jesus"—as supremely important as this is—or only of retrieving "the historical Jesus who preached the Kingdom," but of restoring "the poor" to whom Jesus preached the Kingdom. For this reason, since the tradition of the Kingdom of God restores the poor better than other New Testament traditions and other theologies past and present—and without the dangers that the latter bring—and since it better expresses their privilege in God's eyes, we need to get back to that tradition. It is a matter of defending the poor, ever defenseless, defending them theologically and theologally. To this end let us recall, briefly, the proclamation of the Kingdom that Jesus made to the poor, concentrating on those features that continue to be fundamental in our world, and that are perennially in danger. To be sure, the poor's centrality is not the only thing that should be analyzed in reference to the Kingdom of God. It is also necessary to analyze the relation between the people of God and the Kingdom of God, what the Kingdom requires of the poor, and so on. But, for reasons that have already been given, in this essay we will concentrate on their centrality.

2.1   The Poor from the Perspective of God

It may be taken for granted, but that does not make it less central that Jesus did not preach himself, and not even God, alone, but rather proclaimed the Kingdom of God. This ought to put us on our guard against a Christology unilaterally focused on filiation and not, along with that, on messiah-hood. Yet, on the other hand, Jesus never said *what* this Kingdom of God is, and not even the so-called parables of the Kingdom clarify what the sovereignty of God means, as such. Neither was Jesus being completely original; rather, he took over from Israel—while making modifications—an idea (or set of ideas) about the Kingdom.[35]

At its most general, and according to a diverse set of biblical ideas, the Kingdom of God was a focused expression of a utopian vision: there can be life, justice, fraternity, and dignity in a world in which history seems to render them impossible. The oppressive reality of the anti-Kingdom will be transformed into the reality of fraternity. The Kingdom expresses the utopia of God and the reality of God. Because of all of this the Kingdom of God is a good news, an *eu-angelion*. Jesus proclaims that the *utopia*, an object of eager expectation, has become *topia*, joy for the whole people.[36] Hence his popularity among the people. "Jesus gave religious expression to the real situation of the great majority of the Jewish people in the first century. The God of the Kingdom expresses the real hope of a people with immense material difficulties, caught up in a crisis of cultural and political identity."[37] When the Kingdom happens it is God who is ruling. Because of this it is necessary to talk about *reign*, about God actively ruling, a reign that is also found when human beings correspond to God in faith and in *metanoia*, in accepting a God who is different from the one inculcated by the religious powers.

The initiative for the Kingdom—grace—is God's. Nonetheless, Jesus—and those who follow him—put themselves at the service of the Kingdom by means of a praxis; consequently, something of what the Kingdom meant to Jesus can be understood from what he did (curing, expelling demons, sharing meals, teaching about the true reality of a God who is Abba). Add to this the well-known fact that Jesus denounced oppression (the anti-Kingdom, to use systematic terms), so that by means of what he condemned (religious, social, and economic oppression, and so on) something will be known of what he proclaimed.

Finally, what must have shocked people in Jesus' time was the unwavering proclamation that the Kingdom "is at hand." Although this is supremely important, J. Jeremias nonetheless asserts that we have not yet said what is fundamental: "To say that Jesus proclaimed the dawn of the consummation of the world is not a complete description of his proclamation of the *basileia*; on the contrary, we have still to mention its most decisive feature . . . the reign of God belongs *to the poor alone*."[38]

This relation between the Kingdom and the poor appears in various ways in the synoptic gospels. In programmatic form, the Kingdom of God is presented as the good news of God (see Lk 4:43), and this, in turn, is announced to the poor (see the inaugural address in the synagogue in Nazareth [Lk 4:18ff.] or Jesus' response to the ones sent by John [Mt 11:5; Lk 7:22]). The original and Jesuanic expression of this relation is evidently the one in the Beatitudes, that, in J. Dupont's well-known reconstruction would go like this: "Blessed are the poor because the Kingdom of Heaven is for them. Blessed are the afflicted, because they will be consoled. Blessed are the hungry (and thirsty) because they will be satisfied. Blessed are you when they hate you and persecute you. . . ."[39] Elsewhere Dupont affirms that "the good news announced to the poor cannot be other than the news that they will cease to be poor and to suffer poverty."[40]

The conclusion is that an intimate relationship exists between the Kingdom of God and the poor. Minimally, it has to be said that Jesus announces the Kingdom to the poor because they are poor. This minimum— which is a maximum—is what has to be continually asserted. With this in mind, allow me some clarifying observations that seem important for our present situation.

In the first place, in the synoptic gospels the poor are those who are stooped over, held in contempt, insignificant. They are characterized in a twofold way. On the one hand, the poor are those who are groaning under some kind of basic and vital need that makes survival very difficult. The most adequate metaphor is that of the *anawim*, the ones bent over under some heavy burden. On the other hand, the poor are those held in contempt by their society, "those whose religious ignorance or moral conduct, according to the conviction of the age, closed the door to salvation."[41]

According to J. M. Castillo they can be grouped for purposes of classification into the sick, sinners/publicans, the dispossessed, and women. Pieris, for his part, groups them thus: "the socially excluded (lepers and the mentally deficient), the religiously marginalized (prostitutes and publicans), those who were socially dependent (widows and orphans), the physically handicapped (the deaf and mute, the blind, and the lame), those psychologically tormented (epileptics and those possessed), the spiritually lowly (simple people who fear God, repentant sinners).[42]

There is then no univocal concept of the poor—nor could there be given the historical situation in which human beings live. Whatever the case, however, the poor are poor in reality, not in intention.[43] However necessary it may be to render the concept more sociologically precise, according to times and places, the conclusion is ineluctable: in Jesus' society there were human beings for whom survival was the greatest challenge, and for whom dignity (overcoming marginalization and contempt) was the greatest hope.

At present there are diverse ways of understanding poverty and even diverse theoretical definitions of it (for example, in the UNDPI). In addition, over the last few years the concept of the poor as it has been used in liberation theology has been under debate, often with a critical overtone, as if liberation theology had reduced poverty to *economic* poverty. If this were true this theology would no longer be relevant today. Because of their importance for our theme, I will reproduce these recent words of Gustavo Gutiérrez, in which he responds to these critiques:

> From its beginnings the theology of liberation has always borne the different dimensions of poverty in mind. To put it in other terms — as the Bible does — it was careful not to reduce poverty to its economic aspect, a key aspect, to be sure. This led to the affirmation that the poor person is the "insignificant" person, the one thought of like a "non-person," someone whose full complement of rights as a human being are not recognized. People without political or individual influence, who count for little in society and in the Church. This is how they are seen, or, more precisely, how they are not seen, because they are well nigh invisible to the extent that they are excluded in our contemporary world. There are many different reasons for this: deficiencies in the economic order to be sure, but also the color of one's skin, being a women, belonging to a despised culture (or one that is considered interesting because it is exotic, which finally amounts to the same thing). Poverty is, in effect, a complex and multifaceted matter; in speaking for decades about "the rights of the poor" (see, for instance, *Medellín*, "Peace," §22) we have been referring to this ensemble of dimensions of poverty.[44]

This long citation casts light on the origin of liberation theology, but it clarifies, moreover, certain fundamental issues. However much it is necessary to be precise about poverty and the way it is grasped in different epochs and places, in the Palestine of Jesus' time, in the Third World of Latin America, Asia, and Africa, and in the Fourth World, at the time of Medellín and at the turn of our century, what cannot be ignored is what is most fundamental: there are hundreds of millions, billions, of human beings for whom life and dignity are their greatest problem and their greatest utopia, since they lack both.

It can be argued, rightly enough, that economic poverty is not the only form of oppression — and not even the cruelest — but that there are other oppressions, cultural, religious, ethnic. It can be asserted that women and children are oppressed, and that these ought to be central today for theology. In all of this it is important to recall that even if these forms of oppression are not exclusive to the Third World, nonetheless the majority of cases happen in the Third World. And this is a world that is still the world of the "economically poor."

In the second place, in the synoptic gospels, *the poor are the majorities, the crowds, the people*. This *dēmos* is the fundamental quantitative datum. In addition, the social status of the poor can be gathered from looking at the language which the New Testament uses to describe the poor as majorities.[45] Four terms are used in the New Testament to refer to "the people": *dēmos* (people, nation), clearly secondary;[46] *laos* (people) with a religious connotation;[47] *ethnos* (multitude, people, nation).[48] The most frequently used term is *ochlos* (people, crowd, throng), a term that only appears in the gospels and in Acts: 175 times.

Focusing just on the people who followed Jesus, the most frequent term to describe them is *ochlos*,[49] which designates *the crowds of people, the throng*. Their situation was extremely hard, and many times desperate; they suffered from sickness and demonic possession; they went around like sheep without a shepherd.

In the Galilee of Jesus' times it is possible to be a bit more precise about the reality of the *ochlos*. There was an abyss between the upper classes—leaders, those who governed, priests, their subordinates, and business persons—and the lower classes: peasants, craftsmen, people held in contempt, "the mob," who made up part of the *ochlos*. From the *religious point of view*, the *ochlos* would include the *'am-ha'ares:* the impure, the contaminated, a category in which the uncouth and the ignorant would be seen in contrast to the cultured, the refined, the spotless ones.

It is to these *ochlos* that Jesus directs his message. This means that the good news is for them. It also means that what is good about the news is to be understood from their perspective. What I want to stress at this point is that the good news is for the majorities, for the poor as a people. The same thing happens today: the majorities are poor and the poor are the majorities.

In the Third World, *the poor are the oppressed, the victims*. In the synoptic gospels the opposition between the weak and the powerful is described more as a difference between *poor* and *greedy*, and not so much (as it is in the Old Testament) as a difference between *poor* and *oppressors*. But this does not mean that it is merely a matter of juxtaposition—of the rich man and Lazarus, for example—and that the Old Testament context does not survive into the New: "the class dialectic in the Old Testament lies implicitly in the background of this understanding of the rich and the poor."[50] The reversal of destinies of the rich and the poor proclaimed by the gospels—see the Magnificat—"would not make any sense if the understanding of poverty as a state of unjust oppression were not still operative in the New Testament."[51]

This means that the Kingdom has an intrinsically conflictive character. Conceptualized in contemporary terms, the Kingdom of necessity opposes, dialectically and combatively, the anti-Kingdom. The poor are *dialectically* poor with respect to the rich and powerful; the poor, the impoverished are victims. It is this conflictive reality of the anti-Kingdom that explains Jesus' conflicts. Along with that of the proclamation of the Kingdom, this conflict is perhaps the most certain historical fact we have. "Putting oneself on the side of life and defending life, as Jesus defended it, is not something that can be done with impunity."[52] If the mediations (Kingdom and anti-Kingdom) are at war, the mediators will be too (Jesus and the oppressors, first and foremost in his own times, the High Priests).[53]

The dialectical dimension of poverty is clear today. According to the UNDPI's reports, the proportion of rich to poor in the world was one to thirty in 1969, one to sixty in 1990, and one to seventy-four in 1997. Even if it were simply a matter of the "juxtaposition" of these two groups the scandal would still be serious, and minimally one would have to talk about a conflict of conscience. But it is not just juxtaposition. As has already been said—and Puebla said it solemnly: "There are rich because there are poor, and there are poor because there are rich." The accumulation of a few is what generates the deaths of others.

Today the poor are ignored, their conflictive character is covered up, and, what is more, "alternative" values are proposed that are good in themselves but can be used to disparage those values that accompany the defense of the poor: work, fortitude, struggle, prophecy, utopia. Expressing this from another perspective, respecting the martyrs who have defended the poor is quite normal, and at times they are praised in all sincerity. But as a whole, the awareness and meaning of the phenomenon of martyrs is carefully controlled by society and also by the Church. And it is largely ignored in theology. The martyrs talk about faith and love, but also about injustice and conflict. The conflict that comes from putting oneself on the side of the poor is expressed in their praxis and in their fate. If so many different ways are sought for hiding the conflictive character of poverty, it is because it is very real.

2.2 *God from the Perspective of the Poor*

If God privileges the poor because they are poor, then God is partial and merciful.

Dealing first with partiality, in the founding event of the faith God reveals God's self to an oppressed people because they are oppressed. It is not that God first reveals God's self to everyone and then shows partiality for the oppressed. Rather, it is in and through partiality toward them that God reveals God's proper reality. This pattern continues throughout the Old Testament. Psalm 68:5 defines God as "Father of orphans and protector of widows." In the Prophets it is not all of Israel that God calls "my" people, but the oppressed in Israel.[54] Yahweh is the defender of Israel, the *Go'el* that "defends the poor." "God is the protector of the orphan and of the poor; God works justice for them against those who oppress them and who take advantage of their weakness."[55]

Partiality also lies at the origins of law in Israel and in the surrounding peoples. The hoped-for king is not just any king, but a king who is partial to the oppressed, those who, without him, most easily fall victim to the powerful. The king's justice does not consist "in issuing an impartial verdict but in the protection that is given to the destitute and to the poor, to widows and orphans."[56] The just king's action is that of "saving the oppressed from injustice."[57]

When it comes to the New Testament, we have already seen in a programmatic way that "the Kingdom is for the poor." This offer of salvation is not conditioned by something in the poor's disposition (their moral quality), but in God's disposition. To this it must be added that God makes our final salvation depend on what we do with the poor. We must not forget Jesus' exultation: "the poor understand the mysteries of the Kingdom" (cf. Mt 11:25; Lk 10:21).

The fact of God's partiality is clear, but the question of "why" remains. What is it that moves God to take up this primordial and undeducible stance in favor of the weak? In this I have insisted again and again that one must "let God be God," that one must maintain God's mystery—although Käsemann rightly points out that "God's will is no mystery, at least in so far as it concerns love and one's brother."[58] But sometimes, to put it thus, God himself gives God's reasons: the reason for partiality is the mercy that God feels for the poor, the small, the victim, without there being anything anterior or posterior to the simple reality of the poor that moves God to compassion.

This, so central to God's self-revelation, seems clear to me, but it is frequently disputed. Recall that the Vatican's 1984 Instruction on Liberation Theology asserted that the reason for the liberation of the Exodus lies in the fact that God wanted to create a people with which God could then, subsequently, make a covenant, so that this people would worship God alone.[59] This purely religious interpretation was rejected by Juan Luis Segundo[60] and by Ignacio Ellacuría,[61] in favor of another more historical and even political interpretation. But what I want to stress here is the reason that God adduces for God's actions in the Exodus. The Yahwist tradition has "I have observed the misery of my people who are in Egypt; I have heard their cry on account of their taskmasters. Indeed, I know their sufferings" (Ex 3:7), and the Elohist, "The cry of the Israelites has now come to me; I have also seen how the Egyptians oppress them" (v. 9). The suffering of an oppressed people has moved God.

This basic mercy toward the oppressed—*ḥesed*—is the reason for God's action, and thus, for God's self-manifestation. This does not mean, as Ellacuría admits, that God does not have a covenant in mind that would humanize the people of Israel and liberate it from other slaveries, those that arise from the human condition and even those that come from the new situation subsequent to leaving Egypt: coexisting with the weak of the people and with the stranger, doing justice to them, humanizing authority, monarchical or nomonarchical, relating to God with confidence and with faith, opening oneself to God and allowing oneself to be accepted by God.

The centrality of mercy appears in the New Testament as well. The miracles demonstrate, above all, Jesus' compassion.[62] It repeatedly says in the synoptic gospels that Jesus felt compassion and mercy for the suffering of others, above all the suffering of the simple majorities (the *ochlos*) that accompanied him.[63] Jesus appears to be profoundly moved by another's pain: "his heart was moved" (Mk 6:34; Mt 9:36). He reacts salvifically, defending them from false shepherds; and he makes of this reaction something basic and ultimate, a criterion for all he does. Jesus sees something ultimate in the pain of these majorities, something that can only find adequate response in something ultimate. The verb with which Jesus' attitude is described is *splanchnizomai*, which comes from the noun, *splanchna:* bowels, guts, heart, everything that symbolizes what is *ultimate to human beings.*

Jesus' mercy, then, is a re-action—an action, therefore—to the pain of the poor and victims, from which it is possible to define what is humanly and divinely ultimate. This is how Jesus himself is described and this is how, in Luke's gospel, he describes the upright person, the Samaritan, who is "moved with pity" (Lk 10:33—and it is certainly clear that the poor fellow here is a victim), and God himself, the Father of the Prodigal Son, who is "filled with compassion" (Lk 15:20). And finally, it is what Jesus requires of everyone: "Be merciful, just as your Father is merciful" (Lk 6:36).

2.3   The Jesuanic Principle: The Theologal Dimension of the Poor

Whether one thinks of it in terms of the "only to the poor," or that being in their presence "stirred up something ultimate" in Jesus, there is something about the poor that puts them in an ultimate relation to God: one cannot talk about God except by means of this ultimate relation that God has with them. In this way the poor are elevated to the theologal realm. God manifests God's reality in relation to the poor. And, moreover, God loves and defends the poor by the simple fact that they are poor, by grace. For theology, as a consequence, the poor belong to the theologal realm.[64] As Puebla reformulated it twenty centuries later:

> For this reason alone the poor deserve preferential attention, whatever the moral or personal situation in which they are found. Made in the image and likeness of God, in order to be God's children, this image is darkened and even mocked. Because of this God takes up their defense and loves them. (n. 1142)

The central element of the Jesuanic principle is the love God has for the poor by grace. I call it *Jesuanic* because it goes back to what Jesus said and did historically, the historical cross being the expression "to the end and in spite of everything" of this love and defense by God of the poor, and the resurrection being the transcendent confirmation of the truth of this option for the poor. As Pieris intuitively expresses it, "Jesus incarnates the defensive covenant between the oppressed and Yahweh."[65]

To understand the Jesuanic principle better it would be good to compare it, in its formal elements, with what—for the sake of linguistic symmetry—we can call the *Paulanic principle* and the *Johannic principle*, both of which express the centrality of grace. In Pauline theology justification is by faith, not by works. God justifies the unrighteous by grace, something that appears in a central way in the cross. Conceptualizing this theologally, "in Christ God was reconciling the world to himself" (2 Cor 5:19). In theologal-christological language, "God proves his love for us in that while we were still sinners Christ died for us" (Rom 5:8). God's love is not a reaction to what human beings are worth, but rather is pure gratuitousness, even when human beings act against God. Johannine theology culminates with the proclamation that "God is love" (1 Jn 4:8); it emphasizes gratuity: "he first loved us" (1 Jn 4:19). The historical-transcendent expression of this gratuitous love is the sending into the world of the Son (1 Jn 4:9, 3:16). God's gratuity is clear, and the consequence is a surprising one: "Beloved, since God loved us so much, we also ought to love one another" (1 Jn 4:11). "Loved in order to love" and "pardoned in order to pardon" is what Johannine theology ends up saying— just as the theology of liberation will say "liberated in order to liberate."

Comparing now the Pauline and Johannine claims with the Jesuanic principle, they all converge on the centrality of a gratuitous good news of God. But there are differences in the ways they express it. What is specific to Jesus is that he does not show God's gratuitous love universally in a direct way (to human beings as such, or to human beings as sinners); rather, he shows it in relation to a specific addressee: the poor. The actions that express this love do not come to us articulated in transcendent language (the sending or handing over of the Son), but in historical language (cures, defense of the poor, denunciation of their oppressors, and so on); not in doxological language ("God first loved us"), but rather in narrative language ("every day the father would go out waiting for the son").

The various ways of conceptualizing and formulating the gratuity of God's love have, to put it thus, different potentialities. Obviously they do not oppose but rather complement each other. This being said, I insist on retrieving the Jesuanic principle for two reasons. One is that in the history of the Church and of theology it would appear to be the case that gratuity is reflected well in Paul and John—this is clear—but much more modestly in the synoptic gospels and in their presentation of Jesus. Revelation would put the human being in a direct relation with God, on the basis of being human, and sinful; but the poor, as poor, would not come into relationship to God so radically.

The other reason is that because it expresses realities that are more historical, the Jesuanic principle can function as a mystagogy into the Paulanic and Johannic principles. That God loves human beings prior to their loving God; that God justifies the sinner by grace; that God, God himself, makes himself akin to the crucified ones of history: all of this is understood—in a first moment, logically speaking—from the vantage of what is historical about Jesus, although it can then be elevated to a transcendent principle. Moreover, if one were not to follow the path from the historical (Jesus) to the transcendent (God) in one way or another, it would be saying that one knows what salvation, grace, and justification are independently of Jesus. The life and historical cross of Jesus would not be strictly necessary in order to understand them. Because of this the Jesuanic principle seems to me to be necessary, on the one hand, and a form of mystagogy, on the other: to understand the gratuity of God it is a good thing to see Jesus exercising it, accepting the poor and oppressed, those spurned, the impure. Since the addressee of the gratuity of God is historical, concrete, quite visible—the poor—and not, in the first instance, universal—every human being—this also makes it easy to understand *better* the God of grace.[66]

Ideally the different New Testament perspectives have to be unified, which is the great lesson of a canon that admits of diversity. Concretely, "the justification of the sinner" has to be put in relation with "the salvation of the poor." In both cases God's reaction is directed toward the weak, toward the one who does not merit anything of him- or herself, something for which the Pauline intuition is certainly helpful. As González Faus says, "the doctrine of justification by faith turns the believer toward the poor of this earth, as the theology of liberation has clearly seen: a person ought to love that one who does not deserve anything, whom God has also loved even though he or she does not deserve it."[67] Yet I think that the converse is also true: God's option for the poor is helpful for understanding justification by faith—it nuances it. The poor person is one who is impoverished, and God's relation with him or her is not only a loving and beneficial one, but a defensive and liberating one.[68]

The poor person is not only the one God loves, simply because he or she is poor, but the one whom God defends from his or her oppressors.

All of this leads to the conclusion that the radicality of God's gratuitous love is worked out quite well in the theologies of Paul and John, but it does not start there; rather, it is already worked out—and with absolute clarity—in what Jesus said and did. Mentioning this can seem obvious, but to me it seems to be important to do so, since this fact tends to be forgotten. "The poor" continue to be a concrete reality that the Church and theology cannot seem to figure out how to handle adequately. To put it thus, they are understood *as a part of* the human universe, but they "*get lost*" in this universe. Other realities of the Christian imagination have had their ups and downs in the course of human history, but some of them—including important ones too—have been restored with greater (relative) facility than the Kingdom of God, and, above all, more easily than the poor. At important points, we have gotten back to the realities of grace and freedom, the Church as sacrament, and even the historical Jesus. Getting back, in a focused way, to the poor is always difficult. Holding on to that focus almost never happens.

3.   The Poor's Contribution to Theology

The poor ought to be put at the center of theology, for their own good, but also for theology's good. They offer a specific place for the doing and understanding of theology, and they offer light for the Christian reformulation of its contents. It is well known that central themes have been retrieved from the vantage point of the poor: among others, the historical Jesus, the Kingdom of God, the Church of the poor, the mystery of a God crucified and risen as the justice that God does for a victim, grace, and structural sin. If I may put it this way, there is some truth to the statement that *extra pauperes nulla salus, nulla ecclesia*, and consequently *nulla* Christian theology as well. I am going to illustrate this with some examples.

a) The Recovery of the Option for the Poor

The Jesuanic principle establishes the relation between God and the poor, and God's option—defense—for them. If this is the way things are then that option should be present in all of theology, being clear all the while that that option is not opposed to universality, but rather emphasizes the necessity of looking at and acting on the whole from a part: the poor.

Besides being a content that theology should analyze and ground, the option for the poor is above all a disposition of the theologian, which can carry over to his or her theological product, and shapes the totality of his or her being and work. Recalling Kant's questions—What can I know? For what may I hope? What ought I to do? to which I would add the question, What is given to me to celebrate?—we can say that this option means that theology will shape its answers to these questions from the perspective of the poor.

What can I know? From the vantage point of the poor theology can know the truth of reality better, certainly important aspects of reality: the truth of God and of the idols, of grace and of sin, of Jesus and of the Church. This specifies what in theology belongs to an *intellectus fidei*.

For what may I hope? From the poor theology can once again piece together and formulate the hope that life, justice, dignity, the human family are possible, the hope that the executioner will not prevail over the victim. In a dialectical form: to hope that life will always be a reality, even when confronted with death. This specifies what in theology belongs to an *intellectus spei*.

What do I have to do? From the vantage of the poor theology has to live and to spend its life so that where there is injustice, deceit, contempt, and death there might be justice, truth, dignity, and life. In other words it must help—from the perspective of the theoretical work proper to it—to bring down the crucified from the cross. This specifies what in theology belongs to an *intellectus amoris*.

What is given to me to celebrate? From the perspective of the poor theology can be thankful for and celebrate the life of the poor, their labors and struggles, their great triumphs (in hope) and their little ones, their witness, their love, their devotion, and even their martyrdom—and from thence it is possible to celebrate the building up of the human family. What is essential to celebration is that it is not an achievement but a gift. This specifies what in theology belongs to an *intellectus gratiae*.

Whether it is easy or difficult to do so, what seems clear to me is that these questions are only answered adequately from the perspective of the poor, and by letting oneself be held accountable to the poor.

b) The Recovery of Liberation

It has taken a lot more for theology to recover liberation than to recover freedom. The two Vatican instructions on liberation theology of 1984 and 1986 recognize liberation as something that is central to revelation—in addition to freedom.[69] This notwithstanding, for centuries "liberation" has been ignored in theology, even in progressive theology, although the Spanish theology of the last few decades (*inter allia*, J.I. González Faus, J.M. Castillo), and German political theology (J. Moltmann, J.B. Metz) have taken it seriously. In a nutshell, progressive theology has talked, and ably, about "freedom," and has found in Paul a legitimate champion. But it has not talked about "liberation," and sometimes it has not even found it in the mission of Jesus.

The attempt has been made in liberation theology to encourage both of these things, making them converge;[70] indeed, Juan Luis Segundo even used to say that liberation theology was in need of a deeper reflection on freedom, as Paul presents it. Yet it is clear that the specific contribution of this theology has been the discovery of liberation. What has made this possible has been in large measure the place where theology has been done: the poor. If liberation has been recovered in Latin America as something central, this has happened because it is a poor continent.[71] This theology has been able to look around at its miserable surroundings—just as Paul was able to look around at his gentile surroundings—and it has grasped God's will for them.

c) The Civilization of Poverty

From the vantage of the poor, utopia exists, and it is absolutely necessary that it be worked out in terms of life: a life of justice and dignity for the poor that is always open to more.[72] From their perspective, and given the dehumanization that has beset our world, Ignacio Ellacuría formulated a notion of utopia in terms of humanization, and, elaborating this, he worked it out from the perspective of the poor: "the civilization of poverty." This is an audacious and provocative phrase, but he chose it consciously and stood by it until the end as the way of making "the civilization of work" real in our contemporary world, and of historicizing a "civilization of love," both of which are necessary formulations of utopia, the second, in very general terms, being acceptable to every-one, but not the first. In various articles, from 1983 up to 1989, he worked this civilization of poverty out conceptually. I am going to sketch a few of the details because of the novelty of his proposal, with its prophetic and utopian character.

The civilization of poverty is, first and foremost, a historical neces-sity, given the global correlation of population to resources. It is also nec-essary because of the failure of the civilization of wealth. It is not a mat-ter of becoming "paupers," but of overcoming in a dialectical way wealth and its dynamism:

> The civilization of poverty is so denominated in contrast to the civi-lization of wealth, and not because it proposes universal pauperiza-tion as an ideal of life. . . . What should be stressed here is the dialec-tical wealth-poverty relationship and not poverty in itself. In a world sinfully shaped by the capital-wealth dynamism it is necessary to stir up another dynamism that will salvifically surpass it. . . . We can only begin to look for another type of culture by relinquishing and liberating ourselves from the lie that Western Culture has already found the way, at least, to genuine human progress.[73]

Ultimately, the civilization of poverty is presented as a possibility that the spirit might increase (unmasking the presupposition that Western Civilization has not failed, at least as far as the cultivation of spirit goes).

> This poverty is what really gives room for the spirit, so that it be no longer stifled by the drive to have more than someone else, by the concupiscent longing to have every kind of superfluity when the largest part of humanity is lacking what is necessary. Then the spirit will be able to flourish, that immense spiritual and human wealth of the poor and of the peoples of the Third World, which today is drowned in misery and stifled by the imposition of cultural models that are more developed in some aspects but not by that fact more fully human.[74]

This overcoming of an alienating culture ought also to involve in turn the recovery of the cultural riches of the peoples. But the point is not to recover these cultural riches so that they can be conserved and shut up in themselves, but rather "in quest of a culture of the majority, and not an elitist culture with lots of style and little life. The motto of the new culture in the new world ought to be "That all, if possible, and not just a few, have life and have it in abundance."[75]

Ellacuría tried to promote utopia as *life*, but also as *civilization*, in such a way that dehumanizing wealth would be overcome and the goods of the spirit would be encouraged. His intuition was to insist that real poverty is the most apt place in which the spirit might flourish, and that is why, in a systematic synthesis of the Beatitudes in Matthew and Luke, he talked about the "poor with spirit."[76] In doing this he got back to the poor, but on the other side of the Jesuanic principle, to put it thus. He stressed that it was both possible and necessary that they exist "with spirit," using the language of the synoptic gospels of *metanoia* and of faith. What Ellacuría added, guided more by theology and by Christian faith than by reason alone, is that in the materiality of poverty there is a greater connaturality with the values of the gospel. But the important thing is the conclusion: the poor and their values can generate a new civilization.[77]

d) Overcoming Ecclesial and Theological Docetism: "Being Real"

Theology and the Church have a tendency and temptation not to be "real." They "exist," of course, but they tend to create their own sphere of reality that separates them from, and sometimes puts them in opposition to, the "most real" reality. This is what I call docetism.

This is a familiar problem in Christology. There is something that makes it difficult to accept Christ's humanity, his "reality." Recall that it took much longer for the Church to define Christ's true humanity, his consubstantiality with us human beings (in Chalcedon in 451), even though this is evident in the New Testament, than it did for the Church to define his true divinity, his consubstantiality with the Father (Nicaea, 325), even though this is not evident. It has taken a lot to accept that this humanity is *sarx*, what is weak about the human.

Well, docetism is not just a christological problem, perhaps the gravest since the Church began; rather, it is a recurrent and omnipresent "heresy." It certainly shows up in the Church, and not even theology is immune. Both of these are realities that "exist," but they can live in an "unreal" world. To be real it is not enough to exist physically in the world; nor is it enough to be in sync with a given situation's patterns of thought; rather, what is necessary is that we be shaped by the reality of the world—what there is in it of *sarx*.

Let us put this in contemporary terms. If our knowing, our doing, our hoping and our celebrating are not shaped by the fifty million people who die of hunger every year, or by El Mozote or Rwanda, or by the economic embargo against women, children, and the elderly in Iraq, or by the horrors that Congolese women suffer; if these things do not move our intelligence and heart, then we are not in reality, and in that case it is not just that we are not human, not ethical, or not Christian; more radially, we are not "real."

To say it again using existential language, if sometimes we have not felt ashamed to live on this planet and to belong to the human species, I doubt that we would be living in reality. We would be warding off that reality by taking refuge in an alternative realm of historical, cultural, religious, and theological reality, fabricated for that purpose. According to Kantian thought, we would still be in a deep slumber, not now a dogmatic one, but one of unreality.

In my opinion it is the poor of this world, the *sarx* of reality, who have the power to make us go from "existing" to "being real." Let me say this with some of Archbishop Romero's words, words rarely, if ever, voiced by a bishop:

> I am happy my brothers that our Church is persecuted.[78]

> In a country where assassinations are going on in such a horrible way, it would be a sad thing if we did not count priests as well among the victims. They are testimony of a Church incarnate in the problems of the people.[79]

These are not the words of a mystic, and certainly not of a masochist. They are the words of a human being and a Christian who wants to be "real" in the midst of his people. "We do not want to be different," Archbishop Romero seems to be saying, challenging centuries of ecclesiastical tradition.

The poor, here in their starkest form as victims, are the ones who make it possible to be real in the Church and in theology. By their very reality they express what reality truly is, and they press us to deal with the disgrace of not belonging to it. They accuse us of docetism, but they also save us from it.

e) The Jesuanic Martyrs and the Crucified People

My final thoughts concern the martyrs, a reality both contemporary and massive in countries like mine. For this reason alone—not to mention the fact that Christianity is founded on the martyr, Jesus—theology would have to take this theme seriously, although normally it does not. I would only like to say in all brevity that the poor of this world have helped theology, forced theology, to make these martyrs present to it and to reformulate the concept of martyrdom. And this in two senses.

In the first place, many Christians (and many human beings in general) have suffered violent deaths. The important thing is establishing that on a fundamental level they lived and acted like Jesus, defending the poor from their oppressors, and have died like Jesus, at the hands of the oppressors and executioners of the poor. I call these people Jesuanic martyrs.

This is a fact that is historically manifest, but it leads as well to a theological reflection. "Martyr" means, in effect, witness; but, more primordially, martyrs are those who have been "defenders" of the poor, who have given their lives—to use a Johannine orientation—because of a great love. What one finds in these deaths is, above all, the love and defense of the poor. If you will, the Jesuanic martyrs, today's martyrs, are "the defenders of the poor to the end."

From the vantage of the poor, then, one's eyes are opened to analyze the extraordinary quality of these martyrs from a Jesuanic perspective. And not just Jesuanically, but theologally as well. The Jesuanic martyrs are martyrs *in* the Church, but strictly speaking they are not martyrs *of* the Church. They are martyrs of the Kingdom of God, of humanity, of a creation that is living through the birth pangs of the passage to humanity.

This last fact introduces us into what is most fundamental. The poor are there before the Jesuanic martyrs. They are the ones who suffer the slow death of poverty; and they are the ones who are often assassinated violently, collectively, and with great cruelty. They are the ones that I call crucified peoples, the suffering servant of Yahweh. They go to their deaths less freely, compared with the Jesuanic martyrs, because sometimes they have no chance at all to escape. Neither do they exercise any violence, not even the violence of a prophetic word, like Archbishop Romero's. But, on the other hand, the sin of the world weighs down on them more cruelly and they are assassinated more defenselessly.

These crucified peoples ought to be an absolutely central theme for theology, although they do not even have a name any more. But, what is more, they are the ones, briefly put, who shed light on the "why" of the Jesuanic martyrs and on the martyr Jesus. The latter have been killed for defending these crucified peoples from the slow death of poverty and the violent death of repression.

But in treating the martyrs too, even from the most contemporary perspectives, it is difficult to make the poor majorities, the victims, the center. The deaths of the crucified people are ignored to a much greater extent than the deaths of the Jesuanic martyrs. In the Church people know what to do—sometimes—with the deaths of the active martyrs, but practically never does anyone know what to do with the crucified peoples. Getting even more to the roots of the question, there can be readings of the synoptic gospels that know what to do with the disciples and followers of Jesus, but not so much with the multitudes who flocked to him from every direction: the poor, the infirm, sinners, women, publicans. Nonetheless, Jesus says that the Kingdom of God belongs to these latter. Sometimes I like to say—not ironically, but in order to shed some light on the mystery that is involved here—that without having made St. Ignatius's *Spiritual Exercises*, two or three billion human beings have been chosen to live in poverty and have been put with the Son.[80] We know what to do with those followers who *ask* to be put with the Son, but frequently we do not know what to do with those who have been crucified with him.

Something like this can happen with the martyrs. At times we know what to do with the "Jesuanic martyrs," but frequently we do not know what do with the "crucified people." And what they ask of us is precisely this: that we stand by their cross, that we show profound respect for its mystery—that both hides the mystery of God and at the same time allows it to be seen—that we let them forgive us, pardon us, save us. And that we go to any lengths, even to the point of giving our lives, to bring them down from the cross.

Translated by J. Matthew Ashley

NOTES

1. Ignacio Ellacuría, "Discernir los 'signos de los tiempos' en la telogía de la liberación," *Diakonía* 17 (1981): 58.

2. Ellacuría's well-known text "The Crucified People," carries the subtitle "An Essay on Historical Soteriology." See *Mysterium Liberationis*, ed. Ignacio Ellacuría, S.J., and Jon Sobrino, S.J. (Maryknoll, N.Y.: Orbis Books, 1993), 580–603.

3. Theologal (*teologal*) is a technical term that Ignacio Ellacuría took over from his philosophical mentor, Xavier Zubiri, and which Sobrino often uses. It must be distinguished from "theological" (*teológico*). The distinction is analogous to that between "social" and "sociological." Just as it is the fact that there is an irreducible *social* dimension to human reality that allows, legitimates, and even demands sociological discourse, the "theologal" dimension of reality, and of specific domains and entities in reality, is that dimension which allows, legitimates, and even requires theological discourse (*Trans.*).

4. In this essay I will use "the poor" to refer to the poor, to victims, and to the crucified people, taken as a whole, although at times I will specify somewhat more strongly their character as victims.

5. J.B. Metz, "Teología europea y teología de la liberación," in *Cambio social y pensamiento cristiano in América Latina*, ed. J. Comblin, J.I. González Faus, and J. Sobrino (Madrid, 1993), 268.

6. Pedro Casadáliga, "El Cuerno del Jubileo," *Carta a las Iglesias* 393 (1998): 8.

7. "Mundialización de la Solidaridad y de la Esperanza," *Carta a las Iglesias* 446–447 (2000): 11.

8. It should be made clear that this condition of the poor and victims does not require and make possible "just" a contextual theology, as some are accustomed to say, intending to minimize its importance, but rather the most universal and least contextual theology, since it grapples with the most widespread reality in our world. As far as this goes there is certainly globalization. See Gustavo Gutiérrez, "Situación y tareas de la teología de la liberación," *Revista Latinoameriana de Teología* 50 (2000): 101–116.

9. González Faus, "Veinticinco años de la teología de la liberación: Teología y opción por los," *Revista Latinoamericana de Teología* 42 (1997): 224, where he adduces texts from Domingo Soto and Bishop Bossuet.

10. See J.B. Metz, "Un hablar de Dios sensible a la teodicea," in *El clamor de la tierra* (Estella, 1996), 7–28.

11. Pedro Casadáliga, "Los indios crucificados: Un caso anónimo de martirio colectivo," *Concilium* 183 (1983): 387.

12. Ignacio Ellacuría, "Pobres," in *Conceptos Fundamentales de Pastoral*, ed. Casiano Floristán y Juan-José Tamayo (Madrid, 1983), 791.

13. María López Vigil, *Muerte y vida en Morazán* (San Salvador, 1989), 119.

14. Hugo Assman, *Theology for a Nomad Church*, trans. Paul Burns, with an introduction by Frederick Herzog (Maryknoll, N.Y.: Orbis, 1975).

15. Jesuanic translates *Jesuánico*, a Spanish neologism. Its meaning will emerge from the usage below. As a heuristic definition to begin with, one may take it to denote a crucial reality or starting point that is specified by what Jesus said and did, and from which the whole of Christian faith and theology can and should be construed (*Trans.*).

16. In this essay I will take a great deal from what I have written in *Jesus the Liberator: A Historical-Theological View*, trans. Paul Burns and Francis Mc-Donagh (Maryknoll, N.Y.: Orbis, 1993) and *La fe in Jesucristo: Ensayo desde las víctimasú* (San Salvador: UCA Editores, 2000).

17. Martin Hengel, *The Son of God*, trans. John Bowden (Philadelphia, Pa.: Fortress Press, 1976), 2.

18. Sobrino, *La fe en Jesucristo*, 212–18.

19. Let us recall that in Gal 3:28 Paul says that "there is no longer Jew or Greek, there is no longer slave or free, there is no longer male and female," although in 1 Cor 12:13 the final member disappears from this triad, probably because it was the most scandalous in the Graeco-Roman world and holding on to it raised serious problems for Paul's evangelical work.

20. J. Comblin, *Pablo, apóstol de Jesucristo* (Madrid, 1996), 94–100.

21. In this gospel the Kingdom of God only appears in the conversation between Jesus and Nicodemus (Jn 3:3, 5), and at the end, in order to say that "my Kingdom is not of this world" (18:36).

22. In the New Testament Jesus' resurrection is spoken of as the beginning of the universal resurrection (1 Thes 4:15, 17; 1 Cor 15:51), and Jesus is consequently "the firstborn of many brothers" (Rom 8:29; 1 Cor 15:13; Col 1:18; Acts 3:15; Rv 1:5).

23. I think that Jesus' resurrection also put the Kingdom of God in the shadows in another more programmatic sense, at least in Paul: "The revelation of the risen Jesus led the apostles to a radical simplification of the whole breadth of the religion that he had cultivated with so much zeal. It turned into his only act, and all the rest ended up being only aspects of this revelation" (J. Comblin, *Pablo, apóstol de Jesucristo*, 71f.).

24. "What also remains intact is the fundamental line, which can be described with the sequence, Gospel-faith-eschatological community–definitive encounter with the Lord, so that for Paul, from 1 Thessalonians through Romans, faith can hope that its relation to Christ will pass from the state of faith and hope to the state of definitive vision" (J. Becker, *Pablo, el apóstol de los paganos* [Salamanca, 1996], 522).

25. Ibid., 525.

26. Ibid., 503.

27. Although in this regard it would perhaps be good to recall Cullman's point. Jesus hoped for the nearness of the Kingdom, and yet right up to the end he maintained a social stance of denunciation of the powerful. See Oscar Cullman, *Jesus and the Revolutionaries*, trans. Gareth Putnam (New York: Harper & Row, 1970), 24f.

28. And something similar would have to be said of John. J.I. González Faus says that John's Christology has a sort of triangular form: God at the apex and at the base a radical christocentrism and the love for the neighbor, also radicalized. And he concludes by synthesizing Paul and John: "the 'work of God in Christ' that Paul will call 'recapitulation' (Eph 1:14) consists for John in the fact that if we love one another we have known God and God is in us (1 Jn, *passim*)." See "Mística de la compasión: mística de ojos abiertos," *Revista Latinoamericana de Teología* 47 (1998): 143.

29. Juan Luis Segundo, *Teología abierta III: Reflexiones críticas* (Madrid, 1984), 314.

30. Juan Luis Segundo, *The Liberation of Dogma*, trans. Philip Berryman (Maryknoll, N.Y.: Orbis Books, 1992), 144.

31. J.M. Castillio, *El Reino de Dios: Por la vida y la dignidad de los seres humanos* (Bilbao, 1999), 23.

32. Ignacio Ellacuría, "Aporte de la teología de la liberación a las religiones abrahámicas en la superación del individualismo y del positivismo," *Revista Latinoamericana de Teología* 10 (1987). See also, Jon Sobrino, "La centralidad del 'reino de Dios' en la teología de la liberación" *Revista Latinoamericana de Teología* 9 (1986): 247–81.

33. Let us also remember that, although it is not necessary to get tangled up in oversimplifications or anachronism, the world of the synoptic gospels and of Jesus' activity are in some type of isomorphism with the Third World and with the activity of the Jesuanic martyrs, for example.

34. Walter Kasper, *Jesus the Christ* (New York: Paulist Press, 1977), 86, 87.

35. "The expectation, in itself traditional, of the Kingdom of God . . . ended up being turned into the uniquely decisive perspective" (Wolfhart Pannenberg, "The Revelation of God in Jesus of Nazareth," in *Theology as History*, ed. James M. Robinson and John B. Cobb, Jr. [New York: Harper and Row, 1967] 103).

36. See Leonardo Boff, "Salvation in Jesus Christ and the Process of Liberation," trans. J.P. Donnelly, in *The Mystical and Political Dimensions of The Christian Faith*, ed. Claude Geffré and Gustavo Gutiérrez, *Concilium*, vol. 96 (New York: Herder and Herder, 1974), 80f.

37. R. Aguirre, *Del movimiento de Jesús a la Iglesia* (Bilbao, 1987), 51.

38. Joachim Jeremias, *New Testament Theology*, trans. John Bowden (New York: Charles Scribner's Son, 1971) 108, 116 (emphasis in original).

39. J. Dupont, *Les Béatitudes: Le probleme littéraire* (Louvaine, 1958), 1:343.

40. Various authors, *Evangelizare pauperibus* (Bresccia, 1978), 183.

41. J. Jeremias, *Theology of the New Testament*, 112.

42. Aloysius Pieris, "Christ beyond Dogma: Doing Christology in the Context of the Religions of the Poor," *Revista Latinoamericana de Teología* 52 (2001).

43. In New Testament Greek the term that is most frequently used to describe the poor is *ptochos*. Of the twenty-five times that the term appears, twenty-two times it refers to those who are economically dispossessed and afflicted. In the three places in which *ptochos* designates the spiritually poor (Mt 4:3; cf. Gal 4:9, Rv 3:17), some further qualification is added. In none of the three cases in which Jesus relates the Kingdom of God to the *ptochoi* (Mt 11:5; Lk 7:22, 4:18, 6:20) is its meaning spiritual. The conclusion is that in the New Testament and in Jesus the term "poor" is a sociological category.

44. Gustavo Gutiérrez, "Situación y tareas de la teología de la liberación," 109f.

45. Here I follow J.M. Castillo, "Jesús, el pueblo y la teología," 111–38.

46. It only appears four times, in Acts (12:22; 17:5; 19:30, 33).

47. This appears 131 times, 84 in Luke-Acts. In the New Testament Israel's title as "*laos* of God" passed to the "Christian Church."

48. This appears 162 times in the New Testament. When it is used in the plural (*éthne*) it is clearly applied to "the gentiles." In Paul's theology it has a noteworthy significance for expressing the vocation and the mission of this apostle: to proclaim the gospel to the gentiles (1 Thes 2:16), as a divine calling that liberates them from Jewish legalisms (Gal 1:16, 2:7–9; Rom 1:5).

49. Fifty times in Matthew, thirty-eight in Mark, forty-one in Luke, and twenty in John.

50. G.M. Soares-Prabhu, "Clase social en la Biblia: Los pobres, ¿una clase social?" *Revista Latinoamericana de Teología* 12 (1987): 228.

51. Ibid.

52. J.M. Castillo, *El Reino de Dios*, 79.

53. The people, the *ochlos*, is not in conflict with Jesus. One need not rule out the possibility of the sorts of psychological-social changes to which large crowds are prone happening in relation to Jesus too, but historically R. Aguirre's conclusions seem valid: "Strictly speaking, Jesus never fled from the people, but from the authorities" ("Jesús y la multitud a la luz del evangelio de Juan," *Estudios Eclesiásticos* 218–219 [1980]: 1071).

54. J.L. Sicre, *Con los pobres de la tierra* (Madrid, 1984), 448.

55. Dupon, *Les Béatitudes*, 2:73.

56. J. Jeremias, *Teología del Nuevo Testamento*, 122.

57. José Porfirio Miranda, *Marx and the Bible*, trans. John Eagleson (Maryknoll, N.Y.: Orbis Books, 1974), 113f. It is clear that this partiality of God for the weak is not exclusive to Israel, but this need not make it less important. In any case, this should not lead us to devalue partiality in itself, or its expressions in other religions, but to value it more highly. In the second place, the historical expressions of this partiality in the Old Testament open up—for the Christian

believer—to "the definitive partiality" of the cross, in which what happens is no longer "alterity," although a partial one, but affinity of God and the poor and victims. Partiality can be a mystagogy into affinity. I have written on this in *Jesus the Liberator*, 233–53, and *La fe en Jesucristo*, 478–98.

58. Ernst Käsemann, *Jesus Means Freedom*, trans. Frank Clarke (Philadelphia, Pa.: Fortress Press, 1970), 26.

59. *Instruction on Certain Aspects of the Theology of Liberation*, 4:3. See Alfred T. Hennelly, ed., *Liberation Theology: A Documentary History* (Maryknoll, N.Y.: Orbis Books, 1990), 397.

60. "The three oldest important sources—the Yahwist, the Elohist, and the Deuteronomist—agree in presenting Yahweh as intervening on behalf of the people that is already his own, due to the mercy that he feels before an inhuman situation (call it political or no) that this people is experiencing because of their oppression and slavery in Egypt, and in order to give to them a land of their own. In the most ancient traditions there is no trace of this alleged goal of the Exodus consisting in 'founding the people of God.'" See *Teología de la liberación: Respuesta al Cardenal Ratzinger* (Madrid, 1985), 62f.

61. In a more nuanced form and in dialogue with Urs von Balthasar, Ellacuría repeats basically the same thesis: "But whatever the origin of these stories, their real basis is very precise: the cult (the covenant itself is a different question) does not give meaning to the liberation from Egypt, but rather the liberation gives its specific meaning to the cult, which celebrates and draws out the explicit consequences of that historical experience, that historical praxis" ("The Historicity of Christian Salvation," in *Mysterium Liberationis*, ed. Ignacio Ellacuría, S.J., and Jon Sobrino, S.J. [Maryknoll, N.Y.: Orbis Books, 1993], 264).

62. See Albert Nolan, *Jesus Before Christianity* (Maryknoll, N.Y.: Orbis Books, 1992), 42–44; J. I. González Faus, *Clamor del reino: Estudio sobre los milagros de Jesús* (Salamanca, 1982).

63. "When he went ashore he saw a great crowd; and he had compassion for them and cured their sick" (Mt 14:14). He was moved to pity for a leper (Mk 1:41), for two blind men (Mt 20:34), for those who had nothing to eat (Mk 8:2; Mt 15:32), for those who were like sheep without a shepherd (Mk 6:34; Mt 9:36), for the widow of Nain, whose son had just died (Lk 7:13). And in at least four miracle stories, Jesus cures after the petition "Have mercy on me" (Mt 20: 29–30 par., 15:22 par., 17:15; Lk 17:13).

64. This is an important difference, to be sure, between the social teachings of the Church and the theology of liberation. The former is more ethical; the latter is more theological and theo-logal. It is necessary to insist on this difference, since treating the poor as a theological and theologal theme is, in addition, the best theological defense of the poor.

65. Aloysius Pieris, *El rostro asiático de Cristo* (Salamanca, 1991), 164.

66. It is also a mystagogy in another sense that we have barely touched on. It is said, and rightly, that the justifying presence of God on the cross of Jesus

is faith and pure faith, not something that can be extrapolated by reason. But there is also faith in accepting the Jesuanic principle. The principle is rational insofar as it establishes that *this* is the way that Jesus thinks, speaks, and acts. But that all of that is something real, and not pure illusion, this is a matter for faith. Moreover, going beyond the Jesuanic principle, but in relation to it, the fact that salvation comes to the poor "in a suffering, scandalous way, in short, in the form of mystery, means that the sphere of faith has to be superimposed on the sphere of reason, in such a way that the latter brackets its rationality, including theological rationality, in order to open itself to the unexpected and startling revelation of the Christian God" (Ignacio Ellacuría, "Pobres," 790).

67. González Faus, *Proyecto de humano: Visión creyente del hombre* (Santander, 1987), 520.

68. It can also be said that the human being has to be *liberated* from him or herself, from his or her desire and *hubris*.

69. *Libertatis Nuntius* (1984) says that "The Gospel of Jesus Christ is a message of freedom and a force for liberation" (Introduction, see Hennelly, *Documentary History*, 393). "The aspiration for liberation repeats a theme fundamental to the Old and New Testaments" (III.4, Hennelly, *Documentary History*, 396). And *Libertatis Conscientia* (1986) says that the gospel "is, by its very nature, a message of freedom and of liberation" (intro., 1, Hennelly, *Documentary History*, 461).

70. See J. L. Segundo, "Freedom and Liberation," 373–91; see also Ignacio Ellacuría, "Liberación," in *Conceptos fundamentales del cristianismo*, ed. C. Floristán and J. J. Tamayo (Madrid, 1993), 690–710.

71. Ellacuría used to say both positively and polemically that the "proper place in which [liberation] appears is the place of the miserable and the dispossessed and not of the rich who dispossess them, who have a tendency, rather, to overlook or even to cover up the justice and necessity of liberation" ("Estudio teológico-pastoral de la *Instrucción sobre algunos aspectos de la teología de la liberaction, Revista Latinoamericana de Teología* 12 [1984]: 150).

72. Sobrino, *Jesus the Liberator*, 131–33.

73. See Ignacio Ellacuría, "Utopia and Prophecy in Latin America," trans. James Brockman, in *Mysterium Liberationis*, ed. Ignacio Ellacuría, S.J., and Jon Sobrino, S.J. (Maryknoll, N.Y.: Orbis Books, 1993), 315, 316, 324; translation slightly emended.

74. This text is from 1983, and was published, years later, as the article: "Misión actual de la Compañia de Jesús," *Revista Latinoamericana de Teología* 29 (1993): 119f.

75. Ellacuría, "Utopia and Prophecy," 325.

76. Ignacio Ellacuría, "Las bienaventuranzas, carta fundamental de la Iglesia de los pobres," in *Conversión de la Iglesia al reino de Dios* (San Salvador, 1985), 151.

77. Puebla too affirms both the Jesuanic principle (n. 1142) and the evangelizing potential of the poor, "insofar as many of them actualize in their lives

the evangelical values of solidarity, service, simplicity, and 'disponibility' to accepting the gift of God" (n. 1147).

78. Homily of 15 July 1979.

79. Homily of 24 June 1979.

80. The reference is to the prayers that Ignatius has a retreatant make in the *Spiritual Exercises* that he or she be "received under Christ's standard," to serve and imitate Christ in "actual poverty." See *Spiritual Exercises*, nos. 147, 157, 167, in *The Spiritual Exercises of St. Ignatius: A Translation and Commentary*, trans. and ed. George Ganss, S.J. (St. Louis, Mo.: Institute of Jesuit Sources, 1992), 67, 69, 73 (*Translator's Note*).

CHAPTER SEVEN

On the Way to a Christology after Auschwitz

JOHANN BAPTIST METZ

Looking at the situation "after Auschwitz" demands not only a painful revision of the relationship between Christians and Jews, but also a critical revision of Christian theology itself. And this is true above all for Christology, which perhaps has been the leading edge of anti-Judaism. This observation should lead us neither simply to do without Christology, nor to a too-easy proscription of Christology. Rather, it should lead to a careful formulation of a Christology that is accountable to the situation after Auschwitz, a Christology accountable to Christians and Jews. I would like to formulate some categorical presuppositions and some perspectives toward this end.

I. Premises

I belong to that generation of Germans who slowly—probably much too slowly—had to learn to conceive of themselves as a generation "after Auschwitz," and to reckon with this fact in their theology. Yet we must be wary of a misunderstanding in the way this phrase "after Auschwitz" is commonly used. It cannot mean the attempt to give this catastrophe some sort of Christian meaning after the fact. What this phrase, "theology after Auschwitz" entails first and foremost is a critical interrogation of

Christian theology itself. This is anything but a transparent instrumentalization of this catastrophe. Rather than talking about the Holocaust or even about the Shoah, I myself have always preferred to characterize this catastrophe as "Auschwitz." For me what we are dealing with here is in some sense a topography of horror. The catastrophe needs to have a concrete historical locus so that it does not end up being fashioned into an ahistorical negative myth, which would relieve us of historical, moral, and above all, theological responsibility.

For all of this, Auschwitz signals to me a horror for which I have found no theological language, a horror that breaks through all the familiar ontological and metaphysical certainties in Christian talk about God. I have always asked myself this:

When we look at history theologically is it not possible that we have used categories that are too "strong," categories that are speculatively immunized, that too quickly cover over every historical wound, every historical decline and catastrophe, and do not allow them to reach into our talk about God and God's Christ? Now, at least, in the face of this catastrophe, would not the question of the place and role in theology's logos of the human history of suffering have to arise? Now, at least, would we not have to bid farewell to every metaphysics of salvation that is blind to situations and devoid of memory? Now, at least, would it not be better for theology to remain metaphysically mute than to base itself on a metaphysics which operates above and beyond the human history of suffering and ignores the juncture between truth and the remembrance of suffering? "The need to lend a voice to suffering is the condition of all truth." Would not this statement of Theodor Adorno's finally have to be recognized as relevant for every theological truth claim too? And would not theology "after Auschwitz" finally have to bid farewell to every confidence in being that is embedded in a forgetfulness of suffering and in mythical daydreaming?

To do justice to these questions would mean investigating the history of theology. In this I am guided by the supposition that this investigation would take us back into the history of the separation of Christianity from the spirit of the Jewish traditions. That is to say, very early there began in Christianity a problematic and fateful institutional and intellectual strategy of "substituting" for Israel. On the one hand, Christianity understood itself too exclusively as the "new Israel," as the "New Jerusalem," as the "authentic people of God." The significance for Christians of their roots in Israel, on which Paul insisted in his Letter to the Romans, was repressed. Israel was reduced to being Christianity's superseded presupposition in salvation history. On the other hand—as Christianity developed theologically—there arose what I call the "halving of the spirit [*Geist*] of Christianity." Christians would certainly appeal to the faith traditions of Israel, but for spirit and thought [*Geist*] they drew exclusively on Athens, or, more precisely, on the later hellenistic traditions. Thus, for example, the dogmatic formulae of the early Church, especially the christological ones, came into being under the categorical influence of the philosophical systems of middle Platonism and by the Neoplatonism heavily influenced by Plotinus.

This in no way means that the Christian doctrines that came to be expressed in this categorical world should be rejected. However, it still needs to be asked whether or not an elementary dimension of Christianity's spirit continues to be covered over or forgotten. Had the biblical faith-traditions nothing intellectual to offer? Had Israel's history of faith no intellectual patrimony? As it spread outward into the "heathen world" was Christianity exclusively left to the Greek-Hellenistic spirit, for which ideas are always more fundamental than memories, and for which time knows no finale? There is this intellectual resource for Christianity and for the European spirit. There is in the biblical traditions thinking as covenantal thinking, there is thinking guided by the a priori of suffering [*Leidens-Apriori*], thinking as the remembrance of suffering, suffering of the others [*Eingedenken fremden Leids*], thinking as the intellectual expression of an anamnestic culture, a culture which teaches us how much forgetfulness can be lodged in what we in our modern world hold to be rational, to be reasonable, to be "objective," and the degree to which cultural amnesia rules our still or post-modern world and its logic.

"The God of Abraham, the God of Isaac, the God of Jacob . . . not the God of the philosophers and the scholars." This famous distinction from Pascal's Memorial must not be heard as if it means that the God of Israel—who after all is also the God of Jesus—is a God of the proscription of thinking. Quite the opposite! Discourse about God, who is not nameless and indefinite, but is characterized by Jewish names from Abraham to Jesus, has left a revolutionary mark on the history of human thought. This discourse about God shifts thinking into the fundamental, speculatively irreducible tension between remembering and forgetting. It temporalizes all logic. Thinking God is rooted in remembering God; the concept of God is rooted in the remembrance of God, and in the sense of God's absence. This way, and not the reverse. Of course, theology owes insights like these not so much to the conceptual world of Athens as to the anamnestic culture of Jerusalem.

II. Perspectives

"Who do you say that I am?" The first answer that a Christology after Auschwitz would have to give to the question is this: You are a Jew, *vere homo Judaeus.* Christ was not a Christian, but rather a Jew. What Julius Wellhausen still knew and stressed remained for a long time completely overlooked among us during the christological discussions that followed the Second World War—that is, after the catastrophe of Auschwitz. *Exempla docent.* One need only think back to the discussion that raged for many years in the Bultmanian school about the Jesus of history and the Christ of the kerygma. Its most striking feature was the attempt to formulate a Christology without (if not against) the Bible of Israel and without (if not against) the faith of Israel. This whole discussion overlooked the fact that the Christ question thematizes the God question, and that with the God question the faith and witness of Israel cannot but come into play. Christology may not be understood as the revocation of biblical monotheism. Whenever someone tries to formulate it over and against its monotheistic background Christology devolves into sheer mythology and confirms anew its implicit anti-Judaism. Have we perhaps forgotten once again that Auschwitz stands for the attempt to annihilate the Jewish people and their religious tradition, that religious tradition in which all the great monotheistic religions—Christianity (as Paul attests), but also Islam—are rooted? Are we not forced to admit, consequently, that Auschwitz was a deadly assault against everything that we Christians too would have to hold as sacred?

What light can be shed on a Christology which holds itself accountable to Israel's history of faith, and which cautiously—conscious of its theological and political failings—tries to formulate itself as a "Christology after Auschwitz"? I will name—very briefly—three perspectives from which to envision it:

1.   A Christology Sensitive to the Theodicy Question

Faced by the catastrophe of Auschwitz what matters most for Christian theology is not primarily the question of guilt and of forgiveness for the perpetrators, but the question of the rescue of the victims, of justice for those who suffer innocently. The main issue, in other words, is not soteriology but theodicy. But is not our Christology so soteriologically overdetermined that it is hardly open anymore to the theodicy question—a question just as irresolvable as it is unforgettable? The question that troubles the faith of Israel, the question about the justice for those who suffer innocently, was in Christianity all too quickly transformed and re-expressed as the question about the redemption of the guilty. The question of suffering fell under a soteriological spell; the theodicy question was silenced by Christology as soteriology. And in this way, from being a religion primarily sensitive to suffering, Christianity became more and more a religion sensitive first and foremost to sin. It was no longer the creature's suffering, but the creature's sin that took center stage. This crippled the elementary sensitivity for others' suffering and clouded the biblical vision of that comprehensive justice of God, for which after all, according to Jesus, we are all supposed to hunger and thirst. Is it not, then, absolutely necessary to bring the theodicy question back into Christology? Can Christology spare itself the apocalyptic uneasiness of calling God to account [*Rückfrage an Gott*] in the face of a human history of suffering that cries out to heaven? Let me summarize this paragraph with a German phrase: "Der erste Blick Jesu galt nicht der Sünde der Anderen, sondern dem Leid der Anderen." Where is the place for this observation for this Christology?

2.   A Christology with an Apocalyptic Conscience

In an early thesis, from 1977, I stated the following (and I apologize for quoting myself): "Christology without apocalyptic becomes an ideology of the victors. Were not those whose apocalyptic traditions were all too triumphantly suppressed by Christianity the ones who had to experience this so painfully: that is, the Jews?" I will try to explain further.

Has not Christology always run the danger of being turned into a triumphalistic theology of history? Is it not the case that Christian theology, in the name of Christ's victory, has washed history clean of all contradictions, and ironed it out nice and smooth? The lightning bolt of danger seems to be past. The thunderstorm is only in the distance, drawing away. We hear only the echoes of its thunder. The darkness and the clouds are all now really behind us. Has not Christology long ago lost its sensorium for negativity in history, for its interruptions and its danger? Is it not tempted to react to these kinds of catastrophes with the apathy of the victors? The ways that we Christians usually deal with the catastrophe of Auschwitz may well serve to illustrate this temptation.

Yet Christology is no ideology of the historical victors! It would be both possible and necessary to make this clear again and again by taking a second look at apocalypticism in Israel's faith history. Ultimately it is Paul himself who insists on this connection. One need only hear "If there is no resurrection of the dead, then Christ has not been raised" (see 1 Cor 15:13, 16). Paul thus ties the resurrection of Christ to the resurrection of the dead, which was a part of the apocalyptically expectant faith of Jewish communities threatened by death. Whoever congenially separates Christology from apocalyptic, whoever, for example, hears talk about Christ's resurrection in such a way that in it the apocalyptic cry of the Son forsaken by God has been rendered inaudible, hears not the Gospel, but rather a myth of the victors.

To guard against such misunderstandings of the Christian message I have in the last few years often referred to a so-called "Holy Saturday" Christology. Do we not perhaps have too much of a pure Easter Sunday Christology, which pampers our faith with the language of the victors and "cures" it of its sensitivity to catastrophe? Would not the atmosphere of Holy Saturday have to be expressed more clearly within Christology itself? Does it not belong to the biblically attested faith in the resurrection? When and where—for example—does the Easter faith of the disciples on the road to Emmaus begin? Easter Sunday has not come on the third day for everyone. Do we not need, then, a language of Holy Saturday in Christology, a Christology whose logos can still shock, and in this shock, be transformed?

3. A Christology from a Synoptic Paradigm

The well-known distinction between two ways of believing comes from Martin Buber. I will take up this usage, but I will go further and state—in contrast to Buber—that there is not only a specifically Jewish, Old Testament way of believing, and a Christian, New Testament way, but that within the New Testament Canon as well there are distinct ways of believing. Thus, in the New Testament one can speak of an expressly synoptic way of believing that is different from a clearly Pauline way of believing, without having to make them mutually exclusive. Clearly the synoptic paradigm is more strongly and lastingly marked by the spirit of the Jewish traditions. Alongside of Paul, should it not become, in consequence, the foundation of a "Christology after Auschwitz"?

In the synoptic paradigm, faith, as obedience before the will of God, is first and foremost a way, a way of being on the way, indeed, of being homeless. What this means in New Testament terms is this: discipleship. Christ is the truth and . . . the way. Any attempt to know him is a going forth, a following. Only by following him do Christians come to know with whom it is that they are dealing and who it is who saves them. Christ may not be thought in such a way that he is only thought. A Christology from a synoptic paradigm is developed not from subjectless concepts and systems, but rather from stories of discipleship. It has a narrative-practical character, not as an afterthought, but from its very foundations. A Christology without this foundation leads to gnosticism, with its latent metaphysical antisemitism.

How does this kind of Christology relate to the Church's christological dogmas, which were formulated under the categorical influence of hellenistic metaphysics? It cannot be a matter of de-emphasizing or even rejecting these dogmatic formulas in the name of a Christology after Auschwitz. Rather, it is a matter of opening up these christological dogmas as formulas of a dangerous and liberating memory in the Church. These dogmatic formulas must, correspondingly, always be tied back narratively again and again to the biblical stories of exodus, of conversion, of resistance and of suffering—and to the synoptic stories of discipleship. In the final analysis, Christianity began as a community of memory and narrative in following Jesus, who gave his attention first and foremost to the suffering of the other. Are we conscious enough of this origin when we talk about God and about his Christ now, in this time "after Auschwitz"?

Translated by J. Matthew Ashley

CHAPTER EIGHT

The Christological Paradox as a Hermeneutic Key to Interreligious Dialogue

CLAUDE GEFFRÉ, O.P.

At the beginning of the third millennium, interreligious dialogue has become a "sign of the times." With Vatican II the Church played an important part in promoting this dialogue because, for the first time in the history of Christian thought, it pronounced a positive verdict on the non-Christian religions. Soon after, the World Council of Churches revised some of its own traditional statements in order to legitimize and encourage such a dialogue. Even if it is less evident one can find the same readiness for dialogue in most of the great religions of the world.[1] One must not forget that the "World Conference of Religions for Peace" was founded in Asia, in Kyoto in 1973, on the invitation of the leaders of the great religions of the East. The "Manifesto for a Global Ethics" proclaimed by the Parliament of the World's Religions in Chicago in September 1993 showed that the members of the different religions are conscious of their common responsibility for the future of humankind.

This readiness for dialogue coincides with a very strong consciousness of a religious pluralism which seems to be insurmountable, and it is the task of a responsible Christian theology to try to understand its significance in God's plan. It clearly is impossible to consider it to be a temporary phase in history which will be slowly overcome through the success of the worldwide mission of the Church. But regardless of any developments of Christian theology, when it comes to the interpretation of God's will for universal salvation, it is very important to note that the novelty of interreligious dialogue corresponds to the historic situation of the human family on the threshold of the third millennium. We have now entered into the planetary age of humankind, which means that we are at the beginning of an age of worldwide civilization and of a global community of nations. Regardless of their original culture or religion, all the members of the human family are conscious of what unites them and, more importantly, of what separates them, or even opposes them to each other. It is even true that most of the great religions have a claim to what is absolute and universal and therefore a clear understanding of their historic particularity.

In this context of globalization and close interdependence of all parts of the world, men and women are asking themselves with mounting anguish what will be their future. Due to the prodigious achievements of science and technology, the basic ethical question is whether human beings can control their own power. For the first time in our history we know that, from now on, the survival of the human race depends on our own wisdom and good will. Therefore, instead of looking after their own interests and jealously defending their own particularity, the great religions begin better to understand their historic responsibility in the service of what is truly human, and in the defense of the destiny of the planet earth.

It is not wrong to speak, with Raymond Panikkar, of an *ecumenical ecumenism* when it comes to the common responsibility of all the members of the common house which this planetary village has become. But it is necessary to reserve the first and original meaning of the word 'ecumenical' for the dialogue between the Christian confessions. And it is particularly important not to confuse the need for the ecumenical dialogue in the real sense of the word with the need for interreligious dialogue. In the case of interconfessional dialogue, the search for visible unity among all the churches is a response to the Lord's commandment and we have the right, and even the duty, to hope that it will happen within the confines of our history. Regardless of the historic causes of the splits between the churches, we share the one faith in the Lord Christ and in the one Baptism. We are beginning to understand ever more clearly that we are not going to return to the unity which once existed. We are working for a unity so far still hidden and unknown, which will integrate the legitimate diversity of each Church, which will be the fruit of a "reconciled diversity" and will lead to a "communion of communions." In contrast, it has to be quite clear that the interreligious dialogue does not aim at producing a visible unity among all religions. The search for such a worldwide super-religion is utopian because it would mean the loss of the essential riches that belong to each religious tradition. As has been said earlier, interreligious dialogue has become necessary because of the gravity of the concerns for which the human conscience has now to assume responsibility. And it is precisely on the basis of the spiritual resources of each religious tradition that interreligious dialogue can become a model and an incentive for what could be a form of the common community's joyful coexistence and cooperation in diversity in this planetary age.

The dialogue of the religions has become a new stage in the religious history of humankind. It demonstrates that it is necessary to show openness and understanding even when coming from different perceptions of the truth. One of the great paradoxes is that Christians are the most ardent advocates of the urgency of this dialogue while, at the same time, belonging to a religion which occupies an *exceptional* position among the world religions. The equality of the partners obviously is the necessary condition for any dialogue. However, Christianity witnesses to a truth entirely based on the mediation of Jesus Christ which coincides with the breaking-in of the "absolute" into history. We therefore have to begin by honestly facing the difficulties of a dialogue with other religions while remaining loyal to Christianity. We have to show that it is in the faithfulness to the very center of the Christian message, which is a religion of incarnation, that there lies a possibility to demonstrate that Christianity is not disqualified from being a partner in dialogue. As we shall see, this is so true that we can define the specificity of Christianity in terms of its necessary links with entities other than itself.

Christianity as a Religious Exception

Interreligious dialogue does not escape the rules for all true dialogue even if the dialogue between Christianity and other religions has its own difficulties. The first rule is respect for the other in his or her difference. I have to show interest in the convictions of my partner particularly if they are culturally or religiously foreign to me. In the past, under the banner of the colonial expansion of the West, the mission of the Church often failed to recognize the real identity of foreign cultures. We must not forget, though, that accepting the stranger is one of the roots of the Judeo-Christian tradition. Many of Jesus' parables show his respect for the stranger in his difference. It is important to remember to distinguish between a dialogue which cultivates a sense of difference and a dialogue which seeks assimilation. There is an old principle which goes back to Parmenides' philosophy of identity, which maintains that "only like can recognize like." This has dominated our missionary strategy for too long. It should be replaced by another principle rooted in the biblical tradition which maintains that the "unlike recognize the other, the stranger in his difference."

The second, obvious principle of any dialogue is that one has to be faithful to oneself. In the case of interreligious dialogue this means that each has to remain faithful to their own commitment to faith and belief. Here we come to the paradox of interreligious dialogue. The absolute commitment required by every religious enterprise has to be reconciled with openness to the conviction of others. There exists an inevitable tension between the deontology inherent in any dialogue and the inner conviction of every religious person to possess the truth. The theology of the future will have to learn to accept this difficult coexistence without sinking into relativism. The usual academic theology always claimed to be based on such an absolute concept of truth that, according to the logic of contradictions it cannot recognize the existence of any other kind of truth without compromising its own claim to the truth. At best it can consider other kinds as being either degraded forms of the truth, or distant echoes of the unique truth of which it has the monopoly. The theology of the future will learn to recognize pluralism in the order of truths without sliding into general relativism. The search for an increasingly comprehensive consensus while respecting differences is the underlying presupposition for an *ethics of discussion* as propounded by the philosopher Habermas. Finally, true tolerance always rests on strong convictions. My argued commitments to the truth which I hold does not necessarily bring with it a feeling of superiority which would compromise any possibility of dialogue when I discover that the truth which, for me, is the object of absolute conviction, is neither exclusive nor inclusive of any other truth. It is relative to the fact of the historic particularity of its origins. And it is always in faithfulness to its concrete particularity that a cultural or religious truth can grow beyond itself and aim at becoming universal. Dialogue requires endless patience, geological patience. But contrary to the most widely held opinion, it does not necessarily lead to skepticism or relativism. It rather leads to a rediscovery of its own truth, and invites us to the search for a truth which is higher and more comprehensive than the partial truth to which each person is witness.

It therefore seems legitimate to say that the truth witnessed by Christianity is neither exclusive nor inclusive of any other truth; it is relative to everything that is true in the other religious traditions. Like any other religion, Christianity is rooted in a historic particularity. Therefore it appears not be to exempt from the necessary condition for any dialogue, which is the equality of the partners. But in fact, in the concert of religions, Christianity finds itself irreversibly in an exceptional position because its message is entirely based on a historic mediation which coincides with the breaking-in of the "absolute," which is God. No other religion claims to have a founder who is not only a prophet, somebody sent by God, or a mediator, but the actual Son of God. This is a permanent difficulty in the dialogue between Christians and members of other religions. However tolerant they may be, as soon as Christians ask about the truth of their religion they will interpret it as being superior, if they want to remain faithful to their true identity. In view of the uniqueness of Christ's mediation, how can one reinterpret the singularity of Christianity without making it immediately seem superior to any other religion? This is the difficult task of a modern theology of comparative religion.

Interreligious dialogue does not exist in the abstract. It is always a dialogue between two concrete persons. It would be easy enough to show how the non-Christian dialogue partners often experience a certain Christian condescendence or secret imperialism. One can see this in the case of the Christian-Jewish dialogue and in dialogue with the Muslims. But it is even more evident in the dialogue with the religions of the East, particularly with Hinduism.

Even if Christian theology has undertaken a thorough revision of its anti-Judaism and accepts that the connection between Church and Israel is an irreducible duality, Christians still find it very difficult to accept the basic lack of symmetry between the two Abrahamic religions: Christianity cannot conceive of itself without its Jewish roots while post-Christian Judaism can perfectly well do without a relation to Jesus Christ or Christianity.[2] Equally, in Christian-Islamic dialogue, the Muslim participants often have the impression that the dialogue is unequal from the beginning. Even if Islam does not recognize Jesus as the Son of God he still is a figure essential to the Muslim faith. He is a very great prophet (tradition calls him the "seal of sanctity") and the Muslims are prepared to recognize his message as Word of God, at least as far as it concerns the worship of the one God. On the other hand, Christians are not prepared to recognize Mohammed as an authentic prophet, sent by God. How can they recognize him as being sent by God if he rejects Jesus' divine sonship as idolatry and professes an anti-trinitarian monotheism?[3] And, finally, in the case of other religions which are not connected with the Judeo-Christian alliance, how can their followers accept the idea that their religious traditions only have salvific value through secret links with Christ who is the only savior of all people? How can one take seriously a spiritual experience in its complete difference if its only value for salvation lies in the fact that it already is implicitly Christian? True, a feeling of mystery is not essential to salvation. But how can one still speak about a dialogue on the basis of equality if, for instance, those Hindus who are most faithful to what is ultimately irreducible in their religion are considered to be, in fact, Christians without knowing it?[4]

The Case for an Inclusive Religious Pluralism

We have noted the tensions in interreligious dialogue between the need for equality and the requirement of faithfulness to a clear Christian identity. Since Vatican II the Church has constantly encouraged dialogue with other religions and does not hesitate to display a positive attitude not only toward the followers of other religions but also to the constitutive elements of those religions. But at the same time the Church continues to proclaim, backed by all its tradition, that Jesus Christ is the only mediator between God and humans, and that Christianity is the only religion which testifies to the fullness of the truth about the mystery of God.

It has been the task of studies in comparative religion, for the past decades, to reinterpret the uniqueness of Christ as the only mediator and the uniqueness of Christianity as the truly salvific religion by trying to do justice to the positive value of other religions. This is only possible by going beyond a problem which still lingers within the confines of a renewed version of the old theology of *salvation of non-believers*, and adopting a true theology of religious pluralism which is concerned with the meaning of the diversity of the various religious traditions in God's plan. This transition from accepting religious pluralism as a fact to the idea of a legitimate pluralism as part of God's mysterious plan represents an important theological step forward. Jacques Dupuis's great book entitled *Toward a Christian Theology of Religious Pluralism* is the best and most official statement on this.[5] From the perspective of a hermeneutical theology which takes account of the irreversible facts of our historic experience, I have been trying for some considerable time to show how the religious history of humankind, despite its basic ambiguity, bears witness not only to the fumbling beginnings of a quest for the mystery of the ultimate reality but also to the plurality of the gifts of God who reaches out to humans. In other words, since its beginnings human history itself is already a history of salvation long before the coming of Christ.[6]

In the light of this new paradigm of religious pluralism the central mystery of the Christian faith needs to be reinterpreted, which means that the identity of Jesus of Nazareth has to be confessed as the Christ. "Who do you say that I am?" Even before Vatican II Catholic theology had outgrown a narrow *ecclesio-centrism* when it concerned itself with the question of salvation for those outside the Church. With the exception of a few Catholic theologians who are close to a pre-Conciliar traditionalism, or of certain representatives of evangelical churches, most theologians have now rejected christological *exclusivity* in favor of a christological *inclusiveness* which is already implicit in many texts of Vatican II, at least in the form of what could be called a *theology of fulfillment*. Despite the many interpretations of inclusiveness it is possible today to discern a widespread tendency to distance oneself from too militant a *Christiano-centrism (Christianity-centeredness)*. Particularly in Asia, faced with the difficulties of mission and in search of a better understanding of the riches of the spiritual heritage of the great religions of the East, many theologians have tried to adopt a so-called *pluralist* position. This is identical with a radical form of theo-centrism which holds that all religions are circling round the sun of the ultimate reality of the universe which may or may not be called God. This is the famous *Copernican revolution* linked with the name of John Hick.[7]

In order to do justice to the legitimate requirements of pluralism and promote interreligious dialogue some theologians understand christological inclusiveness in a very weak sense. This leads to a reinterpretation of the divine sonship of Jesus who is inseparably both man and God. For instance, theologians speak of *normative* rather than *constitutive* inclusiveness, e.g., Roger Haight in his recent book *Jesus, Symbol of God*.[8] Jesus is the symbol of the perfect mediation between God and man. He is the criterion for the truth about God, humanity, and the world but he is not the exclusive cause of salvation since he has to give place to other forms of mediation. Haight is right to emphasize that it is *God* alone who saves. Since, historically, there were in fact other mediations of salvation apart from Jesus he refuses to consider Jesus Christ to be the exclusive and constitutive cause of salvation for all humans. He does not see how Christ's salvific acts count for all of human history before the coming of Jesus as incarnate Word. Jesus as savior is normative for all Christians, but it is the action of God as unique savior which is at work in the other religious traditions. In his book on Christology, Haight tries to reinterpret the traditional faith of the Church for what he always calls our *post-modern* age, characterized by a historic consciousness and by the end of metaphysics. He confesses Jesus as symbol of God who is both *manifestation* and *embodiment* of God. But one has to note that his refusal of christological inclusiveness is closely linked to his rejection of a *high* Christology which he condemns as out-dated and abstract. In place of a Christology of the Logos which stresses the consubstantiality of Jesus with the Father he develops a Christology from below, a *Spirit Christology* which mainly emphasizes the consubstantiality of Jesus with every human being.

I cannot here enter into a debate about the different Christologies of the New Testament and about their links with doctrinal statements of the later traditions. In view of the insurmountable limits of the formulations of Chalcedon and faced with a mystery which will always be beyond our grasps I am not sure whether, in the light of all the scriptural witness, it is really correct to see a *high* Christology and a Christology *from below* as utterly opposed to each other. I certainly do not see why a *high* Christology should be disqualified in the post-modern age because of being ontological. One could question the term *post-modernity* which Haight uses all the time. With even more reason one could, instead, agree with Paul Ricoeur's reservation about modernity, when he said that "I doubt whether there is an unequivocal criterion for this essentially present-day term."[9] In any case it is true that although the language of incarnation remains a metaphoric language, the New Testament bears unambiguous witness to the fact that Jesus is the only son of God. Regardless of all discussions about the titles "Son of Man" and "Son of God," the gospels confirm that God's presence in Jesus is something Jesus himself claimed. He himself knew that, in fact, the eschatological kingdom, the Kingdom of God, had come in him.

With a theologian like Jacques Dupuis it is possible, I think, to conceive of a *constitutive christological inclusiveness* which is at the same time also an *inclusive pluralism*. This does not lead to a *Christo-monism*. It is an invitation to look beyond a false opposition between Christo-centrism and theo-centrism. It is always God who saves, and it is important to keep a distance between Jesus and God. But, according to God's eternal plan which has been revealed to us in these later days, Jesus is the unique mediator between God and humans only because he is the beloved Son of the Father. According to 1 Timothy 2:5: "There is one God, and also one mediator between God and men, Christ Jesus, Himself man, who gave Himself in ransom for many." This mediation of Jesus does not exclude other mediations, and certain religious traditions can in their own way have salvific value, but it is always in connection with the event of Jesus Christ in the mystery of his death and resurrection. "The multiplicity of mediations of different orders and kinds is not excluded but they derive their meaning and value only from Christ's mediation, and cannot be considered as parallel or complementary" (*Redemptoris Missio* 5).

While accepting absolutely that Jesus Christ is the constitutive cause of salvation for all humankind I want to take seriously the intrinsic value of other religions as mysterious ways of salvation. In the perspective of the interreligious dialogue, the uniqueness of Christ as Word incarnate and the uniqueness of Christianity as a historic religion have to be reinterpreted. In order to do so, Jacques Dupuis uses as his hermeneutic key a Trinitarian Christology. He states that the Word and the Spirit are always at work in history and, in a certain way, confirm the historic particularity of the event of Jesus of Nazareth. I myself prefer to draw the consequences from the christological paradox.[10] When we confess that Jesus Christ is the only source of salvation, it is the paradox of the Incarnation itself, i.e., the manifestation of the absolute in and through a historic particularity, which invites us not to absolutize Christianity as the only way of salvation, excluding all others.

The Christological Paradox

In order to demonstrate the non-imperialist nature of Christianity and promote interreligious dialogue I think it is preferable to return to the very center of the Christian faith, i.e., to the mystery of the Incarnation in its most realistic and non-mystic sense. To use the beautiful words of Nicholas of Cuse, all the implications of the mystery of Christ must be deployed and understood to be *universally concrete.* Since Apostolic times Christians have confessed Jesus as Christ. This means that Jesus has revealed to us God's universal love for all men and women, not only through his message but by and in his concrete humanity. This identification of God as a transcendent reality based on the concrete humanity of Jesus of Nazareth is the distinctive characteristic of Christianity. According to St. Paul's very strong affirmation that "it is in Christ that the complete being of the Godhead dwells embodied" (Col 2:9), Jesus can be recognized as the face of God's absolute love. But God can only manifest himself in non-divine ways, which means in the contingent humanity of a particular man. We confess that the fullness of God dwells in Jesus. But this identification leads us both to the mystery of God himself which is beyond any identification. Given our human limited perception, the particular humanity of Jesus cannot be the adequate translation of the riches which are contained in the fullness of the mystery of Christ. If it were so, Jesus would no longer be God's icon but already an idol. This is another way of expressing the warning of Chalcedon, *without confusion or separation.*

In agreement with the traditional understanding of the Church fathers it is possible to consider the economy of the Word incarnate to be the sacrament of a larger economy, the economy of the eternal Word of God which coincides with the religious history of humankind. According to the French title of one of Edward Schillebeeckx's books, it is "the history of humankind which *tells* God."[11] For the Christian faith Jesus is the identification of the personal God. But this identification leads straight back to a transcendent God who is beyond any identification. Jesus therefore does not exclude other historic figures from the realms of culture or religion who have a different way of identifying the ultimate reality of the universe. According to the happy formulation of Christian Duquoc, "God does not absolutize a particularity; on the contrary, He shows that no historic particularity is absolute, and because of this relativity God can be reached in our real history."[12] The present task of our theology of religions therefore is not to gloss over the scandal of the incarnation, on the pretext of responding better to the requirements of interreligious dialogue, but to show that it is the paradox of the Incarnation itself, i.e., the presence of the absolute in a historic particularity, which compels us to refuse the claim of Christianity to be absolute and exclusive of other religions. To use the vocabulary of the philosopher Stanislas Breton, one should avoid speaking about the uniqueness of Christianity in terms of *inclusive* or *exclusive* but rather call it a *relative* uniqueness.[13]

I think it is possible to speak about the exceptional situation of Christianity among the religions of the world. It is by insisting on the *difference* of Christianity that one can best contribute to its *de-absolutizing*. I have shown elsewhere that Paul Tillich in his *Dogmatics* of 1925 produced a critique of Christian absoluteness, not only, like Ernst Tröltsch, in the name of the history of religions but in the name of faith itself, and of the principle of justification.[14] The absolute paradox consists of the absolute "no" and the absolute "yes" which God says to the same human person. This law is verified in Christianity because, whenever the Church depends on its faith in the absolute it has also to accept the "no" addressed to it by the one who is unconditional, who is God.

The law of the absolute paradox is also verified by the mystery of Christ being inseparably both man and God. The person of Jesus as the historic manifestation of the invisible and universal Logos makes real the identity between what is absolutely universal and what is absolutely concrete. Here we have to refer to Tillich's doctrine of Christ as the New Being. In his *Dogmatics*, he advances the following thesis: "The being who appeared in Jesus Christ is at the same time part of history and also carries history; he both enters into history and is supra-historic."[15] The paradox is that Christ as a fully historic being is in an unbreakable union with God while history itself, according to Tillich, stands under the Fall, is caught up in opposition between essence and existence, in the separation from God. Christ as a historic event which coincides with the breaking-in of the ultimate revelation by God therefore triumphs over the ambiguity of everything that is historic. This daring vision is interesting because it shows that, far from being opposed to universal significance, the historic particularity of the event of Jesus Christ is the condition which makes it possible. Christ does not only give a meaning to history but he carries history, he is in the center of history as the salvation event.

Such a Christology does not speculate about the union between the two natures in the person of Christ along the lines of thinking started in Chalcedon, and Tillich distances himself from a vocabulary for the incarnation which has nothing to do with the language of the New Testament. He would never accept that the divine sonship of Jesus is only a *metaphoric* way of speaking. This would mean compromising the identity of Jesus as the Christ, and Christology would become "Jesu-ology." If Jesus is confessed as Christ he is identified with the Logos and he is the place of identification between what is absolutely concrete and absolutely universal. The doctrine of Christ as the *New Being* is a commentary on the Johannine affirmation of the "Logos made flesh," and Tillich thinks he can find a scriptural basis for it in Paul's teaching about "our new being in Christ" (2 Cor 5:17). It is clear that, for him, Christ as a historic event can only hold such power over all of history because of his unique union with God. Later, he writes in his *Systematic Theology* that "the doctrine of the Logos as the doctrine of the identity between the absolutely concrete with the absolutely universal is not just one theological doctrine among others; it is the only possible basis for a Christian theology which can claim to be *the* theology."[16]

If one takes the consequences of the christological paradox for the understanding of interreligious dialogue to their full conclusion one has to remember that the doctrine of Christ the New Being, who brings about the union between the absolutely concrete with the absolutely universal, only attains its full significance in the light of the theology of the cross. Death is the presupposition for life, the cross is the presupposition for glory, renouncing a particularity the precondition for a concrete universality. Tillich expresses it in terms of a paradox: "Christ is Jesus and the negation of Jesus." According to his understanding of the Christ-event as the breaking-in of the absolute or the unconditional into history, Christ is only Christ because he has sacrificed his historic existence as the existence of him who was simply Jesus. Tillich writes: "A Christianity which does not affirm that Jesus of Nazareth sacrificed Himself to Jesus the Christ is nothing more than a religion among other religions."[17] The risen Christ liberates the person of Jesus of Nazareth from a particularism which would have turned him into the property of a particular group, i.e., the first community of disciples. Since early times the shape of the cross has been given a universal significance. It is the symbol of a universality which is always linked to the sacrifice of a particularity. Jesus dies to his historic particularity in order to be reborn as a figure of concrete universality, the figure of Christ.

Particularly with reference to the mystery of Christ's *kenosis* it is possible to affirm that Christianity carries within itself its own limitations. One can exorcise all totalitarian venom from the Christian religion and measure the exact extent of its claim to universality. The French Jesuit, Michel de Certeau, has an idea which recurs frequently in his works. He maintains that one could say that Christianity is only faithful to its own particular singularity if, far from being an imperialist and comprehensive religion, it defines itself by what it *lacks*, and by comparison with what it is not. It is Christ's *kenosis* in his equality with God which *allows* the resurrection in its widest sense (cf. Phil 2:6–8). But it is also the empty tomb, the absence of the founder's body which is the condition for the existence of the body of the Church and the body of the Scriptures. Christianity is founded on an original absence. Just as there can be no profound spiritual experience without the consciousness of its origin being absent, so there is no Christian practice without the knowledge that something is *missing*. This is the necessary presupposition for any relation with other people, with strangers, with those who are different. In his work as historian of mysticism, Michel de Certeau has emphasized the category of *permission*, understood in Heidegger's sense of *"Not without"* (*Nicht ohne*). Certeau comments that "rather than the presence, it is the absence which makes things happen; actions occur because of what is lacking."[18]

I am convinced that here we have a very precious hermeneutic key to the understanding of the way Christianity can engage in interreligious dialogue without compromising its own identity. It does not mean that Christianity has to abandon its claim to be a witness to the ultimate revelation but rather that it has to show that it carries its own principles of self-limitation within itself. In this way the expression *relative uniqueness* can make sense, an expression which I used earlier following Stanislas Breton who tried to get away from the idea of a *uniqueness of excellence and of integration*. The term *relative* must be understood to mean the opposite of *absolute*, but in a *relational* sense. The practice of interreligious dialogue forces us to define Christian singularity more in terms of a *relation to an otherness*.[19]

The Christian experience is primarily the experience of an origin which is not there, which is the *otherness* of God. But it also is the experience of the otherness of the person who becomes one's neighbor. Christian identity always lies in the process of *becoming*, of accepting the other in his difference. It is an *Easter existence* which, opposed to any form of imperialism of knowledge and practice, must witness to what it lacks. In the field of knowledge the most unconditional faith carries in itself its own limitations because it cannot encompass the totality of the mystery of God. In the field of practice we know that Christian actions are not the same as any other human actions. Christian practice is rather a kind of displacement, a *radically transforming rupture* (M. de Certeau) with a person who has his own consistency. In other words, the Christian experience is no substitute for other authentic human experiences, whether they are religious or not, but gives them a sense which was previously unknown. One can guess at the consequences if one thinks about the need to inculturate Christianity in cultures which are foreign to it. The Gospel has a universal value and can become the property of every person. But I would say that a Christianity which, when faced with different cultures and religions, does not witness to a certain lack cannot really encounter the otherness of these cultures and religions, and will not be faithful to its universal vocation.

The practice of otherness is a duty for Christianity which arises out of its very nature, if only because it confesses the otherness of a God who is always larger. Because of our Christian identity we are called to recognize the other, the stranger, in his or her difference, and accept the limits this imposes on us. Finally, Christian identity is not defined in terms of perfection which has already been attained but in terms of a process, of *becoming*, of a transition, of accepting the other, and of service. This is what is meant by an *Easter existence*.

I particularly emphasized the kenotic dimension of Christianity, and I think I have shown that this is not a strategy to help interreligious dialogue but a natural requirement. However I am not forgetting all the basic affirmations about the mystery of Christ who is the ultimate fulfillment of the promises of the first Covenant, and about Christianity which is the final gathering of all the seeds of truth, goodness, and holiness which were sown throughout all human religious traditions. For this reason I would like to explain in conclusion how the traditional concept of fulfillment needs to be reinterpreted.

A Non-Totalitarian Fulfillment

The Second Vatican Council did not go as far as qualifying non-Christian religions as *ways of salvation* but it recognized that despite their errors and imperfections these religions could contain positive values. One could quite correctly say that one of the new elements in the teaching of the Council over against a simple theology of salvation for the unbelievers, was that it applied the famous theory of the *seeds of the Word* to the great religious traditions of the world, a theory which the church fathers had reserved for the wisdom of the nations, i.e., for Greek philosophy. Elements of *truth and grace* are discovered not only in the hearts of men and women of good will but also in the constitutive elements of other religions. The text of *Nostra Aetate* says: "The Church considers with sincere respect these ways of acting and living, these rules and doctrines which, although different at many points from what the Church itself holds and preaches nevertheless often shed a ray of truth which enlightens the people" (No. 2). In a similar vein, the decree *Ad Gentes* speaks of "all the good which is sown in the heart and soul of people, or in particular rites" (No. 9). Finally, the document on *Dialogue and Proclamation* of 1991 affirms even more clearly that "Concretely, when sincerely practicing what is good in their religious traditions and following the promptings of their conscience, the followers of other religions respond positively to God's call and receive salvation in Jesus Christ even if they do not know Him or confess Him as Saviour" (No. 29).

The official so-called theology of fulfillment often holds that all those positive values are implicitly Christian values which find their perfect fulfillment in Christianity.[20] I think that this way of understanding the question of promise and fulfillment does not sufficiently take account of the irreducible center of each religious tradition which can reveal the secret presence of the Spirit of God which blows where it wills. The concept of fulfillment needs to be reinterpreted in a completely non-totalitarian way which shows that the seeds of truth, goodness, and even sanctity will find their fulfillment in the fullness of the mystery of Christ, but in such a way that the irreducible core of every religion is respected.[21] I will therefore no longer speak about the implicitly Christian values which will find their perfect development only in the Christian religion. I prefer to speak about "*Christic*" values which, in the time of history, can enrich our understanding of the Christian singularity but which cannot necessarily be integrated into Christianity. It is important not to confuse the universality of the mystery of Christ with the universality of Christianity as a historic religion. Christianity must not try to bring together all the truths scattered during the course of the religious history of humankind. And if Christianity wanted to integrate them all it would be in danger of compromising what belongs to its proper identity and spirit. If one takes seriously the principle of religious pluralism, one has to accept the historic contingency of Christianity. But at the same time I maintain the existence of a certain universal principle, of what could be loosely called "*Christendom*"[22] in which every man and every woman share, as part of God's plan of creation and salvation. Ultimately, God wishes to bring all things together in Jesus Christ. At the end of this essay it will have become clear that, although I utterly refuse to sacrifice Christocentrism to an indeterminate theo-centrism, I also distance myself completely from the frequently found notion of *Christiano-monism*.

I have tried to show how the christological paradox itself is an invitation to overcome a false way of absolutizing and universalizing Christianity. Finally I repeat that we have to reinterpret the singularity of Christianity in the midst of a religious pluralism which appears to be insurmountable. This reinterpretation will have to be done in the light of a still very tentative reflection on the relations between Judaism and early Christianity. Since the last Council most theologians are prepared to recognize in Judaism, as a religion of election, an irreducible core which cannot be integrated into the Church on the level of our continuing history. Even if it is only an analogy, one can find in the relation between Judaism and the early Church a kind of paradigm for the presentday relations between Christianity and the other religions. Just as the Church neither integrates nor replaces Israel so it does not integrate or replace any part of the authentic religious truth which another religious tradition can contain.

Revelation as the coming of the Word of God in Jesus Christ is the fullness of revelation, but it is a qualitative, not a quantitative fullness. As the coming of the Word of God in Jesus Christ, revelation is definitive and unsurpassable. But its content of truth is necessarily historic and therefore limited. It is therefore quite legitimate to consider other sacred writings and other religious experiences as *rays of truth*, incomplete but precious, which in their own way bear witness to the unfathomable mystery of God. The Qur'an itself despite its omissions, its errors, and its denial of the Christian revelation can, paradoxically, bear witness to certain riches like the sense of God's greatness, and the worship which humans owe him. In that part which does not contradict the biblical revelation of the uniqueness of God it may be a genuine piece of prophecy which challenges both Judaism and Christianity.

Only on the last day will we see the manifestation of the mysterious convergence of all religions, and understand their place in the unique design of God. Meanwhile, in the time of our history, it will always be the Church's task to announce to all human beings, be they members of other religions or not, that God's salvation has come in Jesus Christ, but on the condition of respecting God's mysterious ways in the heart of each person.

NOTES

1. For the history of the initiatives in the field of interreligious dialogue see the first part of Jean-Claude Basset, *Le dialogue interreligieux* (Paris: Ed. du Cerf, 1996).

2. See, for instance, Martin Buber, *Deux types de foi: Foi juive et foi chrétienne* (Paris: Ed. du Cerf, 1991).

3. I already deal with this difficulty in Muslim-Christian dialogue in my study, "La portée théologique du dialogue islamo/chrétien," *Islamochristiana* 18 (1992): 1–23.

4. In a lecture given recently in Paris, Father Almadaloss said: "In the light of our appreciation of other religions, any idea that a good Hindu is really an anonymous Christian is unacceptable."

5. J. Dupuis, *Toward a Christian Theology of Religious Pluralism* (Maryknoll, N.Y.: Orbis, 1997); originally published as *Vers une théologie chrétienne du pluralisme religieux* (Paris: Ed. du Cerf, 1997). Apart from its examination by the Congregation of the Faith in October 1998, the book has called forth a number of reactions. Fr. Dupuis has answered most of the criticisms at some length in "The Truth Will Make You Free: The Theology of Religions Revisited," *Louvain Studies* 24 (1999): 211–63.

6. Cf. particularly my article "La singularité du christianisme à l'âge du pluralisme religieux," in *Penser la foi: Recherches en théologie aujourd'hui*, ed. J. Doré and Ch. Theobald (Paris: Ed. du Cerf-Assa, 1993), 351–69.

7. Among other works cf. at least John Hick, *God Has Many Names* (Philadelphia, Pa.: Westminster Press, 1980).

8. Roger Haight, *Jesus, Symbol of God* (Maryknoll, N.Y.: Orbis Books, 1999). Cf. especially chapter 14: "Jesus and the World Religions," pp. 395–423.

9. P. Ricoeur: "Réponses au critiques," in *Temps et récit de Paul Ricoeur en débat*, ed. C. Bouchindhomme and R. Rochlitz (Paris, 1990). He adds: "Any attempt to stabilise the concept of modernity seems to me to come from a hidden philosophy of history, condemned to being up to date and contemporary while not contemporising, to the point where one does no longer know whether what some people call post-modern is not rather what others, following Beaudelaire, would precisely call modern."

10. While basically agreeing with Jacques Dupuis, I am more concerned with showing the universal character of the coming of Jesus Christ as a historic event. I explained this in my book, *Profession théologien: Quelle pensée chrétienne pour le XXI siècle*, Entretiens avec G. Jarczyk (Paris: Albin Michel, 1999), esp. 205–214.

11. E. Schillebeeckx, *L'histoire des hommes, récit de Dieu* (Paris: Ed. du Cerf, 1992). The original Dutch title is *Mensen als verhall van God*.

12. Ch. Duquoc, *Dieu différent* (Paris: Ed. du Cerf, 1978), 143.

13. Cf. this book which is both more philosophical and more theological, Stanislas Breton, *Unicité et monothéisme* (Paris: Ed. du Cerf, 1981).

14. Cf. Cl. Geffré, "Paul Tillich et l'avenir de l'oecuménisme interreligieux," *Revue des sciences philosophiques et théologiques* 77 (1993): 3–22.

15. I quote here thesis No. 63 from the *Dogmatics* of 1925, p. 348 in the new French edition: P. Tillich, *Dogmatique*.

16. P. Tillich, *Systematic Theology* (Chicago: University of Chicago Press, 1954), 1:17.

17. Ibid., 1:135.

18. M. de Certeau, *La faiblesse de croire* (Paris: Ed. du Seuil, 1987), 112.

19. In an essay about the original theological work of Michel de Certeau, I was able to say that, according to him, Christianity is entirely defined as a religion of otherness. Cf. "Le non-lieu théologique selon Michel de Certeau," in *Michel de Certeau ou la différence chrétienne*, ed. Cl. Geffré (Paris: Ed. du Cerf, 1991), 159–80.

20. This was the usual theology developed by authors like Henri de Lubac, Yves Congar, Jean Daniélou, and, partly, also by Karl Rahner before Vatican II.

21. I already tried to apply this necessary reinterpretation to the concept of fulfillment in various works. Cf. particularly my study: "La verité du christianisme à l'age du pluralisme religieux," *Angelicum* 74 (1997): 171–92.

22. I take this expression from Raymond Panikkar, and I explained how I understand it in my book *Profession théologien* (see note 10 above).

CHAPTER NINE

Jesus and the Qur'an

The Word of God among Us

DAVID BURRELL, C.S.C.

As one who has been immersed for twenty years in trying to understand the interaction of Jewish, Christian, and Muslim thought and faith, I present the following remarks as an exercise in comparative theology. They rely on the groundbreaking work of Jean Daniélou and Karl Rahner which has established the potential fertility of comparative inquiry in matters of faith. These remarks seek to bring that work to a fine point by displaying how the perspective of the third millennium, in which people have at last responded positively to the invitation to share in different faiths, can illuminate central issues in Christian life and thought. The one issue on which we shall focus can be gleaned from the words which John puts into Peter's mouth at the end of his lengthy discourse on God's word as flesh to be eaten and blood to be drunk: "Lord, to whom can we go? You have the words of eternal life. We have come to believe and know that you are the Holy One of God" (Jn 6:68–69). If we replace Peter's final confession with words he would not have been able to say (so they would not fit the narrative), yet lifted from the opening verses of that same gospel, we could hear ourselves say: "You have the words of eternal life; we have come to believe that you are the Word of life." That Jesus is himself the creating and redeeming Word of God places revelation squarely in the person of Jesus, who is the person of the Word, and so properly relativizes scripture for Christians. It will prove ironic how a comparative perspective with Islam, whose scripture is God's very Word, can help us clarify issues which have bedeviled Christian accounts of revelation, notably since the Reformation. But that again will reinforce Rahner's prescient point that a more accurate periodization of the history of Christian thought ought to place the crisis points elsewhere than in the sixteenth century.

Each of the faiths which traces its origin to Abraham has a triadic structure which can be characterized as Revealer, Word, and Receiving Community. The One who reveals is identified with the Creator of all-that-is, while the Word spoken is the same Word by which the universe is created. Yet in each case of explicit divine speech, that Word is spoken so that human beings will receive it, and those who receive it will be formed by that same Word into a distinctive community. Indeed, any Jew, Christian, or Muslim will find this description familiar, and also recognize that many failures to understand the contours of their religious faith often fail by neglecting one or another of these three realities, or in missing the creative interaction among them. So, for example, "fundamentalists" tend to focus on the Word itself, abstracted from the One who speaks it as well as the community which receives it, while revisionists typically concentrate on the Word-as-received, in an effort to adapt it to the culture in which they reside.[1]

It is crucial to our thesis that these three—Revealer, Revealing Word, Receiving Community—are internally related once the Revealer has decided to reveal God's way to a people. As with creation itself, the initiative is totally with God, so the community has no claims to identity prior to its being called forth by the revealing Word, nor need God speak that Word. In this sense, all is *grace*. Yet once spoken, it is equally crucial that it be received freely by the intentional beings to whom it is addressed, so each of these traditions has identified that intentionality with the divine image bestowed in creation. Moreover, free reception gives the ensuing community a sense of ownership of that Word, which creates a tension with the way in which it must also allow itself to be shaped and re-shaped by that same revealing Word. For as God's own Word, this Word is not itself part of creation, even though its mode of expression must be. So the revealing Word will in one way stand over against the community which it shapes, yet that very community will also need to establish that Word's coherence with respect to the intellectual world it inhabits, as well as employ the resources of the revealed Word to illuminate the world in which it lives. Whether one calls it *interpretation* or *theology*, as "faith seeking understanding" this effort represents the responsible dimension of humans' freely receiving the revealing word of God.

Once this scenario is in place, it becomes clear how a Christian understanding of revelation is internally tied to God's original choice of Israel. Early attempts (by Marcion) to sever God's revelation in Jesus from the Hebrew scriptures were deemed heretical, linked as they were to a dualistic picture of creation and redemption, as well as opposing the two covenants to one another. There is, as we shall see, a "new" element in God's revelation in Jesus, so contrasts will be in order, but never opposition. I was reminded of this forcibly when attending a celebration of seventy-five years of Catholic Christianity in Mbarara Uganda in 1975. Startled to think that 1900 had represented a clean slate for introducing this divine revelation to this people in this portion of the globe, I wondered how the original missionaries had gone about their task. Indeed, how does one begin to talk about Jesus? I was told that these French White Fathers had listened to the people's stories. That gave them two initial good marks: they had learned the language, and they had listened. When they heard these stories, they remarked that they had similar stories: there was this man Abraham. . . . So Paul's celebrated image of God's revelation in Jesus being grafted onto the trunk of Israel (Rom 11:17), the parent tree planted by God's original word to Abraham and fertilized by subsequent words to Moses, came to life in this account. On reflection, of course, how else could one begin to "talk about Jesus" except in terms set by the covenant under which he was born?

How, indeed, did the earliest believers in Jesus—Jews all—speak of him? By the seamless account of Luke-Acts, as one who continued to astound them with the way he taught—"as one with authority," in contrast with their own certified teachers. And then their disillusion attending his shameful demise, followed by exultation at his presence to them risen. Here, in Acts, begin the proto-affirmations of his unique identity before God: "there is no other name under heaven by which human beings can be saved" (Acts 4:10). Invoking the name of anyone other than "the Holy One" as a way of gaining access to "salvation" would be idolatry; not so with Jesus' name. Jesus' *name* may be invoked as God's own name is invoked because he himself is God's revelation. As has often been remarked, there is little that is novel in Jesus' words; what is striking is his presence, presented throughout the gospels as a healing presence. As the first letter of John begins: "This is what we proclaim to you: what was from the beginning, what we have heard, what we have seen with our eyes, what we have looked upon and our hands have touched—we speak of the word of life" (1 Jn 1:1).

Here the triadic structure shared by all the Abrahamic faiths is stretched to a limit, for the *Word* whereby God reveals the way for rational, responsive creatures to return all that we have received is himself a *person*, with the result that the community shaped by that Word to receive it will be constituted as children of God, brothers and sisters of Jesus. Indeed, to belong to that community is to be reborn "in Christ," as Leo the Great announces in a Christmas sermon:

> Though each and every individual occupies a definite place in this body to which he has been called, and though all the progeny of the church is differentiated and marked with the passage of time, nevertheless as the whole community of the faithful, once begotten in the baptismal font, was crucified with Christ in the passion, raised up with him in the resurrection and at the ascension placed at the right hand of the Father, so too it is born with him in this Nativity, which we are celebrating today. (PL 54, 213–16)

And lest that language be nothing more than a cascade of metaphors, we are reminded by Cyril of Alexandria, commenting on the Gospel of John, that this community is constituted by "the Spirit" which Jesus received at his baptism, accompanied by the divine words: "You are my Son; today I have begotten you" (Mt 3:17). Yet since Jesus is "Son of God," what sense have these words as though announcing an event? Cyril explicates:

> The Father says of Christ, who was God, begotten of him before the ages, that he is 'begotten today', for the Father is to accept us in Christ, in so far as he is man. So the Father can be said to give the Spirit again to the Son, though the Son possesses the Spirit as his own, in order that we may receive the Spirit in Christ. . . . The only-begotten Son receives the Spirit, but not for his own advantage, for the Spirit is his, and is given in him and through him. . . . He receives it to renew our nature in its entirety and to make it whole again, for in becoming man he took our entire nature to himself . . . , for it is through Christ that all gifts come to us. (PG 73, 751–54)

This is overwhelmingly rich, indeed metaphysical fare, yet the predilection of Christianity for such exposition stemmed directly from the fact of God's revelation being *in* Jesus, and not simply *from* or even *through* him. That God's Word is divine should go without saying, yet early Islamic thought wavered on the issue whether the Qur'an was created or not, anxious as it was to safeguard the distinction of Creator from everything else. Not for long, however, for a Creator who is mute (or uncomprehending) proved intolerable. Yet to find the *Word* transmuted into a *person* suggests that what is being revealed is more than a way, but God's own self; while the personal relation with this person Jesus (which the gospels call "faith") is one which invites us into a comparable relation of filiation with God. So this community is an ontological one, reflecting an inner transformation of human beings into children of God. Again, John:

> In the beginning was the Word and the Word was with God. All things were made through him; without him was made nothing that was made. . . . He came into his own . . . and to those who received him, who were born not of the will of the flesh or of man, but of God, he gave the power to become children of God. And the word was made flesh, and dwelt amongst us, and we have seen his glory, as of the Father's only son, full of grace and of truth. (Jn 1:1, 4, 10–14)

So it was inevitable, one might say, that the identification of Jesus with God's Word would take the triadic structure common to all the Abrahamic faiths, and transmute it into a trinitarian divinity with names derived from the new revelation—Father, Son, and Spirit; a divinity ready to receive into its rich inner life all those "who believe in Jesus." Yet the fact remains that it took this community four centuries to clarify the issues surrounding the affirmations of Jesus' divinity, already implicit in Acts. The explanation seems clear: nothing could contradict the defining affirmation of one God which constituted the original covenant ("Hear, O Israel, the Lord your God is one"), and would also form the clarion call of Islam. A God who is Father, Son, and Spirit could not thereby be any less One! Moreover, the fact that the controversies should turn on the ontological constitution of Jesus, rather than a direct explication of the scriptural language of "Father, Son, and Holy Spirit," serves to incorporate the relation between creation and redemption, since the human and divine natures united in the one person of the Word (in the culminating formula of Chalcedon in 451) reflect both creature and creator.

We have also seen, however, how the language of Father and of Son will be filled out by that of Holy Spirit, as the one incorporating all believers into the inner life of God so effectively displayed in the person of Jesus. So trinitarian reflection has always been more than an exercise in higher ontology, for the Spirit's role has ever been one of "divinization," of effecting the transformation of believers into children of God "in the Son." Indeed, the defining characteristic of the new covenant, already implicit in the manner of revelation in the person of the Word made human in Jesus, becomes explicit in the transformed community of faithful. It is this founding fact which accounts for the ubiquity of the language of "grace" in Christianity, a term with both personal and ontological undertones. Yet I would also call attention to its presence in Islam, where the formula for the divine reality of the Qur'an runs parallel to that of Jesus: as Christians believe that the Word of God is made flesh in Jesus, so Muslims contend that the Word of God is made Arabic in the Qur'an. Indeed, the Sufi Islamic tradition attests that meditative recitation (*dhikr*) on these words can effect in Muslim believers the same quality of transformation which Christians associate with reception of the body and blood of Christ in the eucharist. In each case, what is said to transpire is an activity of God transforming the person ("grace"), effected via the mode of revelation proper to each community: the Word of God made human in Jesus, and the Word of God made Arabic in the Qur'an.

That the revealing activity of God takes place in a person, then, calls forth all the intellectual resources of philosophy to try to express this creator-creature relation in a way which respects the reality of both. Indeed, the relation of creator with creature within the person of Jesus also marks that person as a *sacrament:* that is, one whose very theandric mode of being reminds us how present the creator is to all creatures, yet present here so that very relation is displayed in a person. Similarly, Islam reminds its faithful that they are only able to notice how created things are *signs* [*ayât*] of the creator once their minds and hearts have been opened by the *verses* [*ayât*] of the Qur'an. Similarly, Christianity finds God's presence in bread and wine, water and salt, because these have been transformed by the very words of the Word incarnate. So two defining features of Christian life—doctrine and sacrament—both stem from the grounding fact that this Word is flesh, or human. Moreover, the third term of the triad, the living community, which we have linked with the Holy Spirit, is also referred to as the "body of Christ." That is, an organic unity prior to the individuality of each of the faithful who make it up, rooted in this person who, in his divine-human constitution, issues to each of us the call to live by God's own life. So Vatican II explains the public prayer of the church:

> Every liturgical celebration, as an activity of Christ the priest and of his body, which is the church, is a sacred action of a preeminent kind. . . . In the liturgy on earth we are given a foretaste of the liturgy of heaven, celebrated in the holy city of Jerusalem, the goal of our pilgrimage. (*Constitution on Liturgy*, pars. 7–8)

Jesus, as the Spirit of Christ, prays in the Christian praying.

Another term for that new life is 'grace', which signifies an adoptive relation to God-the-Revealer which mirrors in creatures the generative relation of God to God's own Word. As noted previously, all these features of Christian life and thought reflect an unimaginable initiative on the part of the Revealer: not just to speak the divine Word, but to become one of us without ceasing to be that Word, and to do so in such a way as to call us "not servants but friends" (Jn 15:15). Features like these will inevitably "give offense," as Kierkegaard remarks (in *Sickness unto Death* especially), yet that must be part of the package. Again, the pattern can be found in biblical revelation in God's choosing this people as God's very own, or in Islam in God's gifting Muhammad with the Qur'an. In each case—election of Israel, Word incarnate in Jesus, Word made Arabic in the Qur'an—the initiative is completely God's, so no reason for it can be forthcoming. Philosophy can discern patterns, as we have here, yet never be able to give reasons, for in each case all is gift, as each of the revelations assures us creation is as well. This is the *ur*-pattern which Augustine discerned in battling Pelagius: while humans can rightly be rewarded for good actions and punished for evil ones, no one can *merit* the gift of new life, or election, or hearing the Qur'an recited. These are as gratuitous as our very lives are, and receiving them as freely given reminds us how our lives also are gift—much as refraining from labor on *shabbat* is designed to remind us that our work of perfecting God's creation is rooted in the gift of creation itself.

Now let us turn specifically to Islam, and to the Qur'an, which Muslims believe to be the Word of God made Arabic, as Christians believe Jesus to be the Word of God made flesh (or human).[2] Rather than compare these two directly, however, as has been attempted by some who have invented the term 'inlibration' to parallel 'incarnation', I would rather focus on the ways in which Christianity and Islam articulate the consequences for the lives of believers: incorporation into the "body of Christ" (for Christians), or into the *umma* [community of faithful] which allows individual Muslims to find the "straight path" offered by the Qur'an. Reflecting again the internal relation of the three terms in our triadic structure, one cannot speak of Jesus (the One revealing) without attending to the community called forth in his name; or as Augustine taught us to put it: the "whole Christ," head and members. The result— to repeat—is an organic unity prior to the individuality of each of the faithful who make it up, rooted in this person who in his divine-human constitution issues to each of us the call to live by God's own life, doing so in such a way that Jesus, as the Spirit of Christ, prays in the Christian praying. If this depiction of the "whole Christ" offers a formulation of the Christian life far more redolent of Orthodox and Catholic thought and practice than of patterns introduced in the Reformation and subsequently adopted in many western cultures by Catholic and Protestant alike, so be it. It faithfully reflects the doctrine of the church over the centuries regarding the relation of believers to the revealing presence of Jesus, however countercultural that may turn out to be. Furthermore, focusing on this understanding of Christ as the "whole Christ" will also reveal uncanny parallels with Islamic understanding of the pervasive power of God's Word to form persons into a community of faith. Indeed, to reflect on this feature of Islam may well recall Christians to a dimension of their life and teaching which modernist sensibilities have eroded.[3]

How does the Qur'an form persons into a community of faith? One might ask as well how the following of Jesus at once effects and proceeds from incorporation into the "body of Christ"? These are not questions to be answered by a set of techniques, nor can the reality which ensues be comprehended in purely empirical terms. Christianity speaks of baptism *incorporating* those who receive it into this community, the "body of Christ," where the nature of the community as well as the manner of incorporation defy direct description. (Baroque theology concocted the pseudo-empirical conceit of baptism conferring an "indelible mark on the soul"—a mode of discourse which confuses more than it clarifies, yet it does serve to make the point that what is going on resists straightforward description.) What is certain is that we are operating within a *supernatural* field of force, where the causalities at work are certainly extensions of God's creative power, yet directed to individual persons with a view to their responding as part of a community which will shape their lives from within. Yet does not that describe what is going on in Islam as well? By virtue of its ritual repetition, the Qur'an, as God's creating Word, forges a kind of "second nature" within the believer, directing people's attention to those dimensions of God's creation which will turn and return them to its creator. Aquinas will use such Aristotelian categories to speak of God's gift of *grace* as a "second nature," while the same Arabic word [*aya, ayât*] doubles for 'sign' and for 'verse' of the Qur'an, reminding us that one will only read natural things as signs of a creator once one has allowed one's "imaginal world" to be shaped by the verses of the Qur'an. Indeed, Ibn al-Arabi will prefer this "imaginal world" to Aristotle's "second nature" as an explanatory category for what is happening as one becomes "incorporated" into a believing community.[4]

The "ritual repetition" at issue refers to the ways in which the Qur'an enters into the lives of Muslim in their public prayer [*salât*], or in repeated invocations throughout the day in answer to diverse situations—invocations which often embody verses from the Qur'an. In this way, the Word of God becomes operative in the lives of the faithful by shaping the way Muslims regard and approach the world. If that operative Word is the same Word by which the universe is called into being ("God said 'be' and it was" [Qur'an 2:117]), then allowing it to shape our perception and our actions aligns us with the God-given order of the universe, thereby directing us how to return everything to the One from whom we have received everything. And that turning and returning of the self offers a far better description of the dynamic of Islam than the one-word lexical rendering of 'submission', for it articulates what Islam proposes in offering human beings the "straight path" (Qur'an 1:6). What results is a community shaped by the same Word by which the universe is created, thus ordered so as to direct human beings toward their proper end. To effect this, the Word revealed in the Qur'an must be the operative Word by which the universe is created, so through its recitation human beings will be swept up into that divine order. Here we have a strict analogue to the patristic teaching of our transformation by being incorporated into Christ. In standard Islamic teaching, this transformation is to be observed by contrasting Muslims with those mired in ignorance [*jahiliyya*], who can neither recognize themselves to be created nor appreciate the destiny that creation bestows on them. Among Sufis, this same transformation is articulated in ways which approximate the Christian teaching of "divinization."[5]

So while it is true that in the Qur'an the Word became Arabic rather than human, as the creating divine Word that Arabic Qur'an nonetheless effects a human community which—when it responds properly—reflects the God-given order of the universe, and so (in human terms) the face of God. Moreover, this divine face of the *umma* will be exemplified in those individuals who most effectively embody this dynamic, so while the Qur'an celebrates the prophets, Islam turns on the saints: those "friends of God" who provide the poles [*qutb, aqtâb*] on which the cultural universe turns.[6] In principle Islam does not countenance "intercession," yet saints' tombs are frequent places of pilgrimage where faithful Muslims seek assistance from God through the presence of the holy man or woman. The role they play is analogous to that played by the Prophet and the other Qur'anic prophets on the last day: "God's mercy comes out most clearly in the question of intercession [*shafa'a*]. . . . When [the Prophet] has finished interceding for the members of his community, the other prophets will be allowed to intercede for their communities."[7] But then any community of faith which is rooted in a communal commitment will celebrate the holy men and women, living and dead, who exemplify that faith. Just as eastern Christians celebrate eucharist in churches with walls and ceiling studded with icons of those who have gone before yet who continue to accompany them in prayer, so Muslims are conscious of this continuing communal presence, and Sufis may even choose as masters those who are no longer among the living. Both "body of Christ" and *umma* body forth the inherent presence and power of that Word "through whom the universe is made" (Nicene Creed). So we can see how it is that the fruitful scheme for comparing Islam with Christianity is not the one suggested by the Muslim honorific to Christians (or Jews) of being "peoples of the Book." For that insinuates that we should align Qur'an with Bible, and Muhammad with Jesus. It is rather the parallel formulae which point us in the right direction: as Christians believe Jesus to be the Word made flesh (or human), Muslims believe the Qur'an to be the Word made Arabic. The obvious disparity between a book and a person, however, might warn one off that tack; yet to speak, as Augustine taught us to do, of the "whole Christ," provides a way of exploiting this analogy to explore cognate dimensions of Islam while rediscovering similar ones in Christianity as well.

That seems to be the proper way of proceeding in comparing religious traditions: one of "mutual illumination" where the differences are as salient as the commonalties.[8] So it is never an issue of syncretism, but rather one of realizing how following out analogies in other traditions can alert one to fresh ways of cognizing one's own. For a Christian, this can mean discovering new faces of the One who is the revelation of God, Jesus, as Jean Daniélou proposed some forty years ago, in his twin works, *Advent* and *Salvation of Nations*.[9] Composed in what Karl Rahner would help us see were the final decades of the "missionary movement," Daniélou suggested replacing the idiom of "bringing Christ" (to Asia or Africa) with that of "finding Christ" there. The point is a simple one, embodied in "reader-response" criticism: to speak of Jesus to people formed in a very different tradition is to invite hitherto unsuspected questions; so to try to answer them will be to discover a fresh way of putting what one came to announce. (The alternative conception means, of course, that we bring all of our own cultural readings with us.) Furthermore, those missions which had instinctively followed his proposed idiom proved to be the ones which were fruitful. Karl Rahner's celebrated 1979 "world-church" lecture, originally entitled "Towards a Fundamental Interpretation of Vatican II" and republished in the leading theological journals in Asia and Africa, proposed a new periodization for western Christian history, identifying 70 and 1970 as key symbolic dates, bracketing nineteen centuries of western European Christianity.[10] The significance of these dates is that each marked, in a symbolic fashion, a "theological crisis" to which the community of faithful had to respond without requisite theological reflection: in 70, whether to circumcise or not the pagans desiring baptism; and in 1970, how to understand Christianity vis-à-vis the other religions of the world in a new post-colonial context. (As a reading of Vatican II, his radical proposal had the advantage of incorporating the accepted interpretation as well: that the council had relativized the opposition between Protestant and Catholic which had dominated theological and ecclesial reflection for four centuries; for if 70 and 1970 become the crucial dates, the sixteenth century becomes a blip on the screen!)

We must also recall that Rahner had identified *Nostra Aetate* as the most significant document of the Second Vatican Council, where his point in doing so was hardly to downgrade the others, but to remind us how— thanks to the *ressourcement* of the French *nouvelle théologie* movement— the major documents of the council had enjoyed a rich theological preparation, while the issue of Christianity's relation to "other religions" had barely been broached. So this document reflected an ecclesial step, taken in the course of the council itself, whose theological significance we are continuing to plumb, and to which this modest effort is meant to contribute. *Nostra Aetate* properly finessed the delicate questions of *truth*, however, so let me offer a word here by way of concluding this discussion and opening that issue for further reflection. Retaining our focus on the "whole Christ," let us begin by linking the gospel's criterion: "by their fruits you shall know them," with John Paul II's recent call for repentance of the part of Christians for our recurrent failures to live up to the call of Christ over the past two millennia. If we had done so, the issue of the truth of Christianity would have been clearly and decisively decided. Moreover, we have no other way of deciding the issue, since the once-popular "extrinsic" forms of apologetics fail to pass the critical test of history. (Jesus' resurrection—often taken as a decisive proof of his divinity—is not itself a historically attested fact, nor could it be; indeed, the only *fact* reported even by the gospels is the empty tomb. So the witness of the fledgling community of believers is our best historical attestation of Jesus' resurrection.)

So what about other communities which have generated holy men and women, people who traced their manifest transformation to another revelation? If we can only come to assess the truth of such revelations by their fruit, then it is the saints who make us take notice. Beyond that, we can only recall Aquinas's sober dictum that in speaking of divine things, our language can *at best* "imperfectly signify" its subject[11] so we are always ready to learn—in the fashion suggested by Jean Daniélou—more about ourselves from other traditions, as we explore the traces of the divine in their teachings as articulated by their intellectuals, but even more saliently, as embodied in their saints.

NOTES

1. I am indebted to Nicholas Lash's prescient exposition of trinitarian thought, *Believing Three Ways in One God: A Reading of the Apostles' Creed* (Notre Dame, Ind.: University of Notre Dame Press, 1993), for suggesting how this triadic structure contributes to a self-correcting exposition.

2. For a brief recent history of this comparison, see James Tebbe, "Comparing Christ and Qur'an," *International Review of Missions* 88 (1999): 414–24.

3. For a sympathetic treatment of those sensibilities, see Charles Taylor, *Sources of the Self: The Making of the Modern Identity* (Cambridge, Mass.: Harvard University Press, 1989), esp. chap. 6.

4. As Henry Corbin puts it, "the Necessary Being, whose pure Essence is incompatible with all form, is nevertheless manifested in a form belonging to the 'Imaginative Presence'" (*Alone with the Alone: Creative Imagination in the Sufism of Ibn 'Arabi* [Princeton, N.J.: Princeton University Press, 1997], 218). In William Chittick's exposition: "only the faculty of imagination perceives God in His self-disclosure. In contrast, reason declares Him incomparable with all forms and all self-disclosures. However, the imagination that truly perceives the real is not just any imagination. The seeker needs the imaginal vision that Ibn al-'Arabi typically refers to as 'unveiling'" (*The Self-Disclosure of God: Principles of Ibn al-'Arabi's Cosmology* [Albany, N.Y.: State University of New York Press, 1998], 54).

5. For a vivid account, see Ruzbihan Baqli, *The Unveiling of Secrets: Diary of a Sufi Master*, trans. Carl Ernst (Chapel Hill, N.C.: Parvardigar Press, 1997); the classical comparative study is that of G.C. Anawati and Louis Gardet, *Mystique Musulmane* (Paris: J. Vrin, 1976).

6. Chittick, *Self-Disclosure*, 22.

7. William Chittick and Sachiko Murata, *Vision of Islam* (Minneapolis, Minn.: Paragon House, 1994), 209.

8. I owe this serendipitous phrase to my Notre Dame colleague, Bradley Malkovsky.

9. Jean Daniélou, *Advent* (New York: Sheed and Ward, 1951); Jean Daniélou, *Salvation of the Nations* (Notre Dame, Ind.: University of Notre Dame Press, 1962).

10. Karl Rahner, "Towards a Fundamental Interpretation of Vatican II," *Theological Studies* 40 (1979): 716–27, reprinted in *African Ecclesiastical Review* 100 (December 1980). For a commentary from the perspective of Jerusalem, see my "Jerusalem and the Future of Inquiry," *Tantur Yearbook* (1981–82): 35–56.

11. *Summa Theologiae* 1.13.4: "[In speaking of God,] the different and complex concepts which we have in mind correspond to something altogether simple which they enable us imperfectly to understand"—an explication on which Herbert McCabe, O.P., expands in "Appendix 3: Signifying Imperfectly," to the Blackfriars edition (New York: McGraw-Hill, 1965).

CHAPTER TEN

Blindness or Insight?

The Jewish Denial of Jesus Christ

MICHAEL A. SIGNER

From Disputation to Dialogue: Past the Stumbling Block

In 1863 Abraham Geiger, the leading rabbi of liberal Judaism in Germany, described the liberating role of scholarly study in the area of religious studies: "The deepest contents of all the spiritual movements is scholarship. Where scholarship turns with its power it brings light to whatever was in chaos. The study of Judaism can proceed hand in hand to build a supportive circle with Christian theologians."[1] From our present perspective we can look back after almost one hundred and fifty years with profound sadness and some hope. The "supportive circle" of Jewish scholars and Christian theologians never emerged during Geiger's day or in subsequent decades. Generations of Christian scholars turned away from the efforts made by liberal Jewish theologians to open collaborative investigations of the history of early Christianity or later periods. The nightmare of the Shoah extinguished the institutions and many of the scholars of European Jewry who might have participated.

However, during the last fifty years there are signs that Geiger's hope for scholarship to "turn with its power" and bring light could be realized. Churches have made significant statements such as *Nostra Aetate* (1965) that support a more positive attitude toward Judaism and the Jewish people.[2] Many of these statements have been brought to life in the on-going activities of Pope John Paul II to move toward reconciliation.[3] His efforts toward reconciliation between Christians and Jews are grounded in his deep theological conviction and have expressed themselves in his actions during his visit to Jerusalem in March 2000. Statements by ecclesiastical groups that encourage individual Christians to ameliorate their relationship to Judaism have been matched by intensified contacts between theologians and scholars—many who appear here in these pages.

We look back wistfully and conjecture that discussions about Christianity and Judaism might have been very different if theologians like Leo Baeck and Franz Rosenzweig would have read Pelikan or Lindbeck instead of Harnack.[4] In the field of New Testament studies John Meier has observed that what distinguishes the scholarly literature of the "third quest for the historical Jesus" from previous efforts has been the fruitful exchange between Jewish and Christian scholars.[5]

In the Jewish community we find the partnership between ecclesial bodies and scholarly investigations to be a most significant component of moving the reconciliation with Christians forward. Whatever misgivings scholars of either faith community may have with their Churches or Synagogues they have discovered that without serious dialogue with those who serve directly in the pulpits, there is little hope that their hard-won scholarly gains will be heard or read by the people in the pews who need them the most. As scholars—historians or theologians—we have come to realize our obligations to our communities of faith and to include them in our deliberations.[6] We realize that religious life occurs not in the pages of learned journals but in the homilies delivered during liturgies; and in the rituals and rites of celebration of our sacred calendars. We want to be bold and see broader horizons than previous generations, and we hope that we can be guides to those who doubt and those who are so certain that they are afraid to doubt.

What motivates me to answer the question "Who is it that you say I am?" is grounded in the praxis of my teaching in a Catholic university and as a rabbi with responsibility to Reform Judaism in North America. I hear a paraphrase of "Who do you say I am?" in my classes at the University of Notre Dame. It usually occurs after the first month of lectures. The topic of the course makes very little difference. One bold soul inquires, "Rabbi, what do the Jewish people think about Jesus?" or "Who is it that you and the Jewish people say he is?" My answer to their question usually evokes some disappointment. They cannot grasp how it is possible that Jesus Christ—so central to their lives and community—could be so marginal in my own Jewish community. Their inquiries resonated with a more positive and hopeful assertion by a theology student at the University of Augsburg. He spoke to me at a seminar with great enthusiasm arguing that Jesus Christ was the bridge between Jews and Christians—between Judaism and Christianity—because only Jesus Christ was simultaneously a Jew and a Christian. When I indicated to this well-meaning student that I hardly thought that the historical life of Jesus would be sufficient to sustain the Christian community he sadly agreed. He conceded that ultimately the question of who Jesus *was* would be an inadequate response to who Jesus *is*.

In reflecting upon my answers to both the American and German students the words of Paul (1 Cor 1:23) came to mind: "We preach Christ crucified, folly to the Greeks and a stumbling block to the Jews." This use of the term '*skandalon*' calls to mind the commandment of Leviticus 19:14 not to put a stumbling block before the blind. Yet it is precisely the image of partial blindness that Paul ascribes to the Jews and which later came to be incorporated into the iconography of the medieval church in the west as "Synagoga."[7] Is it possible for Jews to speak with Christians about the question of Jesus Christ and turn the image of the stumbling block into a positive image—as a boundary marker, perhaps—that will encourage further discussion rather than close down discourse?

Over the past thirty years Christians and Jews have come to understand each other in their own integrity—within the wholeness of their assembled communities and traditions. In the course of those discussions many negative perceptions of Judaism have been removed.[8] Can this new effort be sustained in a dialogue between the two communities about how Christians approach the ineffable? Is it possible to examine the negation of Jesus Christ in the Jewish tradition as insight rather than blindness?

In the discussion that follows I would, first, like to suggest a framework for Jewish discussions with Christians about the nature of Jesus Christ. Second, I will survey some of the most significant responses of the Jewish tradition with respect to Jesus Christ and demonstrate a remarkable continuity from antiquity to modernity. Finally, I will set out an agenda that outlines what stake the Jewish community has in future Christian theological deliberations about Christology.

From Silence to Speech:
The Two Horizons of the Christological Discussion

Let us begin with the christological question before us and search for a framework where a Jewish response might contribute to a deeper conversation. The question "Who is it that you say I am?" has a particular resonance for the Jewish reader. The final linguistic unit: "I am" recalls the ineffable name, YHWH, in the book of Exodus that God imparts to Moses (Ex 3). While the question in the book of Exodus is a divine response to a question raised by Moses, the inquiry by Jesus in the gospel demands a human response from the apostles to a divine query. In either case the Jewish reluctance to utilize the *nomina sacra* immediately sets the boundary of what might be articulated in human speech. From the late biblical period and into the rabbinic literature the Jewish tradition discovered euphemisms for the use of the divine name. Nouns such as "the heavens" "the place" "the Holy One" replaced the Tetragrammaton YHWH and Elohim.[9]

Rabbinic and medieval Hebrew literature referred to Jesus, the inquirer, as "oto ha-ish" ("that man"). The name of Jesus Christ, as we will see further on, was removed from many rabbinic texts as an act of self-censorship.[10] However, if we inquire why self-censorship was important to these earlier generations two distinct answers are plausible. The first answer would be that once Christianity became the majority religion in the West it began to diminish the legal status of Judaism.[11] In order to avoid further danger the Jewish community encoded references to Jesus by the derisive term "that man."

An alternative answer to the development of the use of "oto ha-ish" or "that man" would follow this line of reasoning. The Jewish tradition holds a great reverence for words and particularly for names. This reverence is clear with respect to the *nomina sacra*, the divine names, where there has been a reticence among Jews even to pronounce them. Therefore for Jews to utter the name "Jesus Christ" would have been an apparent validation of belief in him. Lest we think that this reticence to utter the name Jesus Christ is relegated to the past, there are many Jews who asserted their youthful religious identity by joining their public school classmates in singing Christmas carols but remaining silent when the lyrics required them to say Jesus or Christ.[12]

The rabbinic proverb "Silence is appropriate for wisdom" has been at the heart of the popular Jewish reaction—from antiquity to modernity—

to public statements about the nature of Jesus Christ.[13] We shall see later in this essay that the Jewish negation of Jesus as Christ went well beyond silence. Within the confines of their own community, Jews had a clearly articulated negation about Jesus. Silence in public discussion and articulate refutation within the privacy of the Jewish community was a strategy for the physical survival of the Jewish community in Christendom. This bifurcated approach was a strategy for physical safety and survival of the community. It began to break down in the second half of the nineteenth century and continued until the beginning of the Shoah.[14]

The changes that have occurred in Christian theology since the Shoah urge an effort to renew a serious discussion between our communities. Christian communities that no longer target Jews for proselytism may open the doors to fruitful discussion about Christology. The discourse should be carefully framed to provide respect for Christian belief and tradition and must accord a presentation of Jewish perspectives that are grounded in the Jewish tradition.[15]

Let me propose two horizons for a dialogue between Jews and Christians about the question, "Who is it that you say I am?" The first horizon for christological discussion is what I call the ontological or existential horizon. The assertions by Jesus in the Gospel of John that "I am the way, and the truth, and the life" and that "he who believes has eternal life" indicate that the person who professes Jesus Christ has a unique ontological status. The believer is transformed from mortality to eternal life because he or she accepts this truth. This truth is affirmed by the speech by Peter after the initial commissioning of the disciples through the power of the Holy Spirit (Acts 2:14–41). That passage indicates that through the death and resurrection of Jesus Christ a change has occurred in the way God offers salvation to humankind. In the Pauline writings there are frequent references to the power of salvation that occurs when the individual becomes part of the community of believers.[16] Subsequent generations of Christian authors have attempted to describe the ineffable change that occurs in the heart, mind, and soul of those who believe.

The ontological or existential horizon can be understood in the deep private experience of a faith community. It requires a commitment of faith in order to comprehend its language. As a Jew I may read the meditations of Teresa of Avila, John of the Cross, or Thomas Merton. However, when they attempt to describe the profound change that Jesus as Christ makes in their lives I can only read them empathetically. When I attend

Christian worship and watch the faces of those who go up to take the Eucharist, I can observe the change in their demeanor and glimpse traces of their inner experience.

The private nature of these experiences creates a language of belief that can at best be appreciated by non-believers but can never fully engage them beyond an appreciation of how they function in the life of the Christian community. Their descriptions invite empathy, but cannot provide a comprehensible account of their inner experience for one who does not share their conviction. Rabbi Joseph Soloveitchik's 1964 essay, "Confrontation," captures the difficulty that Jews might have in understanding the ontological/existential horizon of Christology. He argues for a strict boundary between faith communities with respect to the discussion of these theological claims. He asserts that the language of faith is a "private language" in the Wittgensteinian mode that can only be understood by those who share common faith commitments.[17]

From my perspective christological discussions have a second horizon that I would call temporal/eschatological. My study of the Christian tradition has taught me that Jesus Christ enters the economy of salvation and transforms history. Jesus Christ, the eschaton or end, enters at the mid-point pointing the way for humanity to the ultimate end when God will be "all in all." St. Augustine's sermon or treatise on the Jews focuses on this very theme of how the reading of God's revelation in Hebrew Scriptures is changed by Jesus Christ.[18] From the Christian perspective Jesus lived in history and demonstrates the way beyond history. The temporal/eschatological horizon provides Jews and Christians with subject matter for very fruitful discussions. Sacred history built on the foundation of the Hebrew Bible forms the main point of convergence and divergence between us. Christians and Jews share the prophetic visions of divine judgment and mercy "in the end of days." The apocalyptic literature promises justification to endure suffering until the eschaton. What Christians and Jews have not and still do not share is the claim that Jesus Christ entered human history as God's incarnation. Debates from antiquity to modernity indicate that it is precisely the temporal/eschatological horizon that has been the platform for disputation between our communities. Of course in the Christian community the ontological and temporal horizons are fused—it is because Jesus is the Christ that he brings triumph over death and a vision of Christian community in love until the eschaton. The Jewish negation of Jesus as Christ, as we shall now discern, begins with the temporal/eschatological horizon. It asserts that there was a man named Jesus, but he was not "the Christ."

"That Man": Jesus as Fully Human

There is a remarkable consistency in the responses by Jewish writers from antiquity to modernity about Jesus.[19] He is portrayed as a historical person who was a member of the Jewish people. Jews knew the details of the life of Jesus as they are narrated in the gospels despite the fact that these documents never held canonical status. Since the fourth century Jews lived in a culture where Jesus was understood as the exclusive savior of the majority Christian community. Until the late twentieth century the Jewish community was—and for some Christian groups remains—a target for proselytization.[20] With this historical and contemporary situation we can understand that the Jewish negation of Jesus Christ was not only a denial of the truth of Christianity. It was an assertion of the continuing validity of God's revelation and commandments that would accompany the Jewish people until *their* Messiah arrived to deliver them from exile and the "yoke of the gentiles." For these reasons the Jewish negation of Jesus was couched in an angry, assertive, and almost scandalous rhetoric.

We turn now to two documents from the early medieval period that reflect the sharp Jewish negation of Jesus: the *Toledot Yeshu* [narrative of Jesus] and *Sefer Nestor HaKomer*. They each represent a different genre: *Toledot Yeshu* is a narrative of negation that retells the life of Jesus. It is filled with detail that demonstrates that Jesus is not the Christ or Messiah.[21] *Sefer Nestor HaKomer* [*The Book of Nestor the Priest*] is written as a philosophical dialogue that demonstrates how Christian proofs about the theological significance of Jesus as messiah do not withstand the scrutiny of reason. *Nestor HaKomer* is the ancestor of many compositions that would be written under the pressure of evangelization by the mendicants in the High Middle Ages.[22]

Toledot Yeshu seems to have been composed in ninth- or tenth-century Europe, most likely in Italy.[23] Though it existed in many manuscripts and several versions Jews never printed it. There is some evidence that the ninth-century bishop Agobard of Lyons knew of its existence. Johann Christoph Wagenseil in his *Tela Ignea Satanae* (1681) printed it in order to demonstrate what calumnies Jews committed against the name of Jesus.[24]

Toledot Yeshu is indeed a parody and biting satire on the life of Jesus. It draws upon passages in the Talmud and from apocryphal gospels that portray Jesus in an unfavorable light. However, if *Toledot Yeshu* is read in light of its rhetorical purpose—to persuade a Jew who might be wavering toward baptism—then we can discern the lines of argument that a minority makes in order to preserve its identity.

Following upon the pattern of the gospels, *Toledot Yeshu* begins with an infancy narrative.[25] Mary was to betroth a scion of the house of David named Johanan who was also a great Torah scholar and a student of Rabbi Shimon ben Shetach. However, during Johanan's absence Mary was raped. In order to preserve her honor and Johanan's it was arranged for them to marry. The oscillation between the Davidic lineage of Jesus and his connection to rabbinic circles is preserved. However, the supernatural conception of Jesus is turned into the calumny of rape.

Toledot Yeshu portrays the young Jesus as a student of Torah and very clever. Difficulties arise when Jesus fails to display appropriate respect for the authority of his teachers. He violated the custom of humility and the document raises the question "Who is the teacher and who is the student?" From this altercation, the circumstances of Jesus' birth are also revealed. The rabbis then sentenced Jesus to death for being one who leads others astray. Yet the work consistently portrays Jesus as a brilliant interpreter of Scripture. He depicts himself as the object of prophecies in Isaiah and Jeremiah. The rabbis offer counter-interpretations.

Jesus is therefore expelled from rabbinic circles and seeks his own group of disciples. He gathers these disciples through his miracles. *Toledot Yeshu* offers an explanation for these miracles. Jesus entered the holy of holies and read the divine name. He wrote it down, cut a slit in his arm where he placed the parchment with the divine name. Afterwards he used the divine name to perform miracles. Once again, *Toledot Yeshu* places the activities of Jesus within a natural realm of explanation. The use of the divine name for magical purposes was known among rabbinic Jews. Jesus was simply part of this tradition and his miracles were not a demonstration of divine favor. In the concluding part of *Toledot Yeshu* the rabbis send Judas Iscariot into the holy of holies to retrieve the divine name and engage in a contest with Jesus before the Roman ruler.

In the *Toledot Yeshu* there is an exchange between Jesus and the rabbinical sages about his name that speaks directly to the question of his identity. Jesus is asked, "What is your name?"

He responds, "My name is Mattai [When]." The Rabbis ask what is the basis in Scripture for this name. Jesus responds, Ps. 42:3 "When shall I come and see the face of God." The Sages responded, "When will he die and lose his name?" Ps. 41:6. Again the sages ask his name and Jesus answers, "My name is Naqi [clean]" When asked the Scriptural basis for this name, Jesus responds, Ps. 24:4 "[I am of] clean hands and a pure heart." The Sages counter with "God will not remit all punishment," Ex. 34:7. Once again the Sages ask for the name and its Scriptural proof and Jesus responds that his name is "Beni [my son]" and the scriptural proof is Ex. 4:22 "Israel, my first born" and the response of the Sages is "I will kill your first born," Ex. 4:23. The final exchange about the name is when Jesus asserts that his name is "Netzer or sprout" and the Scriptural proof is Is 11:1 "He shall grow out of the stump of Jesse." To this name the Rabbis responded with Is. 14:9, "Then you were sent from your grave like a hated sprout."

Toledot Yeshu thus presents its audience with a disputation over the biblical proof of Jesus' identity. The names begin with the wisdom literature or psalms. Jesus is not the subject of "when" he will come to see the face of God, but the very opposite—he will lose his name. He is not of clean hands and pure heart, but the one whom God will not hold guiltless despite his mercy to the thousandth generation.

The center of the exchange, regarding passages from the book of Exodus, is over whether or not Jesus can assert that he is "beni," my son. Here the *Toledot Yeshu* places two succeeding verses against one another. Jesus asserts that he is Israel's God's first-born while the rabbis put his sonship among those of the Egyptians whom God will smite. Any hope that Jesus might assert his name as the sprout of Jesse is dashed by the assertion of the sages that he will be sent from his grave like a hated sprout. This negation of Jesus' claim to messianic prophecy is at the midpoint of the narrative and foreshadows his death by crucifixion for "misleading the generation."

The concluding parts of *Toledot Yeshu* focus on the death and burial of Jesus. There is no resurrection but simply a misplacement of his body so that the grave would not be robbed. After the death of Jesus the disciples continue to dispute with the sages. The disciples claimed, "You have killed the messiah of God and Israel," while the sages asserted, "You believe in a false prophet." In some versions of the *Toledot Yeshu* the separation of

Jesus' disciples from Israel is the result of the machinations of the sages. They convince a great sage named Elijah [in the ms. Strasbourg version] that he should lead the Christians out of the community of Israel. Elijah agrees to their request and tells the followers of Jesus that they must change their worship; cease to observe the Sabbath and change the day of their worship to Sunday; no longer observe Passover but celebrate the feast of the resurrection. He claims that circumcision is a decision that is up to them. The Christians call this Elijah "Paul" and it was he who brought about the separation between Jews and Christians. Arguments then ceased within the household of Israel.

Contemporary Christian readers might want to approach the *Toledot Yeshu* with the same perspective that Jews now read some of the more assertive rhetoric in the early Christian authors. Robert Wilken has taught us that even John Chrysostom's paschal sermons are an assertion of Christian identity.[26] Surely, the *Toledot Yeshu* stamps the life of Jesus with a Jewish narrative. All supernatural elements of Jesus' life are given natural explanations. Biblical messianic prophecies are refuted by utilizing the rabbinic hermeneutic technique of *gezerah shavah* (the use of the same word in another context). Surprisingly from our modern perspective where so much violence has resulted from the charge of deicide by Jewish hands the *Toledot Yeshu* affirms that Jews did put Jesus to death. For the sages it was not a deicide but simply the death of a rebellious Jewish student. The narrative about Jesus in *Toledot Yeshu* is not about one who "is" in the profound sense of the Christian tradition—but about a man who "was" and whose existence brought sadness and sorrow to the house of Israel. *Toledot Yeshu* is, therefore, an internal document, filled with passion and pathos, and it had a profound influence in the folkloric life of the Jewish people.

In the *Book of Nestor the Priest* we discover a framework much more suitable for academic debate. It originated in the Islamic East and was composed in Arabic. In the ninth or tenth century it was translated into Hebrew. When comparing the Arabic version with the Hebrew, Stroumsa and Lasker point out that the latter version is more acerbic and describes Christian arguments with more derisory terminology. Removing the debate from the cultural sphere of Islam where Judaism and Christianity were both minority religions to the realm of Christendom motivated the translator to "strengthen the weak knees" of his co-religionists.[27]

Nestor is described as a priest who converted to Judaism and debated with pagans and sages. This literary motif descends from antiquity but no doubt had verisimilitude in both the Islamic and Christian worlds of the Middle Ages. The composition is set in a series of propositions or questions which are then systematically refuted.

Rather than rehearse the responses to each of these questions I think that it is more useful to gain some understanding of how *Nestor HaKomer* frames the discussion. It begins with the question of the incarnation: How could God take on human form and guide humanity? A comparison of Jesus with figures from the Old Testament consistently reveals the superiority of the latter [par. 4]. A description of the Christian argument for the trinity follows the problem of the incarnation [par. 25–26]. A discussion of the religious practices of Jesus follows. It raises the question: Should Christians follow the Jewish practices that Jesus did? [par. 33–36, 63–69]. Nestor raises the issue about the validity of Jesus' divinity based on the premise that he did not demonstrate the attribute of omnipotence. It asks why it was necessary for Jesus to pray to God to relieve his burden of suffering or why he permitted people to mock him before his crucifixion [par. 51–53]. Indeed, why did Jesus need to eat and sleep if he was divine [108]?

The framework of these questions and responses is significant for the history of many Jewish-Christian debates in the Middle Ages and modernity. When later polemical treatises asserted that reason could ultimately convince Jews of the truth about Jesus Christ and Christianity, the arguments offered by Nestor appear.

In its arguments Nestor covers much of the same ground as *Toledot Yeshu*. However, it adds an important additional dimension. Nestor indicates that Christianity itself stands in opposition to the life and teachings of Jesus. For Nestor, Jesus was an ordinary Jew who followed the law. As we have seen the assertion that Jesus was human and lived within history forms the basis of the Jewish negation of Jesus. At times they were reluctant to speak about Jesus at all as Nachmanides asserted in his 1263 debate with Pablo Christiani, "We will not discuss Jesus but whether or not the messiah has come."[28] On other occasions, particularly with the approach of modernity Jewish authors fell back on the human Jesus theme as Moses Mendelssohn did when he averred, "Jesus of Nazareth observed not only the laws of Moses but also the teachings of the Rabbis . . . and you, dear brothers and fellow human beings who follow the teachings of Jesus, should you be so angry with us when we do what the founder of your religion did and which was preserved through his authority."[29]

In the nineteenth and early twentieth centuries the Jewish negation of Jesus Christ came to focus more and more on the distinction between Jesus and Paul.[30] While Abraham Geiger asserted that Jesus should be placed within the Pharisaic context, he argued that it was Paul who was influenced by paganism. Leo Baeck distinguished between the classical religion of ethics as practiced by Jesus and the Pharisees and the romantic religion of abandonment asserted by Paul.[31] Joseph Klausner and Samuel Sandmel both argued that Jesus was a loyal Jew, while Paul was the founder of a Christianity that was harmonious with paganism.[32] More recent historical scholarship by Jews examines Jesus and Paul within a broader historical context reclaiming both of them into a pluralistic Judaism of the period and some have asserted that there is a co-emergence of Judaism and Christianity as distinct religions only in the fourth century.[33]

It is important to remember after rehearsing the specific Jewish negations about Jesus as the Christ that they apply only to members of the Jewish community. Rabbis in the Talmud had already developed the concept of the "Noachide commandments" that opened God's loving kindness to all the nations of the world.[34] Some medieval rabbis thought that Christian belief in Jesus and the Trinity was permissible for Christians because it brought them under the wings of the God of Israel. From antiquity through modernity Jewish theologians have been prepared to assert the independent validity of Christianity for Christians.[35] Does this assertion put Jewish theologians beyond any interest in future christological discussions?

Toward a Future Agenda:
The Jewish Interest in Continued Christological Discussion

In these concluding remarks I will argue that Jews have a profound interest in the internal debates by Christians. Our position as serious interlocutors will oscillate between silence and intense discussions with Christians. There is no question that Jewish attempts at reclamation of Jesus have foundered within the Jewish community. Martin Buber's assertion that Jesus was his elder brother did not earn him accolades among his co-religionists.[36] Rabbi Maurice Eisendrath's admonition to the Union of American Hebrew Congregations that Jews name Jesus as one of our great teachers received no enthusiastic response among some of his most ardent followers.[37] The ontological horizon—the change in the spirit and being of the individual believer—that Jesus brings to Christians as their Christ stops at the door of the rabbinic assertion that Torah is God's living covenant with the Jewish people. The "metanoia" among recent Christian theologians that the covenant with God and the Jewish People has never been revoked surely reinforces the trust the Jewish theologians will develop in our future discussions.

Perhaps the time has come to recover Franz Rosenzweig's assertion about his own life and paraphrase it as a general rule: Jews do not come to God through Christ but as Jews—and Christians come to God through Christ as Christians. This axiom leaves us as a Jewish community with an opportunity to engage in conversation and deliberation with the Ecclesia, those who constitute the "body of Christ." It is precisely with Christians, through whom Christ acts, that Jews can enter into profound discoveries about the way that God acts in our lives and how our traditions make demands upon us to help in the establishment of divine sovereignty in the world.[38]

As Jews we have an interest in what you believe and how it transforms you. It has been the appreciation of Jesus Christ as human and his capacity for human suffering, as described by Professor Metz in his contribution to this volume, which has brought Christians to a deep appreciation of Jewish loss during the Shoah.[39] The Trinitarian reflections in the writings of Catherine LaCugna and Elizabeth Johnson that emphasize interrelationship rather than hierarchy open believing Christians to positive relationships with those who live beyond the household of the Ecclesia.[40] Christologies that emphasize Jesus Christ as one who lived with the poor, the suffering, the alien—as we find in Liberation theologies—have found sympathetic ears and outreaching arms from members of the Jewish community whose religious identity is founded upon the fusing of rite, ritual, and prophetic justice.[41]

In this essay I have attempted to reverse the perspective that Jews and Christians have had about the Jewish negation of Jesus Christ. Jesus Christ remains a stumbling block, but not one that causes the downfall of either community. The presence of Jews and Christians in the world of the twenty-first century will be very different from the previous two millennia. After witnessing a near annihilation of those who denied Jesus Christ, many Christians have made radical metanoia about those to whom they have been so intimately and separately bound through the temporal horizon. The images of Ecclesia and Synagoga have found two new iconographic expressions in recent publications. The German edition of Cardinal Ratzinger's book about the Jewish-Christian relationship and world religions has cleverly repositioned the medieval Ecclesia at the arm of Synagoga in a supportive gesture.[42] Sister Mary Boys' book *Has God Only One Blessing?* bears a photograph of her newly commissioned sculpture where Ecclesia and Synagoga sit side by side.[43] The temporal/eschatological horizon of Christology has opened opportunities for productive new conversations between our communities. The ontological horizon of the Christian experience of Jesus Christ in this new era may provide Jews an opportunity to listen and learn without fear.

NOTES

This essay is dedicated to the memory of Rev. Leonard E. Boyle, O.P., professor in the Pontifical Institute of Medieval Studies at Toronto and Prefect of the Vatican Library, who was my first mentor in Catholic-Jewish dialogue, and to my colleagues in the Department of Theology at the University of Notre Dame who daily renew my belief that continuing dialogue will yield profound insights.

1. Quoted in Susannah Heschel, *Abraham Geiger and the Jewish Jesus* (Chicago: University of Chicago Press, 1999), 149.

2. The statements and relevant commentaries may be found in Helga Croner, *Stepping Stones to Further Jewish-Christian Relations* (London and New York: Stimulus Books, 1977) and *More Stepping Stones in Jewish Christian Relations: An Unabridged Collection of Documents: 1975–1983* (New York: Paulist Press, 1985) and Roger Brooks, ed., *Unanswered Questions: Theological Views of Jewish-Catholic Relations* (Notre Dame, Ind.: University of Notre Dame Press, 1988). More recent statements can be accessed through www.jcrelations.net.

3. Eugene J. Fisher and Leon Klenicki, eds., *Pope John Paul II: Spiritual Pilgrimage Texts on Jews and Judaism 1979–1995* (New York: Crossroad, 1995). See also Tad Szulc, *Pope John Paul II: The Biography* (New York: Scribner, 1995); Darcy O'Brien, *The Hidden Pope* (New York: Daybreak Books, 1998); and George Weigel, *Witness to Hope: The Biography of John Paul II* (New York: Cliff Street Books, 1999). The relationship between Christians and Jews with respect to theological speculation and public gesture in the papacy of John Paul II requires further study.

4. Jaroslav Pelikan, *The Christian Tradition: A History of the Development of Doctrine* (Chicago: University of Chicago Press, 1971–1989), 1:22–23 indicates that "the victory of Christian theology overcame more by default than by conquest." Pelikan's examination of the history of doctrine pays careful attention to relations with Judaism and Jewish ideas. This irenic approach can be contrasted with that of Adolph Harnack whose ideas about Judaism as thoroughly surpassed by Christianity were questioned by Leo Baeck in *The Essence of Judaism* (New York: Schocken Books, 1961). See Samuel Sandmel, *Leo Baeck on Christianity* (New York: Leo Baeck Institute, 1975); Albert Friedlander, *Leo Baeck: Teacher of Theresienstadt* (Woodstock, N.Y.: Overlook Press, 1991); and Walter Homolka, *Jewish Identity in Modern Times: Leo Baeck and Modern Protestantism* (Providence, R.I.: Berghahn Books, 1995), for the development of Baeck's refutations of Harnack's ideas about Judaism.

5. John P. Meier, "The Present State of the 'Third Quest' for the Historical Jesus: Loss and Gain," *Biblica* 80, no. 4 (1999): 459–87.

6. The balance between theoretical and praxis-oriented issues in Jewish-Christian dialogue is examined by Martin Cunz, "Pastoral Aspects of the Jewish-Christian Dialogue" and my own essay, "Communitas et Universitas: From Theory to Praxis in Judaeo-Christian Studies" in *When Jews and Christians Meet*, ed. Jakob J. Petuchowski (Albany, N.Y.: State University of New York Press, 1988).

7. Romans 11:25 ascribes partial blindness to the Jews [*caecitas ex parte*] that will be removed when the fullness of the gentiles come in. 2 Corinthians 3:14 describes the Jews as being "of hardened minds" and unable to understand the reading of Scripture.

8. The removal of anti-Jewish stereotypes from Christian catechesis has been described by Eugene Fisher, *Faith without Prejudice: Rebuilding Christian Attitudes toward Judaism* (New York: Crossroads, 1993) and Philip A. Cunningham, *Education for Shalom: Religion Textbooks and the Enhancement of the Catholic-Jewish Relationship* (Collegeville, Minn.: Liturgical Press, 1995). The work of the Vatican Commission on Religious Relations with the Jews has encouraged this work in its 1985 document, "Notes on the Correct Way to Present Jews and Judaism in Preaching and Catechesis."

9. On the paraphrase or substitution for biblical names for God in the rabbinic period see George Foot Moore, *Judaism in the First Centuries of the Christian Era* (Cambridge, Mass: Harvard University Press, 1958) and E. E. Urbach, *The Sages: Their Concepts and Beliefs*, trans. Israel Abrahams (Jerusalem: Magnes Press, 1979).

10. Self-censorship in rabbinic literature is the subject of study by Asher Finkel, *The Pharisees and the Teacher of Nazareth* (Leiden: Brill, 1964); William Popper, *The Censorship of Hebrew Books* (New York: B. Franklin, 1968); Moshe Carmilly-Weinberger, *Censorship and Freedom of Expression in Jewish History* (New York: Sepher-Hermon Press, 1977); and Robert Travers Herford, *Christianity in Talmud and Midrash* (New York: Ktav, 1975).

11. The history of the diminution of Jewish legal status beginning with the conversion of Constantine is narrated by James Parkes, *The Conflict of the Church and the Synagogue* (London: Soncino Press, 1934) and the important study by Marcel Simon, *Verus Israel: A Study of the Relationships between Christians and Jews in the Roman Empire (135–435)*, trans. H. McKeating (New York: Oxford University Press for the Littman Library of Jewish Civilization, 1986).

12. The charming story "The Loudest Voice" by Grace Paley provides an illustration of the ambivalence of the community of twentieth-century Eastern-European Jewish immigrants in America to permit their children to say the name of Jesus in public in Grace Paley, *The Collected Stories* (New York: Farrar, Straus, Giroux, 1994).

13. *Mishnah*, Tractate Aboth.

14. The breakdown of this two-pronged approach began with Moses Mendelssohn's response to Johann Christoph Lavater and continued through the writings of Abraham Geiger, Martin Buber, and Franz Rosenzweig. For a history of the public presentation of the negation of Jesus Christ see Hans Joachim Schoeps, *Jüdisch-christliches Religionsgespräch in neunzehn Jahrhundert* (Koenigstein: Judischer Verlag Athenaeum, 1984); Walter Jacob, *Christianity through Jewish Eyes: The Search for a Common Ground* (New York: Hebrew Union College, 1974); Fritz A. Rothschild, *Jewish Perspectives on Christianity* (New York: Crossroad, 1990); Heschel, *Abraham Geiger and the Jewish Jesus*.

15. An appropriate approach to dialogue between Jews and Christians is suggested by the Pontifical Commission for Religious Relations with Jews in their document "Guidelines and Suggestions for Implementing the Conciliar Declaration *Nostra Aetate* (n. 4)" (January 1975). David Novak offers a description of a Jewish approach to dialogue in *Christianity in Jewish Terms*, ed. Tikva Frymer-Kensky, David Novak, Peter Ochs, David Sandmel, and Michael A. Signer (Boulder, Colo.: Westview Press, 2000), 1–6. The editors of the volume offer a new Jewish theological framework for dialogue on pp. xvii–xx. The statement, also known by the Hebrew name "*Dabru Emet*," was signed by more than two hundred rabbis, scholars, and theologians and is available at www.icjs.org.

16. The narrative of Paul's conversion Acts 9 with its sensory deprivation and restoration illustrates the phenomenon. See Alan F. Segal, *Paul the Convert: The Apostolate and Apostasy of Saul the Pharisee* (New Haven, Conn.: Yale University Press, 1990). For Paul's soteriology within the historical context of first-century Palestine, see E. P. Sanders, *Paul and Palestinian Judaism* (Philadelphia, Pa.: Fortress Press, 1977); David M. Stanley, *Christ's Resurrection in Pauline Soteriology* (Rome: Pontifical Biblical Institute, 1961).

17. Joseph B. Soloveitchik, "Confrontation" in *A Treasury of Tradition*, ed. Norman Lamm and Walter Wurzburger (New York: Hebrew Publishing, 1967), 55–80. For a response to Soloveitchik see David Novak, *Jewish-Christian Dialogue: A Jewish Justification* (New York: Oxford University Press, 1989) and David Ellenson, "History, Memory, and Relationship" in *Memory and History in Christianity*

and Judaism, ed. Michael A. Signer (Notre Dame, Ind.: University of Notre Dame Press, 2000), 170–81.

18. *Adversus Judaeos* PL 42:51–64. The principal study has been B. Blumenkranz, *Die Judenpredigt Augustins* (Basel: Helbing and Lichtheim, 1946). His analysis has been challenged by Paula Fredriksen, "*Excaecati Occulta Justitia Dei:* Augustine on Jews and Judaism," *Journal of Early Christian Studies* 3, no. 3 (1995): 299–324, and Jeremy Cohen, *Living Letters of the Law: The Idea of the Jew in Medieval Christianity* (Berkeley and Los Angeles: University of California Press, 1999), 23–65.

19. Avigdor Shinan has compiled an anthology in Hebrew of Jewish authors who have written about Jesus Christ from antiquity through modern Israeli literature, *'Oto ha-'Ish: Yehudim Misapperim 'al Yeshu* [Jesus through Jewish Eyes] (Tel Aviv: Yediot Aharonot and Dvir, 1999). This anthology makes available a series of texts about Jesus that have not been available to the Israeli public. Read together with the Open University Course compiled by Ora Limor, *Beyn Yehudim leNotserim: Yehudim veNotserim beMa'arav Europa 'ad Reshit ha-'Et ha-Hadasha* [Jews and Christians in Western Europe: Encounters between Cultures in the Middle Ages and the Renaissance], 7 vols. (Tel Aviv: Open University 1993); and Israel Jacob Yuval, *Shnei Goyyim be-Bitneych: Yehudim ve-Notserim-Dimuyyim Hadadiim* (Two Nations in Your Womb: Perceptions of Jews and Christians] (Tel Aviv: 'Am Oved, 2000), a remarkably unapologetic perspective on Jewish approaches to Jesus Christ emerges. Samuel Sandmel, *We Jews and Jesus* (New York: Oxford University Press, 1965) reviews the Jewish attitudes toward Jesus that emerge from the modern quests for the historical Jesus. Paula Fredriksen, *From Jesus to Christ: The Origins of the New Testament Images of Jesus* (New Haven, Conn.: Yale University Press, 2000), and *Jesus Christ: King of the Jews: A Jewish Life and the Emergence of Christianity* (New York: Knopf, 1999) lucidly describe the historicist approach to Jesus as the background for the development of Christian theological ideas.

20. The Southern Baptist Convention has made direct approaches to convert the Jewish community in North America and has provided financial support for the group called "Jews for Jesus."

21. All references to the *Toledot Yeshu* are from Samuel Krauss, *Das Leben Jesu nach jüdischen Quellen* (reprint, Hildesheim: Georg Olms, 1977). Johann Maier, *Jesus von Nazareth in der talmudischen Überlieferung* (Darmstadt: Wissenschaftliche Buchgesellschaft, 1978) provides a form-critical analysis of the Talmudic passages that form the material for *Toledot Yeshu* as well as providing important bibliographical information. It is also appropriate to note that some modern Christians object to the name "Yeshu." They understand it as a truncated form of the name "Yeshu'ah" which means "salvation." During the medieval period—and in some versions of the *Toledot Yeshu*—the name "Yeshu" is an acronym for "Yemach Shemo U'zikhrono" [May his name and memory be blotted out!], an anathema against Jesus.

22. Daniel J. Lasker and Sarah Stroumsa, *The Polemic of Nestor the Priest*, 2 vols. (Jerusalem: Ben Zvi Institute, 1996), presents the text in Arabic and Hebrew together with extensive commentary and notes. A comparison of both *Toledot Yeshu* and *Nestor HaKomer* can be found in Ora Limor, "Polemos Nestor Ha-Komer ve Toledot Yeshu [The Polemics of Nestor HaKomer and Toledot Yeshu]," *Pe'amim: Studies in Oriental Jewry* 75 (1998): 109–28.

23. On the earliest texts of the *Toledot Yeshu*, cf. Jacob Deutsch, "'Eduyot 'al Nusah Qadum shel Toledot Yeshu," *Tarbitz* 69, no. 2 (2000): 177–97.

24. Krauss, *Das Leben Jesu*, 27–153.

25. The account of *Toledot Yeshu* in this essay follows the version of ms. Vienna in Kraus, *Das Leben Jesu*, 64–88.

26. Robert L. Wilken, *John Chrysostom and the Jews* (Berkeley and Los Angeles: University of California Press, 1983).

27. Lasker and Stroumsa, *Polemic of Nestor*, 13–38.

28. On the Barcelona debate and its background cf. Robert Chazan, *Barcelona and Beyond: The Disputation of 1263 and Its Aftermath* (Berkeley and Los Angeles: University of California Press, 1992).

29. Moses Mendelssohn, *Jerusalem, or, On Religious Power and Judaism*, trans. Allan Arkush, introduction and commentary by Alexander Altmann (Hanover and London: University Press of New England, 1986), 135.

30. On nineteenth-century debates between Jews and Christians cf. Heschel, *Abraham Geiger and the Jewish Jesus*, 186–242; Uriel Tal, *Christians and Jews in Germany* (Ithaca, N.Y.: Cornell University Press, 1975); Hans Joachim Schoeps, *Jüdisch-christliches Religionsgespräch in neunzehn Jahrhunderten* (Königstein: Judische Verlag Athenaeum, 1984); and Walter Jacob, *Christianity Through Jewish Eyes* (Cincinnati: Hebrew Union College Press, 1974).

31. Leo Baeck, *The Essence of Judaism* (New York: Schocken Books, 1961) and *Judaism and Christianity: Essays* (Philadelphia, Pa.: Jewish Publication Society of America, 1958). For an evaluation of Baeck's writings on Christianity cf. Albert Friedlaender, *Leo Baeck: Teacher of Theresienstadt* (Woodstock, N.Y.: Overlook Press, 1991); Walter Homolka, *Jewish Identity in Modern Times: Leo Baeck and German Protestantism* (New York: Berghahn Books, 1991); Samuel Sandmel, *Leo Baeck on Christianity*, Leo Baeck Memorial Lecture 19 (New York: Leo Baeck Institute, 1975).

32. Joseph Klausner, *From Jesus to Paul* (London: Allen and Ulwin, 1942) and *Jesus of Nazareth: His Life and Teaching* (London: Allen and Ulwin, 1925). Rabbi David Sandmel is currently writing an evaluation of Klausner's intellectual background and contributions to the study of early Christianity and Judaism. Samuel Sandmel, *The Genius of Paul* (New York: Farrar, Strauss and Cudahy, 1958); *The First Century in Judaism and Christianity: Certainties and Uncertainties* (Oxford: Oxford University Press, 1969). An evaluation of Samuel Sandmel's contribution to Jewish understanding of Christianity is a *desideratum*.

33. Daniel Boyarin, *Dying for God: Martyrdom and the Making of Judaism and Christianity* (Stanford, Calif.: Stanford University Press, 1999); Guy G. Stroumsa, "From Anti-Judaism to Antisemitism in Early Christianity" in *Contra Iudaeos: Ancient and Medieval Polemics between Christians and Jews*, ed. Ora Limor and Guy G. Stroumsa (Tübingen: J. C. B. Mohr, 1996), 1–26.

34. A thorough treatment of the Noachide commandments can be found in David Novak, *The Image of the Non-Jew in Judaism: A Historical and Constructive Study* (New York: E. Mellen Press, 1983). The primary discussion of these laws is found in the Babylonian Talmud, *Sanhedrin* 50-60, and they are codified by Maimonides in his *Yad HaHazakah*, Laws of Kings 8:10; 10:12. The traditional enumeration of the seven commandments would include the prohibitions of idolatry, blasphemy, bloodshed, sexual sins, theft, and eating from a living animal as well as the injunction to establish a legal system.

35. Jacob Katz, *Exclusiveness and Tolerance: Jewish-Gentile Relations in Medieval and Modern Times* (New York: Schocken Books, 1962) is the best summary of the development of traditional Jewish law with respect to Christianity.

36. Excerpts from Martin Buber's most significant writing about Christianity can be found in *Jewish Perspectives on Christianity*, ed. Fritz Rothschild (New York: Crossroads, 1990), 111–55. My opinions here are anecdotal and not the result of empirical research.

37. I have been unable to locate the text of Eisendrath's address to the Biennial Assembly of the Union of American Hebrew Congregations. However, I remember the issue discussed with great intensity during my youth.

38. These ideas echo the following point in *Dabru Emet: A Jewish Statement on Christians and Christianity:* "The humanly irreconcilable difference between Jews and Christians will not be settled until God redeems the entire world as promised in Scripture. Christians know and serve God through Jesus Christ and the Christian tradition. Jews know and serve God through Torah and the Jewish tradition. That difference will not be settled by one community insisting that it has interpreted Scripture more accurately than the other, nor by one community exercising political power over the other. Jews can respect Christians' faithfulness to their own revelation just as we expect Christians to respect our faithfulness to our revelation. Neither Jew nor Christian should be pressed into affirming the teaching of the other community" (*Christianity in Jewish Terms*, xix). George Lindbeck's response from a Christian perspective can be found in *Christianity in Jewish Terms*, 357–66, where he coins the felicitous phrase "Appropriation: Sharing Israelhood" as an appropriate new Christian theological response to Judaism.

39. Cf. Ekkehard Schuster and Reinhold Boschert-Kimmig, *Hope against Hope: Johann Baptist Metz and Elie Wiesel Speak Out on the Holocaust* (New York: Paulist Press, 1999) and J. Matthew Ashley, *Interruptions: Mysticism, Politics and Theology in the Work of Johann Baptist Metz* (Notre Dame, Ind.: University of Notre Dame Press, 1998).

40. Catherine M. LaCugna, *God for Us: The Trinity and Christian Life* (San Francisco, Calif.: HarperSanFrancisco, 1991). Elizabeth A. Johnson, *She Who Is: The Mystery of God in a Feminist Theological Discourse* (New York: Crossroad, 1992).

41. *Judaism, Christianity, and Liberation Theology: An Agenda for Dialogue*, ed. Otto Maduro (Maryknoll, N.Y.: Orbis Books, 1991) and Mark Ellis, *Toward a Jewish Theology of Liberation: The Uprising and the Future* (Maryknoll, N.Y.: Orbis Books, 1989) focuses almost entirely on the Intifada and the Israeli-Palestinian conflict. Its perspective is rather narrow and has not resonated within the Jewish community. Dan Cohn-Sherbok, *On Earth as It is in Heaven: Jews, Christians, and Liberation Theology* (Maryknoll, N.Y.: Orbis Books, 1987) is a survey of possible areas of convergence between Jews and Christians. To capture the spirit of a Jewish theologian whose writings have inspired many to work in collaboration with Christians on areas of social justice one should read Abraham Joshua Heschel, *Moral Grandeur and Spiritual Audacity: Essays*, ed. Susannah Heschel (New York: Farrar, Straus and Giroux, 1996).

42. Joseph Kardinal Ratzinger, *Die Vielfalt der Religionen und der Eine Bund* (Hagen: Verlag Urfeld, 1998). Dr. Rudolph Pesch, who arranged for the publication of Ratzinger's lectures, told me that the repositioning of the classical figures of Ecclesia and Synagoga was exactly his purpose. On the development of Ecclesia and Synagoga as Christian artistic motifs cf. Heinz Schreckenberg, *Die christlichen Adversus-Judaeos-Texte 11–13 Jh.* (Franfurt-am-Main: Peter Lang, 1997), 447–636; Wolfgang Seiferth, *Synagogue and Church in the Middle Ages: Two Symbols in Art and Literature* (New York: Ungar, 1970); and Ruth Mellinkoff, *The Horned Moses in Medieval Art and Thought* (Berkeley and Los Angeles: University of California Press, 1970).

43. Mary C. Boys, *Has God Only One Blessing? Judaism as a Source of Christian Self-Understanding* (New York: Paulist Press 2000).

CHAPTER ELEVEN

Jesus as Bridegroom and Lover

Critical Retrieval of a Medieval Metaphor

ELIZABETH A. DREYER

In a 1994 address, "Jesus and Salvation," Elizabeth Johnson refers to a number of theological issues that need to be raised in our attempts to interpret the narrative of Jesus in the contemporary world. These issues include theologies of God, of Christ, Christian anthropology, theologies of the cross, and consideration of world religions.[1] Under "anthropology" she notes:

> As the ministry and resurrection of Jesus regain their rightful place in the soteriological narrative, they propel greater inclusiveness regarding the dimensions of human life wherein salvation occurs. If Jesus fed, healed, soothed, and otherwise cared about persons precisely as embodied, and if his resurrection affirms the body's participation in the shalom of the reign of God, then salvation concerns not just the soul but also the body; not just the individual but also society; not just humanity but also the whole of nature. . . . Redeemed bodiliness, along with new appraisal of the sexual and erotic long denigrated in Christianity, still needs to be integrated into soteriology.[2]

The medieval mystical tradition, with its avid interest in the Song of Songs and its abundant use of intense, erotic metaphor to describe the

God-human relationship, is an excellent resource for the task of integrating the sexual and the erotic into Christology. Even within a post-Freudian, postmodern, and some would say post-Christian culture, with its many, variegated attitudes toward sexuality and erotic love, I believe there is a place for the answer "Jesus is Lover" to the question "Who do you say that I am?"

At the outset, it is important to note the necessary ambiguity and elusiveness of topics such as the erotic, the nuptial, and the sexual. In an article arguing for the integration of *Eros* and *Agape* in marriage, Paul Ricoeur suggests that sexuality and its many complex components may remain basically impermeable to reflection and inaccessible to human mastery—reabsorbed only symbolically by whatever mythical element remains in us.[3] He points to the

> vivid yet obscure feeling that sex participates in a network of powers whose cosmic harmonies are forgotten but not abolished; that life is much more than . . . the struggle against death, or delaying the time when the debt must be paid; that life is unique, universal, everything in everyone, and that sexual joy makes us participate in this mystery; that man does not become a person, ethically, juridically, unless he also plunges again into the river of Life—such is the truth of romanticism as well as the truth of sexuality. But this vivid feeling is also an obscure feeling. . . . The enigma of sexuality is that it remains irreducible to the trilogy which composes man: language, tool, institution. Even when it makes itself expressive, it is an infra-, para-, superlinguistic expression. It mobilizes language, true, but it crosses it, jostles it, sublimates it, stupefies it, pulverizes it into a murmur, an invocation. Sexuality demediatizes language; it is Eros and not Logos.[4]

This elusive, mysterious quality of sexuality, juxtaposed with the further elusive quality of mysticism, should serve to keep us humble and circumspect, but it cannot deter us from attending anew to the interplay of intimate love relationships with human and divine beloveds, and to argue that the particular, concrete ways in which such love is expressed can serve as a resource for theology. Erotic power is an indispensable part of life, a force that creates and sustains connectedness—intimacy, generosity, and interdependence—and without which life is not truly life.[5]

In addition to the elusive nature of this task, one can name a host of other cautions that must be taken into consideration in retrieving the language and imagery of Jesus as Lover. For some, speaking about Jesus as Bridegroom/Lover smacks too much of a private, individualized, "me and God" spirituality. It fails to make room for the wider community and for the demands of justice, so pressing in our time. Advocates of women are bothered by the possibility that the traditional way of presenting this material does not take into account the very complex and often negative experience of spousal relationships today. A metaphor that views the divine in male terms and the human in female terms has too often worked against women struggling to overcome disempowerment and marginalization.[6] Still others worry that bridal mysticism tends toward pantheism and the obliteration of the Creator-creature distinction. In terms of contemporary culture, the metaphor seems soft-headed, sentimental, and impractical in a fast-moving, hard-hitting, pragmatic world. More conservative groups worry that religious metaphors that are sensual and erotic in tone can be too easily confused with secular versions that use similar language, but that are regarded as too intimate to be discussed, or simply sordid and destructive—clearly not a way anyone would want to speak about God.

Of course, the point of exploring ways to speak about God in lively, compelling metaphors is to make the faith attractive and credible in imaginative ways that will lure persons to become engaged. That is why theologians need to entertain new metaphors for God as well as to reconsider traditional metaphors to see if they can be recast in ways that make sense to, and serve, each subsequent age.[7] Critical recovery of spousal imagery also contributes to the larger project of maintaining religious language that is concrete, poetic, and image-laden.[8] If the Incarnation transforms *all* things human into sacraments of God, giving substance and meaning to human existence and identity, then surely the experience of lovers and bridegrooms qualifies as a sacrament that both has intrinsic value and points to powerful new ways of being human. This metaphor, as used in the medieval mystical tradition, also tells us something about Jesus and about the Trinity.

I am confident we can retrieve elements of this medieval mystical tradition even though they are embedded in a Neoplatonic thought world with its preference for spirit over body, and written for the most part by and for celibate monastics.[9] I suggest that the metaphor of bridegroom/

lover can provide a destabilizing, disorienting truth to shock a cynical age into a new recognition of the identity of Jesus and insight into his unqualified love. It can remind us of our potential to respond to the invitation to relate to this Jesus in intimate loving ways. Most importantly, the metaphor of bridegroom/lover can affirm and give value to the ways in which we already open ourselves to the risk of intimate love for each other and for the world, as well as call us to ever greater heights of love in the future.

The Bible and Tradition: God As Love

In the other chapters in this volume, we have seen how biblical authors have responded to the question "Who do you say that I am?" (Mk 8:29) with a wide range of christological names. The early communities of disciples used what Elizabeth Johnson calls a "dazzling variety of imaginative metaphors" to interpret their experience of salvation in Jesus—financial, legal, cultic, political, personal (in terms of forgiveness), medical, existential (in terms of freedom), and familial (in terms of being sons and daughters of God).[10] Absent from these lists, however, is the christological name, "Lover" and the metaphoric categories of the nuptial and the erotic.

The primary biblical grounding for the particular language and imagery of lovers is, of course, the Song of Songs. It was this most-commented-upon book in the Middle Ages that captured the imaginations of so many medieval thinkers and mystics.[11] They turned to this storehouse of erotic love imagery as a resource through which to express the truth of their experience of God. Origen's commentary set the stage for subsequent allegorical interpretations of this text in which the bride is seen in terms either of the Church or of the individual soul.[12] In what follows, I focus on the individual, realizing that for the mystics, the individual is always situated in a complex web of community relationships.

But biblical language about the intimacy of God's presence is not limited to the imagery of the Song of Songs. From Exodus to Isaiah, we read how God chooses to pitch a tent among his people, how Yahweh longs for them with tender affection. Throughout the scriptures, God is experienced not in distant, abstract ways, but in specific, concrete, historical contexts, speaking, acting, wooing, commanding, reprimanding.[13]

The New Testament continues this trajectory with its language about the intimacy of the divine and the human.[14] Paul waxes eloquently on themes of living "in Christ" and of love—both the love of God and the love that he hopes will be present in the newly converted Christian communities.[15] The synoptic focus on the Kingdom of God speaks of God as near, about to break into the flow of history in dramatic, freeing ways.[16]

Thus, we can point to a Judeo-Christian biblical culture in which linguistic patterns employ love language and imagery—only some of which are explicitly spousal—that reflect aspects of the divine-human relationship that are intense, intimate, and passionately engaged.[17] Later Christian creeds and doctrinal statements exchanged the language of love for imagery that runs more in the direction of the almighty, omnipotent one, Creator of heaven and earth, redeemer, sanctifier, *pantokrator* (2 Macc 8:18; Rom 11:36; 2 Cor 6:18; Rv 1:8 and 4:8). But other aspects of the tradition carry forward and develop this affective biblical language. In particular, the Christian mystical tradition takes up the language of love, frequently specifying particular forms of love—the love of brides, bridegrooms, wedding banquets, and stormy, passionate, intimate relationships.[18]

The list of those who turned to the affections, to human desire, and spousal metaphors to speak about God is long. It includes Augustine, Gregory of Nyssa, Bernard of Clairvaux, Bonaventure, Hadewijch of Antwerp, Mechthild of Magdeburg, Julian of Norwich, Catherine of Siena, Teresa of Avila, and John of the Cross—to name a few of the most prominent. In various ways they used erotic, spousal imagery and the language of desire to describe the goodness of God and the ways in which this goodness attracts the human will. Let us examine a sampling of texts from this tradition.

Medieval Mysticism

Medieval mystics, male and female, plumbed the depths of encounter with Jesus Christ and answered the question, "Who do you say that I am?" in various imaginative, intriguing, and compelling ways.[19] One might ask why the mystics described their encounter with God in the language of human love, when, as celibate monks, they continually cautioned against confusing mystical love with human, sexual love in all its spiritual, psychological, and physical intimacy? One answer is that erotic, spousal human love is such a basic and primordial experience that it was inevitable that Christians would turn to this experience—and the language and imagery surrounding it—to speak of intense, intimate relationship with God. Other explanations point to the cultural context in which this literature was written. In the twelfth century, monasteries accepted a growing number of individuals who had experienced marriage prior to becoming monks. Other authors were aware of the poetry of the courtly love tradition, a literature that was borrowed to help express the intricacies of mystical experience. Still others felt compelled to defend marriage in light of heretic movements such as the Cathars who disparaged bodiliness, sexuality, and procreation.

For the most part, scholarly analysis of this material has focused on how physical love was appropriated by the mystics to describe spiritual love. Less attention has been paid to how the language of spiritual love can serve to highlight the goodness of sexual love, endowing it with both human and divine value. Irving Singer suggests that the first Christian writer to take this approach was seventeenth-century poet, John Donne.[20] From the Jewish tradition, Bernard McGinn calls attention to certain strains of mysticism in which marital intercourse plays a necessary role in the mystical life. Unlike the Christian tradition, some "Kabbalists consecrate sexual activity in order to restore true conjunction both above and below."[21]

As we explore the possibility of retrieving critically the medieval mystical tradition that speaks of Jesus as Bridegroom/Lover, I find the following themes to be most helpful: 1) the human capacity for intense, engaged, intimate relationship with God; 2) aspects of love that are described with metaphors of suffering, struggle, pain, war, and death; 3) the tension between reason and passion; 4) the image of spiritual nakedness; 5) the tension between the presence (joy) and absence (sadness) of the beloved ; 6) the role of desire; 7) explicit use of erotic, sexual metaphors; 8) ways in which the language of eros and desire are attributed to God; 9) the role of the neighbor as recipient of the fruits of this love. I am able to develop here only two of these themes—the human capacity for God and the ways in which intense suffering is described as an integral element of spousal love—as they appear in a select number of texts.

Human Capacity for Spousal Love

A central element of the anthropology of many mystical writers is the conviction that the human soul has the capacity for intimacy with God that is beyond imagining (Phil 4:7). In fact, one might say that the entire life of the mystic is based on this presupposition and that a key *desideratum* of much mystical writing is to communicate this truth to readers. That human beings are to be understood primarily as *capax Dei* is expressed forcefully in the works of Teresa of Avila. In the First Dwelling Places of *The Interior Castle*, Teresa builds a case for what will follow based on how she understands the identity of the human person:

> . . . what I shall now speak about, that which will provide us with a basis to begin . . . is that we consider our soul to be like a castle made entirely out of a diamond or of very clear crystal, in which there are many rooms, just as in heaven there are many dwelling places. For in reflecting upon it carefully, Sisters, we realize that the soul of the just person is nothing else but a paradise where the Lord says he finds His delight.[22]

Teresa links the structure of the human person with the paradise of the creation story in Genesis and the paradise of heaven, commenting that she cannot find anything "comparable to the magnificent beauty of a soul and its marvelous capacity."[23]

Teresa goes on to make two seemingly contradictory points. Since the sisters are made in God's image, there is no point, she says, in their tiring themselves trying to comprehend this beauty—"it is almost impossible for us to understand the sublime dignity and beauty of the soul," she writes.[24] But then she immediately laments that the sisters do not realize who they are. "It is a shame and unfortunate that through our own fault we don't understand ourselves or know who we are."[25] She continues, "The things of the soul must always be considered as plentiful, spacious and large; to do so is not an exaggeration. The soul is capable of much more than we can imagine, and the sun that is in this royal chamber shines in all parts."[26] In this way, she maintains her quite exalted anthropology without letting go of the utter transcendence of God.

Teresa turns to the metaphor of marriage reluctantly. In the Fifth Dwelling Places she says, "You've already heard that God espouses souls spiritually. . . . And even though the comparison may be a coarse one I cannot find another that would better explain what I mean than the sacrament of marriage."[27] She wants to make sure that the sisters know that spiritual marriage is far removed from the corporal, and that the joys of their life are "a thousand leagues distant"—and superior to—the joys of their married brothers and sisters. With some negotiation, however, we can still hear and make use of Teresa's anthropological point reminding us of the immense value of human existence based on the presence of God as Spouse at its deepest center.[28]

In the Seventh Dwelling Places, Teresa describes the marriage. The difference between two who are betrothed and two who are married is that the latter can no longer be separated. The union is like rain falling into a river or like the light that streams into a room through two windows.[29] Teresa experienced this marriage not only as christological but also as trinitarian. "Each day this soul becomes more amazed, for these Persons never seem to leave it any more. . . . In the extreme interior, in some place very deep within itself, the nature of which it doesn't know how to explain, because of a lack of learning, it perceives this divine company."[30] And long-time lovers will recognize what Teresa describes as "rejoicing together in the deepest silence."[31] Failure to notice and celebrate this light results from our inability to "see ourselves in this mirror that we contemplate, where our image is engraved."[32]

Teresa's experience of betrothal and marriage is not a static affair. A mirror image of life, the soul moves back and forth and from side to side in the endless sequence of rooms in the castle.[33] But there is progress and development. Toward the very end of her treatise, she writes,

> I repeat, it is necessary that your foundation consist of more than prayer and contemplation. If you do not strive for the virtues and practice them, you will always be dwarfs. And, please God, it will only be a matter of not growing, for you already know that whoever does not increase decreases. I hold that love, where present, cannot possibly be content with remaining the same.[34]

The practice of virtue and love of neighbor are always Teresa's litmus test. The marriage is not an exclusive affair but just the opposite. When love turns in on itself, we do not fulfill our human capacity for God but remain stunted.

Although Teresa's time and culture prompt her to call God "His Majesty," she has no difficulty coupling this royal imagery with the language of love: "the soul lives with a remembrance and tender love of our Lord."[35] While at Eucharist, Teresa was told that she was to consider as her own what belonged to Christ and to know that Christ would take care of what was hers. Love moves the lover to focus on the beloved, freeing both for self-forgetfulness.[36] Christian anthropology must take account of this paradox—that lovers communicate to each other that they are infinitely valuable and precious *and* that this knowledge allows them to forget themselves, since their only concern is the "other."

Teresa's capacious anthropology tells us something not only about the human person but about God as well. Teresa reminds the reader that there is no end to talk about God because the greatness and the works of God are without limits. "Who will finish telling of His mercies and grandeurs?" she writes.[37] The more we know about God's communication to creatures, the more we will praise this grandeur. People are valuable because the Spouse delights in them. This truth causes us not only to praise the grandeur of God but also to be in awe of others whose beauty we are able to see. Teresa writes, "For just as in heaven so in the soul, His Majesty must have a room where He dwells alone. Let us call it another heaven."[38] She continues, "Thus we are not reflecting about something restricted to a corner but about an interior world where there is room for so many and such attractive dwelling places, as you have seen; and indeed it is right that the soul be like this since within it there is a dwelling place for God."[39]

Bernard of Clairvaux also speaks of this capacity in *On the Song of Songs*, a series of conferences written for monks who had reached maturity in the spiritual life.[40] In addition to describing what it is like to be kissed "with the kiss of his mouth" (Song 1:1), Bernard goes on to make a further point, that this human capacity for intimacy with God is always available in spite of all obstacles. He offers an exhaustive list, most of which would be familiar to ordinary Christians—sin, vice, pleasure, exile, imprisoned in the body, distracted by business, afflicted with sorrow, and anxious forebodings. Indeed, he says, every soul standing under condemnation and without hope

> has the power to turn and find it can not only breathe the fresh air of
> the hope of pardon and mercy, but also dare to aspire to the nuptials

of the Word, not fearing to enter into alliance with God or to bear the sweet yoke of love (Matt. 11:30) with the King of angels. Why should it not venture with confidence into the presence of him by whose image it sees itself honored, and in whose likeness it knows itself made glorious? Why should it fear a majesty when its very origin gives it ground for confidence?[41]

Indeed, it is the very origin of human existence, a birthright described by Bernard as an indestructible beauty, that empowers the bride to desire the kiss, to be bold in her demands and expectations of the Beloved. The soul is like the Word by nature and in the exercise of the will, "loving as she is loved."[42]

As with Teresa, also for Bernard, this nuptial relationship is a trinitarian affair. In Sermon 8 of *On the Song of Songs*, he speaks of the third and supreme kiss, the kiss of the mouth in which the soul is invited to share in the deepest love of the trinitarian persons which he equates with the gift of the Holy Spirit (Jn 20:22), "the imperturbable peace of the Father and the Son, their unshakable bond, their undivided love, their indivisible unity."[43] This kiss involves more than just a single aspect of the human person. While unable, as a twelfth-century monk, to include the physical body as indeed we must today, Bernard embraces affective as well as intellectual fruits of the kiss. It bestows not only the light of knowledge but also lights the fire of love (Rom 5:5).[44] Bernard ends this sermon with a comparison between human and spiritual marriage that avoids painting the former unfavorably. "For if marriage according to the flesh constitutes two in one body (Gen. 2:24), why should not a spiritual union be even more efficacious in joining two in one spirit (1 Cor. 6:16)?"[45]

Again in the following century, Mechthild of Magdeburg uses erotic imagery to describe not only Jesus but also the entire Trinity. She describes the Trinity as a "playful flood of love," bringing together the force of the Trinity's love and the erotic exchange between it and the soul.[46] Throughout *The Flowing Light of the Godhead*, Mechthild describes how the Trinity chooses a bride who in God's words will "greet me with her mouth and wound me with her appearance," so that love will occur.[47] The mission of love is to bind God and the human soul together.[48]

Mechthild is well known for her rejection of the mediation of Mary and the infant Christ. She writes, "That is a child's love, that one suckle and rock a baby. I am a full-grown bride. I wish to go to my Lover."[49] The deeply trinitarian nature of this mystical literature extends the use of erotic, spousal imagery beyond the second person to the entire Trinity. As theologians seek to recover the trinitarian dimensions of the doctrine of God, Christology, and pneumatology, it would be well to keep in mind the ways in which the mystical tradition has applied metaphors of spouse and lover to the God who is three in one.

Struggle and Pain

The language of suffering love[50] is found throughout medieval mystical literature.[51] Subthemes include: the cosmic battle between the forces of good and evil reflected in one's love affair with God; links with Jesus' suffering on the cross; the pain of unfulfilled desire; the merit to be gained from suffering willingly and with joy; the ways in which suffering purifies love; the value of remaining silent in the face of suffering; the praise of disinterested love; the demand to love faithfully in spite of hardship and pain.

The poetry of a thirteenth-century Beguine, Hadewijch of Antwerp, comes immediately to mind as an example of a vivid portrayal of the slings and arrows of a love affair with God. Her words echo Hebrew psalms of lament and the book of Job, as well as elements of the medieval courtly tradition. We know almost nothing about her life, although scholars conjecture that she may have been the superior of a group of young Beguines who asked her to leave the community, possibly because of her unyielding desires that they attain the heights of nuptial love that was her own call. It is clear that she experiences the deep pain of exile at God's hands. She writes,

> Alas, poor me! I cannot cause
>   Myself to live or die!
> O sweet God, what has happened to me
> That these people bring me to ruin?[52]

Hadewijch describes her longing as "violent";[53] Love's power is a tyranny[54] and the chains of love bind her.[55]

Taking a cue from the Song of Songs (3:1) she speaks of the pain of losing the beloved. "So greatly has the pain of love worn me out / That

I am now unfit for anything / . . . I sought her wise secrets, / . . . she has withdrawn them from me since then / And has hidden many things from me. / Yet I will gladly suffer all things, / For Love has never revoked / The promises she held out to me."[56] Love withdraws but never for good.

Bernard of Clairvaux also struggles to explain why the Bridegroom is absent, an absence he describes as a "long, unrelenting disappointment, which induces weariness, foments suspicion, inflames impatience, acts as a stepmother to love and a mother to despair." In the end, the pain attendant upon the loss of the beloved serves to enkindle the infinite longing for God and to teach the soul that she may seek him as she can, "provided she remembers that she was first sought, as she was first loved; and it is because of this that she herself both seeks and loves."[57]

The image of the "wound of love," sometimes described as both painful and pleasurable, was an image well established in secular love poetry and frequently taken up into the devotional tradition. Isaiah (49:2): "he made me a polished arrow/in his quiver he hid me away"; lines from the *Song of Songs:* "You have wounded my heart" (4:9), and "they beat me, they wounded me, they took away my mantle" (5:7) provide biblical motifs. Hadewijch writes,

> However cruelly I am wounded,
> What Love has promised me
> Remains irrevocably.[58]

At one point Hadewijch uses an especially vivid metaphor from the courtly tradition to describe this wound of love. She imagines herself as a knight, warding off Love's blows with a shield. She writes, "that she [Love] would consider my sorry plight, / I should regain courage none too soon: / For my shield has warded off so many stabs / There's no room left on it for a new gash."[59]

In a dialogue between Love and the soul at the beginning of *The Flowing Light of the Godhead*, Mechthild of Magdeburg employs violent language to speak of this wounding.

> Love: That I hunted you was my fancy.
> That I captured you was my desire.
> That I bound you made me happy.

When I wounded you, you were joined to me.
When I cudgel you, I take you into my power.[60]

And later:

O Lord, you pamper to excess my dank prison,
In which I drink the water of the world and eat in great misery
The ash cake of my frailty,
And am wounded to the death
By the beam of your fiery love.
Now you leave me, Lord, lying in my misery,
My wounds untended, in great torment.

To which the Lord replies:

Queen dear to my heart,
Must you always be so impatient?
When I wound you most deeply,
I immediately apply salve most tenderly.
The abundance of my riches is yours alone,
And even over me you hold sway.
You are very dear to my heart.
If you have the scales, I have the gold.
All that you have done for my sake, renounced or suffered,
I shall balance off completely and shall give myself to you forever
Expecting nothing in return, just as you will.[61]

Central to Mechthild's reflection on her experience of the Christian life is her call to participate in the contempt, exile, suffering and death of Christ.[62] Her text becomes a record of "alternation of ecstasy and alienation."[63]

Perhaps the most celebrated image of wounding is Bernini's sculpture, *Ecstasy of St. Teresa*.[64] In *The Interior Castle*, it is in the Sixth Dwelling Places that the soul is wounded with love for its Spouse. Teresa speaks of impulses deep within the soul by which God acts like a "falling comet" or a "thunderclap" to recall the soul from distraction. The soul "feels that it is wounded in the most delightful way, but it doesn't learn how or by whom it was wounded."[65] Bernini's sculpture is linked more directly by Teresa's account of her experience of wounding in *The Book of Her Life*:

> It seemed the angel plunged the dart several times into my heart and that it reached deep inside within me. When he drew it out, I thought he was carrying off with him the deepest part of me; and he left me all on fire with great love of God. The pain was so great that it made me moan, and the sweetness this greatest pain caused me was so superabundant that there is no desire capable of taking it away, nor is the soul content with less than God.[66]

Teresa captures in clear and powerful language the recognizable but elusive human experience in which the joy of intimate, committed love can be simultaneously tinged with profound sorrow.

In medieval mystical literature, the suffering experienced by Jesus on the cross reveals the true nature of divine love and stands as a model by and through which humans are to understand the pain and suffering that is almost always a consequence of deep, genuine love between spouses and lovers. The desire to imitate the way of Jesus, even to stand with him at the cross is the omnipresent backdrop to this literature. As with Jesus, so in the lives of the mystics, a life of love and single-minded fidelity leads to suffering and eventually to death.

This sense of love leading to death may stem in part from the passage in Matthew's gospel in which Jesus, in the garden of Gethsemane, says, "My soul is sorrowful unto death" (26:38). Such mortal sorrow is a consequence of loving to the end those who reject him. This mystical death is experienced in many forms. Hadewijch speaks of the death in which there is a loss of self.

> To sublime Love
> I have given away all that I am.
> Whether I lose or win, let all
> That is owed her be hers without diminution.
> What has happened now?
> I am not mine:
> She has engulfed the substance of my spirit

Her fine being
Gives me the assurance
That the pain of Love is all profit.[67]

And in the final, moving paragraphs of the *Itinerarium mentis in Deum*, Bonaventure describes the mystical death of the soul who dies in a conflagration of love, a spousal union made possible by Christ's own Passion.

> If you wish to know how these things may come about, ask grace, not learning; desire, not understanding; the groaning of prayer, not diligence in reading; the Bridegroom, not the teacher; God, not humans; darkness, not clarity; not light, but the fire that wholly inflames and carries one into God through transporting unctions and consuming affections. God Himself is this fire, and *His furnace is in Jerusalem* (Isa 31:9); and it is Christ who enkindles it in the white flame of His most burning Passion. This fire he alone truly perceives who says: *My soul chooses hanging, and my bones, death* (Job 7:15). He who loves this death can see God, for it is absolutely true that *Man shall not see me and live* (Exod. 33:20).
>
> Let us then die and enter into this darkness. Let us silence all our care, our desires, and our imaginings. With Christ crucified, let us pass *out of this world to the Father* (John 13:1), so that, when the Father is shown to us, we may say with Philip: *It is enough for us* (John 14:8).[68]

Teresa of Avila equates death with living in fear of losing Christ forever. She writes in *The Interior Castle*'s Third Dwelling Places: "If it is your will, my God, may we die with You, as Saint Thomas said; for living without You and with these fears of the possibility of losing You forever is nothing else than dying often."[69]

Thus, pain, suffering and death of the beloved are real, but never have the last word. The power of this spousal love wins out over the pain, transforming it into joy. The fidelity of God the lover enables the beloved to be faithful in return. Hadewijch writes,

Since I have followed in her train with strong fidelity,
That Love might stand me in good stead,
I have renounced all alien sadness,

And I am firm in confidence
  Through which I know
  That Love one day
  Will embrace me in oneness.[70]

Pierced by Love's arrow, Hadewijch is willing to do without everything "Until Love wills to place me / In possession of the magnificence with which she satisfies me."[71]

The paradox that in the end (and often in the moment) the wound of love brings joy is tangibly present in this literature. Suffering may be everywhere, but joy is never far behind and always has the last word. For most readers, the message of texts replete with talk about anxiety, exile, wounding—physical and spiritual suffering of all kinds—is surprisingly not morbid but hopeful since it is clear that for the beloved, suffering is not for its own sake. These mystics experience suffering as a difficult, but joyful *imitatio Christi*, and they write powerfully of the creative aspects of this paradox. Again we turn to Hadewijch:

What is sweetest in Love is her tempestuousness;
Her deepest abyss is her most beautiful form;
To lose one's way in her is to touch her close at hand;
To die of hunger for her is to feed and taste;
Her despair is assurance;
Her sorest wounding is all curing;
To waste away for her sake is to be in repose;
. . . .
Her sorest blow is her sweetest consolation;
Her ruthless robbery is great profit;
Her withdrawal is approach;
Her deepest silence is her sublime song;
Her greatest wrath is her dearest thanks;
Her greatest threat is pure fidelity;
Her sadness is the alleviation of all pain.[72]

The model for this pain that is "shot through" with joy is Jesus, the divine-human lover. Julian of Norwich also discovers that the joy God experiences in bringing redemption far outweighs the suffering of the cross. The Lord says to Julian: "It is a joy, a bliss, an endless delight to me that ever I suffered my Passion for you; and if I could suffer more, I should suffer more."[73]

It is impossible for us to understand the various kinds of suffering endured by medieval people, much less the meaning they attached to it. We can be sure that physical suffering was common and virulent; life tenuous and fragile. The psychological meaning of suffering for medieval persons is equally elusive. And we must confront head-on the extremes of asceticism that can only be judged as aberrant elements in the spiritual life—elements that we must not mindlessly admire or emulate in the critical retrieval of this tradition. There are always dehumanizing as well as humanizing influences in any social setting and the mystics were not exempt from absorbing strains of both. But an overall evaluation that these descriptions of pain and suffering are masochistic and motivated by self-hate is difficult to defend.

We do not need to compare or measure degrees of pain (an impossible task, in any case) to know that there has never been a time in history when the human race has not experienced unimaginable suffering. But might we today be too limited in the ways in which we assign meaning to pain? The Christian tradition, grounded in Judaism, invites us to understand human suffering, not as something merely to be endured because it cannot be avoided, but as a vehicle by which to encounter ourselves and God more fully. Instead of a license for cynicism, suffering can be experienced as a humbling, "radical reassessment, a turning once again back to the metaphorical road from which, in our salad days, we may have strayed. It means turning back to God."[74]

But one cannot emphasize enough that texts about the suffering of lovers are not a recipe, much less a prescription, for suffering, but rather a way to speak, and make sense of, the choice to love deeply and the suffering that inevitably comes in its wake. These descriptions of the suffering of the beloved hold a key to the meaning and dignity of human suffering that is an inevitable part of being deeply, passionately committed to the beloved. And for Christians, the paradigm of this suffering love is Jesus of Nazareth. The cost of true love and genuine discipleship is high.

Thus, I suggest that these mystical texts can provide a wellspring of images and language that can assist us in risking deep, intimate love, in celebrating its joys, and coping with its pain. Of course, spousal love is not the only kind of love which demands suffering and loss of self. But the metaphor of Jesus as Bridegroom/Lover offers a vision of love, a horizon of meaning in which "to lose oneself is to find oneself." The ideal of the marriage promise "for richer, for poorer, in sickness and in health" cannot be relegated to the dung heap of outworn clichés. The lover *does* recognize that love can indeed transform burdens that are heavy, even seemingly unbearable, into yokes that are light.

Conclusion

Few will argue against the centrality of incarnation for Christian faith and theology. And it is undeniable that the Christian mystical tradition is christological and theological at its core. But have we plumbed the depth and breadth of its mystery adequately? Are we guilty, in Ronald Rolheiser's words, of "under-understanding" this mystery—meaning that we have grasped but the tip of the iceberg? "We miss it," he says, "by not seeing its immensity."[75] Is it possible that by marginalizing the metaphor of Jesus as Spouse and Lover, we are guilty of what Walter Brueggemann similarly describes as "under-living" when it comes to our experience and language about Jesus?[76]

It is a truism to say that the faith of the community informs Christian theology and that, in turn, theological language influences the life of faith. Every name or image that we use to point to Jesus presents and evokes distinct spiritual emphases. If the theological community does not speak of Jesus as Bridegroom/Lover, it is less likely that believers will think of Jesus in these terms. And if believers do not recognize and embrace Jesus as Lover, then all the theology in the world will not make it so.[77] Our awareness of the ways in which contingent historical contexts affect how we experience, think, and talk about Jesus, reinforces the conviction that naming Jesus is a dynamic, fluid enterprise that involves testing and creative innovation to respond to the variety of contexts in which Christians relate to, and speak of, the Jesus of history and the Christ of faith.

If we think of the Christian vocation as a call to open oneself to God's embrace in Jesus, and to be the continuing epiphany of God in all the concrete, ordinary events of our lives, is it outlandish to suggest that we think and talk about Jesus as Bridegroom/Lover in light of our experiences of passionate, erotic, nuptial love, and allow such talk about Jesus to influence those human loves? If God is love and we are made in the image and likeness of God, are not then *all* forms of love potential places for us to become the Word we speak and profess? In particular, the present chaos in sexual mores and attitudes makes it imperative that Christian theologians confront those aspects of the tradition that cast an unnatural and unfounded eye of suspicion on bodiliness.

The names of Jesus found in scripture and tradition are both rooted in experience and intended to transform both our lives and our images of God. Metaphoric associations such as "doors" and "shepherds" have invited Christians to encounter Jesus in terms familiar from their daily lives.[78] But we must be courageous not only in conserving and understanding anew familiar theological language for Jesus, and in some cases abandoning it—but also in *expanding* it—in this case by recovering aspects of the mystical tradition.

Thus, why should our response to the question, "Who do you say that I am?" not include Jesus as Bridegroom/Lover? This broadening of our language about Jesus through the critical recovery of aspects of the tradition suggests the following. First, the mystics' experience of Jesus as Lover provides to skeptical believers who are willing to allow it, a glimpse into the possibility of intimacy with God. To those who suggest that an incarnational Christology is no longer a possibility,[79] I want to ask: Is it only the saints and mystics of old who found themselves touched by "divine madness," or might this kind of relationship be a possibility in the present? If so, what are the contours, the context, the language, and the feelings that will reflect the distinctive ways in which we in *this* time encounter Jesus as Bridegroom/Lover?

Second, speaking of Jesus as Lover sheds light on the reality of God inasmuch as we see Jesus as the authentic embodiment and reflection of God. Jesus as Bridegroom/Lover tells us something about a God who is willing: to become vulnerable; to enter into the joyful transformation that intimate love makes possible; to experience the newness that comes with seeing oneself accepted and embraced; to risk the peaks and valleys of a faithful, committed relationship; to abandon and sacrifice oneself in Jesus even to the cross, for love of others.

Third, speaking of Jesus as Lover not only complements christological discussions about the Jesus of the cross, but deepens their meaning.[80] Indeed, many of the mystics experienced the enormity of God's love precisely in the cross.[81] To oppose the spouse and the cross is to short-circuit the depth and totality of the meaning of Jesus' life and death. For it is precisely in the cross that many mystics witnessed the kind of love that swept them up into the intimacy and ecstasy of spousal relationship. Contemporary interest in the human Jesus is enhanced by the addition of Jesus as Lover to current discussions about Jesus' suffering, his caring relationship to others as servant/minister, his outreach to the marginalized. Pleas to see history not as an abstraction but as concrete reality need to include not only the history of suffering victims, but also the history of lovers.

In his very existence, Jesus is the reality and symbol of the intimacy that is possible between the divine and the human and the wellspring of such love among humans. It is not necessary to sacrifice the truth of God's transcendent otherness in order to acknowledge and announce with confidence that our humanities (and divinities) can indeed touch in profound and life-giving ways. Intimacy develops through a highly interactive process of mutual recognition, communication, and acceptance, and erotic power is the force that creates and sustains this connectedness—intimacy, generosity, and interdependence.[82]

Calling Jesus Bridegroom/Lover need not be interpreted as an invitation to individualism; to a sexual cheapening of our image of Jesus; nor to a sentimental, self-centered "me and God" kind of spirituality. We are heir to an understanding of love that has psychological and physical as well as spiritual dimensions. We understand genuine love between persons to be the foundation and source of love for others. Indeed loving and being loved in a personal, intimate way is, for many, the condition for the possibility of loving the neighbor—a truth to which the mystics witness splendidly. Genuine spousal love can lead to heroic self-sacrifice and radical self-giving, which, because they are grounded in passionate love, are experienced not as burden, but as joy.

Finally, to speak of Jesus as Bridegroom/Lover is to bring the possibility of new dignity and grace to the authentic experience of human lovers. Speaking and encountering Jesus as Lover could serve to redeem and reduce the violence of rape and sexual abuse; to free us from sexism and injustice in our most intimate relationships; to offer an alternative to intimate relations that are narcissistic, obsessive, and exploitative; to fire our imaginations to transform our intimate connections with others into loves that are not only tender, respectful, and faithful, but also out-going, generous, and committed to bringing about justice for the world.[83]

Since the tradition turns so consistently to the experience of human lovers to speak about spiritual intimacy with God, it seems appropriate to underline the incarnational nature of our talk about God by allowing the mystical tradition to shed a favorable light on the graced nature of erotic love. And authentic, intimate human love provides a window through which we glimpse what it is like to be intimate with God—the experience of being loved unconditionally, accepted in our bodiliness and in our nakedness, as well as in our spiritual, psychological, and intellectual dimensions—with all our warts as well as our gifts; the discovery that we do not need to strive for radical independence, but can rather embrace interdependence and at times, even a radical dependence in all spheres of life; the joy of knowing that genuine love is not ultimately private, but gives birth to generous and joyful behaviors on behalf of others (Mt 25:31–46); glimpsing the potential for new life that love inevitably brings; tasting the reality of the Spirit's promise that all things will be made new; celebrating the profound sense of gratitude and humility that accompanies the awareness that love is ultimately gift.

In Wendell Berry's novel, *Remembering*, Andy Catlett's life has been devastated by the loss of his hand in a corn picker. He now views the world in a dark, distrustful way that has seeped into his once-vibrant relationship with his wife. But he can remember what that relationship used to be like and his description reminds us of the heights to which intimate, nuptial love can soar.

> It was as though grace and peace were bestowed on them out of the sanctity of marriage itself, which simply furnished them to one another, free and sufficient as rain to leaf. It was as if they were not making marriage but being made by it, and, while it held them, time and their lives flowed over them, like swift water over stones, rubbing them together, grinding off their edges, making them fit together, fit to be together, in the only way that fragments can be rejoined. And though Andy did not understand this, and though he suffered from it, he trusted it and rejoiced in it.[84]

Andy's love affair with his wife was larger and stronger than their individual selves, a source of profound grace and truth. For Christians, intimate, loving, self-sacrificing nuptial love is one, concrete, incarnate expression of who God is. Amidst the chaos of broken, violent, and abusive nuptial relationships, the mystics call out to us, reminding us of new possibilities, sparking our imaginations, inviting us to see Christ and ourselves as lovers— if only in fleeting moments.

And yet mature Christians are aware of what Rowan Williams calls the "tantalizing inadequacy of human intimacy."[85] It is but one aspect of human existence. And to say that Jesus is like a Bridegroom or Lover is also to acknowledge that Jesus is *not* like a Bridegroom or Lover. But it is no longer necessary or appropriate to bracket erotic love when we think about Jesus or reflect on the hallmarks of love, so beautifully expressed in chapter thirteen of Paul's first letter to the Corinthians. The contemporary vision of the human person in her or his erotic fullness can and should be wedded to our understanding of the Christian life and to our understanding of the many faces of Jesus, who is at the center of that journey.

NOTES

1. Elizabeth A. Johnson, "Jesus and Salvation," in *Proceedings of the Catholic Theological Society of America*, ed. Paul Crowley, vol. 49 (Baltimore, Md.: 9–12 June 1994), 12–16.

2. Ibid., 12. Johnson cites as support for this discussion Karl Rahner, "The Body in the Order of Salvation," in *Theological Investigations*, trans. Margaret Kohl (London: Darton, Longman, and Todd, 1981), 71–89; Paula Cooey, "The Redemption of the Body: Post-Patriarchal Reconstruction of Inherited Christian Doctrine," in *After Patriarchy: Feminist Transformations of the World Religions*, ed. Paula Cooey et al. (Maryknoll, N.Y.: Orbis, 1993), 106–30. I would add: Kathleen O'Grady, Ann L. Gilroy, and Janette Patricia Gray, eds., *Bodies, Lives, Voices: Gender in Theology* (Sheffield, U.K.: Sheffield Academic Press, 1998); Sallie McFague, *The Body of God: An Ecological Theology* (Minneapolis, Minn.: Fortress Press, 1993); Lisa Isherwood and Elizabeth Stuart, *Introducing Body Theology* (Sheffield, U.K.: Sheffield Academic Press, 1998); Susan Ross, *Extravagant Affections: A Feminist Sacramental Theology* (New York: Continuum, 1998); Peter Biller and A. J. Minnis, eds., *Medieval Theology and the Natural Body* (Rochester, N.Y.: York Medieval Press/Boydell Press, 1997); Jane Marie Law, ed., *Religious Reflections on the Human Body* (Bloomington, Ind.: University of Indiana Press, 1995); Elisabeth Moltmann-Wendel, *I Am My Body: A Theology of Embodiment* (New York: Continuum, 1995); Paula Cooey, *Religious Imagination and the Body* (New York and Oxford: Oxford University Press, 1994); Elizabeth Alvilda Petroff, *Body & Soul: Essays on Medieval Women and Mysticism* (New York: Oxford University Press, 1994); Linda Lomperis and Sarah Stanbury, eds.,

Feminist Approaches to the Body in Medieval Literature (Philadelphia, Pa.: University of Pennsylvania Press, 1993); Karma Lochrie, "The Language of Transgression: Body, Flesh, and Word in Mystical Discourse," in *Speaking Two Languages: Traditional Disciplines and Contemporary Theory in Medieval Studies,* ed. Allen J. Frantzen (Albany, N.Y.: State University of New York Press, 1991); Ulrike Wiethaus, "Sexuality, Gender, and the Body in Late Medieval Women's Spirituality," *Journal of Feminist Studies in Religion* 7, no. 1 (1991): 35–53.

3. Paul Ricoeur, "Wonder, Eroticism, and Enigma," *Cross Currents* 14, no. 2 (spring 1964): 140.

4. Ibid., 140–41.

5. Rita Nakashima Brock, *Journeys by Heart: A Christology of Erotic Power* (New York: Crossroad, 1988), 35–37.

6. Brock sees problems with the Bridegroom motif to the extent that it propagates and maintains hierarchical marriage ingredients detrimental to the community (Brock, *Journeys by Heart*, 4). See also Haunani-Kay Trask, *Eros and Power: The Promise of Feminist Theory* (Philadelphia, Pa.: University of Pennsylvania Press, 1986); Susan Griffin, "The Way of All Ideology," *Signs* 7, no. 3 (spring 1982): 641–60, and *Pornography and Silence: Culture's Revenge Against Nature* (New York: Harper & Row, 1981); Audre Lorde, "Uses of the Erotic: The Erotic as Power," in *Sister Outsider* (Trumansberg, N.Y.: Crossing Press, 1984), 53–59.

7. See Mark S. Burrows, "Naming the God Who Is Beyond Names: Wisdom from the Tradition on the Old Problem of God-language," *Modern Theology* (January 1993): 37–53.

8. Sallie McFague refers to this process as "remythologization," i.e., theologians must "search in contemporary life and its sensibility for images more appropriate to the expression of Christian faith in our time." Such metaphorical theology, according to McFague, "encourages non-traditional, unconventional, novel ways of expressing the relationship between God and the world" (*Models of God: Theology for an Ecological Age* [Philadelphia, Pa.: Fortress Press, 1987], 32–33, 35).

9. In addition to Brock and McFague, other feminist theologians criticize what they see as an entrenched "spiritualizing" tendency in the tradition, flowing in part from a dualistic Neoplatonic worldview that devalues the material and the particular, especially when it comes to bodies, sexuality, and the erotic. I propose that, while the critical reappropriation of spousal/lover imagery does not necessarily demand the wholesale rejection of "spiritualized" meanings of love language in the medieval mystical tradition, it does require that one attend to the context of this literature, which was overwhelmingly monastic and celibate, and ask critical questions about how it can be authentically reappropriated, corrected, or complemented in other, very different contexts. See Rosemary Radford Ruether, "The Liberation of Christology from Patriarchy," in *Feminist Theology: A Reader*, ed. Ann Loades (London: SPCK; Louisville: Westminster John Knox, 1990), 138–48.

10. Johnson, "Jesus and Salvation," 3–4.

11. There are nearly one hundred extant commentaries and homilies on the Song of Songs written between the sixth and the fifteenth centuries (E. Ann Matter, *The Voice of My Beloved: The Song of Songs in Western Medieval Christianity* [Philadelphia, Pa.: University of Pennsylvania Press, 1990], 3).

12. Origen, *Commentary on Song of Songs* (written *ca.* 240), trans. R.P. Lawson, Ancient Christian Writers, vol. 26 (Westminster, Md.: Newman Press, 1957).

13. In the space allowed, I can but give a few examples: "But I will be with you" (Ex 3:12); "a young woman shall conceive and bear a son and shall call his name Immanuel" (Is 7:14); "With all my heart I long for you in the night, I seek you eagerly when dawn breaks" (Is 26:9); "Your walls are always before my eyes, I have engraved them on the palms of my hands" (Is 49:16); "And so my heart yearns for him, I am filled with tenderness towards him" (Jer 31:20).

14. See Bernard McGinn, *The Foundations of Mysticism*, vol. 1 of *The Presence of God: A History of Western Christian Mysticism* (New York: Crossroad, 1991), 66–79.

15. A few examples: Paul's famous paean of love in 1 Cor 13; Paul's linkage of "divine" jealousy with betrothal imagery (2 Cor 11:2); the phrase "in Christ" occurs 164 times in all the letters ascribed to Paul (e.g., 1 Thes 4:17; 2 Cor 5:8; Gal 2:19–20, 3:27, and 4:19; Phil 1:23); Paul also speaks of the Spirit living and making his home in Christian believers (Rom 8:1, 9). Divine-human intimacy is reflected especially in the community's love for each other. The community is like a body with all its diverse organs (1 Cor 12). Paul wants the Word to take root in real communities whose members have faces and names— people who are immersed in the whole range of earthly existence as sinners, listeners, speakers, learners, victims, prophets—and lovers.

16. The link between human and divine love is pointedly and poetically expressed in 1 John 4:7–13: "Beloved, let us love one another; for love is of God, and he who loves is born of God and knows God." See also Jn 1:14; 15:4; 17:20–23, etc.

17. Explicit biblical language referring to brides and bridegrooms is not abundant. It is used to describe Israel's relationship to Yahweh in both its faithful (Is 49:18; 61:10; 62:5) and faithless forms (Jer 2:32; 7:34; Hos). The Bridegroom's faithfulness is constant. "The Lord has acknowledged you a wife again, once deserted and heart-broken, your God has called you a bride still young though once rejected. On the impulse of a moment I forsook you, but with tender affection I will bring you home again" (Is 54:6–7). In the New Testament Jesus speaks of himself as bridegroom in response to criticism that his disciples do not fast (Mt 9:15; Mk 2:19; Lk 5:34) and John the Baptist refers to Jesus as bridegroom (Jn 3:29). John places the first of Jesus' signs at the wedding feast of Cana (Jn 2:1–11). Matthew speaks of the Kingdom of heaven as a wedding banquet, lamenting that those who were invited were not worthy (Mt 22:2) and for which the bridesmaids must prepare and be ready (Mt 25:1–13). And in the

final verses of the Book of Revelation those who thirst are invited to drink at the eschatological feast—"The Spirit and the Bride say, 'Come'" (Rv 22:17).

18. For a historical treatment of this and other mystical themes, see Bernard McGinn, *The Presence of God: A History of Western Christian Mysticism*, 3 vol. (New York: Crossroad, 1991, 1994, 1998); and "The Language of Love in Christian and Jewish Mysticism," in *Mysticism and Language*, ed. Steven Katz (Oxford: Oxford University Press, 1990), 202–35.

19. There are a number of "hermeneutic hurdles" to be addressed in retrieving this material. One must ask about the relationship between experience and language. How do time, historical setting, geography, and genre affect the use of bridal imagery? One must also distinguish the voices of the saints from their interpreters and ask about differences between the voices of women and men. Given the predominantly male imagery used for God in the Middle Ages, one might expect women to use nuptial imagery more frequently than men in self-representation. Analysis shows, however, that this is not the case in the writings of Clare and Francis; Hildegard of Bingen and her hagiographer, Theoderic of Echternach; Christine of Stommeln and Peter of Dacia. See Catherine M. Mooney, ed., *Gendered Voices: Medieval Saints and Their Interpreters* (Philadelphia, Pa.: University of Pennsylvania Press, 1999), 1–15. For a summary of feminist analyses of female medieval mystics' use of the vocabulary of erotic, sexual love to express their intense relationships with the divine, see Julie B. Miller, "Eroticized Violence in Medieval Women's Mystical Literature," *Journal of Feminist Studies in Religion* 15, no. 2 (fall 1999): 25–49, esp. 25 n.1.

20. Irving Singer, *Courtly and Romantic*, vol. 2 of *The Nature of Love* (Chicago: University of Chicago Press, 1984), 195–205.

21. McGinn, "Language of Love," 232.

22. Teresa of Avila, *The Interior Castle*, I.1.1 (New York: Paulist Press, 1979), 35.

23. Ibid.

24. Ibid., I.1.1, p. 36.

25. Ibid., I.1.2, p. 36.

26. Ibid., I.2.8, p. 42.

27. Ibid., V.4.3, p. 103.

28. Ibid., VII.2.9, p. 181.

29. Ibid., VII.2.2–3, p. 178–79.

30. Ibid., VII.1.7, p. 175.

31. Ibid., VII.3.11, p. 186.

32. Ibid., VII.2.8, p. 181.

33. Ibid., Epilogue, 3, p. 196.

34. Ibid., VII.4.9, p. 191.

35. Ibid. VII.3.8, p. 184.

36. Ibid., VII.2.1; VII.3.2, pp. 177, 183.

37. Ibid. VII.1.1, p. 172.

38. Ibid., VII.1.3, p. 173.

39. Ibid., VII.1.5, p. 174.

40. Bernard of Clairvaux, *On the Song of Songs*, 4 vols. (Kalamazoo, Mich.: Cistercian Press, 1971, 1976, 1979, 1980). For a provocative treatment of how the Song of Songs functioned as a theological matrix for the shaping of an erotic Christology in Bernard, see Mark S. Burrows, "Foundations for an Erotic Christology: Bernard of Clairvaux on Jesus as 'Tender Lover,'" *Anglican Theological Review* 80, no. 4 (1998): 477–93.

41. Bernard of Clarivaux, *On the Song of Songs*, 83.I.1, 4:180–81.

42. Ibid., 83.I.3, 4:182.

43. Ibid., 8.I.2, 1:46.

44. Ibid., 8.II.5, 1:48; see also 8.IV.6, 1:49.

45. Ibid., 8.VII.9, 1:52.

46. Mechthild of Magdeburg, *The Flowing Light of the Godhead*, trans. Frank Tobin (New York: Paulist Press, 1998), VII.45, p. 314. See also Margot Schmidt, "'Die spilende minnevluot? Der Eros als Sein und Wirkkraft in der Trinität bei Mechthild von Magdeburg," in *"Eine Höhe, über die nichts geht": Spezielle Glaubenserfahrung in der Frauenmystik?* ed. Dieter R. Bauer and Morgot Schmidt (Stuttgart-Bad, Cannstatt: Fromann-holzboog, 1986), 71–133. Cited in Amy Hollywood, *The Soul as Virgin Wife: Mechthild of Magdeburg, Marguerite Porete, and Meister Eckhart* (Notre Dame, Ind. and London: University of Notre Dame Press, 1995), 241 n.6.

47. Mechthild, *Flowing Light*, III.9, p. 115.

48. Ibid., IV.19, p. 164.

49. Ibid., I.44, p. 61. See Edith Scholl, "To Be a Full-Grown Bride: Mechthild of Magdeburg," in *Peace Weavers*, vol. 2 of *Medieval Religious Women*, ed. John A. Nichols and Lillian Thomas Shank (Kalamazoo, Mich.: Cistercian Publications, 1987), 223–37.

50. For a very different interpretation of suffering in women's mystical literature, see Julie B. Miller, "Eroticized Violence." Miller is right to demand that scholars ask whether this material and contemporary interpretations of it support or protest actual violence against women. However, I disagree with her suggestion that both these literatures might be consciously or unconsciously supporting a patriarchal structure in which women are not only abused but are seen to take pleasure in suffering. Elements central to this discussion include: the role of suffering in mystical literature written by men; the experience of violence in medieval culture from war, weather, family feuds, disease, etc.; the fact that men were able to suffer with and for Christ in their public ministries in ways denied to women; the role and meaning of the cross, etc. While one must be alert to the ways in which this material has been used to support the status quo against women, I am suggesting that this material can be put to other uses that are beneficial to women. Scientific research on the brain may also shed light on

this question. Scientists at the University of California, San Francisco, found that the sensation of pain triggers the same brain circuits that are involved in pleasure (Jerome Burne, "Pain, Pleasure and Phantom Limbs," *Financial Times*, 3–4 June 2000, 2).

51. Of course, the medieval tradition is heir to the patristic tradition of martyrdom in which martyrdom was seen as a second baptism of blood that united the martyr with Christ in his passion. See for example, Origen's *Homilies on Judges*, 7.2; *Commentary on John*, 6.281; and *Exhortation to Martyrdom*. And in *Sermon* 131.2, commenting on John 6:44, Augustine writes, "*Nobody can come to me, unless the Father who sent me drags him* [John 6:44]. He didn't say 'leads,' but 'drags.' This violence happens to the heart, not to the flesh. So why be surprised? Believe, and you come; love and you are dragged. Don't regard this violence as harsh and irksome; on the contrary it is sweet and pleasant" (cited by P. Gorday and J. Cavadini in *The Cross in Christian Tradition: From Paul to Bonaventure*, ed. Elizabeth A. Dreyer [Mahwah, N.J.: Paulist Press, 2000], 116, 161).

52. Hadewijch of Antwerp, Poems in Stanzas, "Vale Millies," 5, in *The Complete Works*, trans. Mother Columba Hart (New York and Ramsey, N.J.: Paulist Press, 1980), 128.

53. Ibid., Poem 7.5, p. 146.

54. Ibid., Poem 9.1, p. 149.

55. Ibid., Poem 10.3, p. 153.

56. Ibid., Poem 2.8, p. 133.

57. Bernard of Clairvaux, *Sermons on the Song of Songs*, ser. 84.2–4, 4:189–91.

58. Hadewijch, Poems in Stanzas, 16.10, p. 171.

59. Ibid., 3.3, p. 135.

60. Mechthild, *Flowing Light*, I.3, p. 42.

61. Ibid., II.25, p. 94.

62. See Hollywood, *Soul As Virgin Wife*, 59.

63. Caroline Walker Bynum, *Jesus as Mother: Studies in the Spirituality of the High Middle Ages* (Berkeley, Los Angeles, and London: University of California Press, 1982), 230; cited in Hollywood, *Soul as Virgin Wife*, 60.

64. See Robert T. Peterson, *The Art of Ecstasy: Teresa, Bernini, and Crashaw* (New York: Atheneum, 1970); Leo Sternberg, *The Sexuality of Christ in Renaissance Art and in Modern Oblivion* (New York: Pantheon, 1982). Andrew Greeley also discusses this sculpture in *The Catholic Imagination* (Berkeley, Los Angeles, and London: University of California Press, 2000), 54, 57, 63–65, 75, 86, 184.

65. Teresa of Avila, *Interior Castle*, VI.2.2, p. 115.

66. Teresa of Avila, *The Book of Her Life*, in *Collected Works*, trans. Kieran Kavanaugh (Washington, D.C.: Institute of Carmelite Studies, 1987), 1:252.

67. Hadewijch, Poems in Stanzas, 16.8, pp. 170–71.

68. Bonaventure, *Itinerarium mentis in Deum*, trans. Philotheus Boehner (St. Bonaventure, N.Y.: Franciscan Institute, 1956), 100–101.

69. Teresa of Avila, *Interior Castle*, III.1.2, p. 56.

70. Hadewijch, Poems in Stanzas, Poem 19.10, p. 178.

71. Ibid., Poem 16.4, p. 169.

72. Hadewijch, Poems in Couplets, 13, in *The Complete Works* (New York and Ramsey, N.J.: Paulist Press, 1980), 344.

73. Julian of Norwich, *Showings* (New York, Ramsey, N.J., and London: Paulist Press, 1978), 216.

74. Paul Mariani, "The Unshapeable Shock Night: Pain, Suffering and the Redemptive Imagination," *America*, 20 February 1999, 17.

75. Ronald Rolheiser, *The Holy Longing: The Search for a Christian Spirituality* (New York: Doubleday, 1999), 75.

76. Walter Brueggemann, *In Man We Trust* (Atlanta, Ga.: John Knox Press, 1972), 40.

77. However, I was encouraged by the comments of an undergraduate who said at the end of a course on medieval women mystics: "One can say that the images of God used in *The Interior Castle* can still apply in today's society. A common image of God was God as the bridegroom. I believe that this is an excellent image of God, one that many can relate to. Since marriages these days foster an equal contribution to the marriage from the husband and wife, married couples know that it takes commitment, determination and respect from both parts to make a marriage work. So it is with a relationship with God."

78. Mark S. Burrows, "Naming the God Beyond Names," 37–53.

79. Mark McIntosh calls attention to this position in order to counter it. "The range of arguments against incarnational conceptions in Christology is fairly wide today. Yet there does seem to be a fundamental consensus among the critics that, simply put, we would not now understand our experience of Jesus in terms of a literal incarnation because a literal incarnation is simply unintelligible today, i.e., we don't understand the world or the human self in ways that could make sense of it. Among many others we might name the analyses of Schubert Ogden, Maurice Wiles, Karl-Josef Kuschel and John Hick as raising a number of objections along these lines." McIntosh turns to the resources of mystical theology to counter three points of opposition to incarnational thought: that divine and human existence are mutually exclusive; that there is insufficient knowledge of Jesus' self-understanding; and that incarnational Christologies are inevitably docetic. See *Mystical Theology: The Integrity of Spirituality and Theology* (Oxford: Blackwell, 1998), 192–208.

80. See Elizabeth A. Dreyer, ed., *The Cross in the Christian Tradition: Paul to Bonaventure* (Mahwah, N.J.: Paulist Press, 2000); and Cynthia S. W. Crysdale, *Embracing Travail: Retrieving the Cross Today* (New York: Continuum, 1999).

81. Prime examples include chapter 7 of Bonaventure's *Itinerarium mentis in Deum* and Julian of Norwich's *Showings*.

82. Brock, *Journeys by Heart*, 35–37.

83. See Joan Timmerman, *The Mardi Gras Syndrome: Rethinking Christian Sexuality* (New York: Crossroad, 1984).

84. Wendell Berry, *Remembering: A Novel* (San Francisco: Point Press, 1988), 34–35.

85. Rowan Williams, *Christian Spirituality* (Atlanta, Ga.: John Knox Press, 1979), 78.

CHAPTER TWELVE

Christos Mystikos

Jesus Christ and the New Millennium

LAWRENCE S. CUNNINGHAM

Let the word of Christ dwell in you richly
—Col 3:16

Karl Rahner once wrote, famously, that the Christian of the future would either be a mystic "who has experienced something or will cease to be anything at all."[1] The burden of Rahner's argument was that the day when Christians (he was speaking of his own experiences as a European) would simply be born into, and assimilated by, the Bavarian piety of his youth and young adulthood had passed, eroded by the traumas of the century, the rapid rise of urbanization, and the decline of insulated islands of traditional Catholic culture. His statement, in short, reflected a sober judgment about the de facto situation in Europe, a situation that had been described by many commentators both within and outside of Germany in particular and Western Europe in general. His words may have appeared alarmist to believers on the other side of the Atlantic, at least in North America, but they were received without quarrel in Western Europe since Rahner was talking about a religious phenomenon at least as old as the warnings found in Henri Perrin's path-breaking book *Is France Pagan?* published during the Second World War.

When Rahner wrote that the Christians of the future had to "experience something" he used a kind of shorthand to describe what elsewhere he called the "church in the diaspora"—those communities of believers who exist along with a secularized culture which views the believing community either with benign indifference or outright hostility. To be a believer in post-war Germany or in a *banlieue* of Paris or in the de-Christianized cultures from Scandinavia to the Iberian peninsula was only possible if those who lived in such communities actually believed in something. There would be nothing substantially nourishing found in the culture itself that would support belief; belief could only be sustained and nurtured by authentic religious experience. In other words, the Christians of the future would have to accommodate themselves to being minority communities in largely unbelieving societies.

One can enlarge Rahner's observation by thinking about those believers who live as a distinct minority in an alien culture (in Pakistan, the Sudan, large parts of India, in the Middle East, Northern Africa, etc.) or in one that is aggressively hostile to believers such as the People's Republic of China. Or, to calibrate the matter somewhat differently, to think of those believers who live in cultures which are nominally Christian but whose political climate is such that deeply committed believers become the object of murderous impulses as the recent lugubrious history of several Latin American and Central American countries testify. What is rather new about martyrdom in those latter countries is, as Javier Limón has written, that "people are not being killed through hatred of the faith or by a militantly unbelieving or atheist world. They are being murdered in culturally Catholic countries belonging to Western civilizations, apparently secular and tolerant."[2]

Whether the country is secularized or shaped by a quite different religious history or hostile or even benignly tolerant, the same question occurs: How is Christ present to that situation? There was a time not too far distant when the answer was simple enough: use the energy, the resources, and the purported superiority of Western culture to make Christ present, i.e., to evangelize with aggressive enthusiasm. That attitude, among certain strains of fundamentalist Christianity, is still regnant as monies, advanced media, and social services blanket the world with one or other particular version of the Gospel. Such a muscular approach to mission does carry with it more than a hint of superiority not unlike the old concept of a colonialism—the *mission civilitrice*—where the Gospel and capitalist expansion went hand in hand. Given the ubiquity of the media today there is more than a suspicion in some countries that aggressive evangelization is another covert attempt at the McDonaldization of the entire world.

The whole issue of mission in a pluralist world is a topic that has engaged the attention of theologians who have addressed a whole spectrum of topics.[3] That spectrum runs from issues about inculturation at the most benign level to the vexatious topic of the degree to which one must preach salvation through Christ as the one way to salvation. That spectrum is so broad and the topics within it so neuralgic that it would be beyond the capacities of this essay to even list them.

My reflections will be much more modest since they will focus on only one fundamental issue: Who is Jesus Christ for today and how is the presence of that Christ instantiated in the contemporary world especially in those parts of the world where Christ is either not known or only understood as a kind of cultural artifact belonging to an age long gone? To put it bluntly: what think ye of the Christ in Oslo or Karachi or Bogota or Chicago or even here in the Middle East? I ask this question as a Christian to Christians since I am not expert enough to ask it in tandem with other religious traditions as the comparative theologian might do. I ask simply how a believing Christian thinks of the presence of Jesus Christ in places and situations where such belief looks either odd or even hostile to the best of the culture.

Some Fundamental Assertions

We might begin with a fundamental truth: Jesus is a person with a history. His life story as a public person does not begin "once upon a time" but "in the fifteenth year of the reign of Tiberius Caesar" (Lk 3:1). Furthermore, this historical person had a history succinctly summed up in an economic phrase written by an ardent follower: Jesus was born at the right time; he was born of a woman; and, finally, he was born into the culture of the Jews ["In the fullness of time God sent his son, born of a woman, born under the law. . ." Gal 4:4]. Not to parse that phrase too carefully we can stipulate that (1) Jesus cannot be understood except against the background of the long history of the Jewish people; (2) from the perspective of his followers, his coming was the culmination of a long period of expectation; (3) he was not an angel or a demiurge but one born of a woman—a man who was understood to be both the son of his mother and the Son of God. (4) Finally, he was born at a particular moment in history and in a particular place so that, humanly speaking, there is a long period "before" and "after" Jesus.

To insist that Jesus was a man with a history does not mean that his meaning is exhausted by grasping him *solely* as a person who lived at a particular moment in time; in other words, the believing community of Christians has never held that the center and wellspring of their belief derives from the mere fact of his historical reality *pace* some popular interpretations of contemporary scholarship on the historical Jesus. The fact that Jesus is a historical person does not mean that his meaning is totally bound to his historical moment. For the Christian community Jesus has a meta-historical significance. To recover Jesus as a historical person only takes us so far. Paul Tillich got it exactly right when he wrote something over fifty years ago that is true both of theological method and the dynamics of belief:

> The historical foundation of theological method does not mean that the theologian has to wait, in fear and trembling, for the next mail which may bring him a new, more critical, or more conservative statement about some important facts of the 'life of Jesus' according to which he has to change his faith and his theology. But it does mean that his theology is determined by the advent of the appearance of the new reality in history, as reflected in the *full* biblical picture of Jesus as the Christ and as witnessed by all biblical writers and the whole tradition of Christianity.[4] (Tillich's emphasis)

Resistance to a reduction of the significance of Jesus to the results of historical scholarship does not mean that such research is without value. To the contrary, such scholarship is a gift to the believing community. Resistance however should reflect an unwillingness to limit the significance of faith as a result of such work. When Tillich spoke about the *full* biblical picture and the witness of the whole tradition of Christianity, he was writing, in effect, about the ceaseless attempt on the part of believers to answer the question which is our theme: "What think ye of the Christ? Whose Son is he?"

It is not to oversimplify to say that the struggle to answer that question at a very deep level involves an attempt to do justice to the historicity of Jesus as a fellow member of the human race and the evolving understanding of his followers from the beginning to reach up to the significance of what the full biblical witness had to say about him. The canonical scriptures themselves reflect that struggle for understanding—the articulation, in other words, of a *theologia* that does full justice to the deepest meaning of that word.

A Historical Perspective

Let me put the issue before us into some kind of perspective. Christians today make up about a quarter of the world's population. To take comfort in that fact is to elide over the other fact that in large parts of the world the Christian presence is minimal. That minimal presence must be set against the universalist claims which Christian faith makes. Not far from this place where we meet, Christians honor the birthplace of Jesus. Our tendency is to think of the message of Jesus radiating out from ancient Palestine toward the North and toward the West following the map of, say, Paul's journeys around the Mediterranean world. That bias toward the West derives, of course, because of the facile identification of Christianity with the West but, as we should know, that is only one way of looking at matters.

Permit me, however, to turn your eyes to the East in order to do a thought experiment.[5] If one were to travel East through Iraq at the time of the birth of Jesus one would pass through ancient Persia already wedded to a religious dualism which would provide in time both Zoroastrian, Mandean, and Mithraic impulses. Voyaging from Persia in an easterly direction one passes through the vast reaches of Central Asia. By taking the southern silk route one would arrive, eventually, in the subcontinent of India. At the time of the birth of Jesus, India had a millennial history of religious practice reflected first in the liturgical texts known collectively as the *Rig Veda* and later in the philosophical corpus of the *Upanishads*. In the time roughly coinciding with the times of Jesus the epic tradition of India was taking shape in the form of both the *Ramayana* and the *Mahabharata* in which is found the exquisite *Bhagavad Gita*. By following the Northern silk route of central Asia one would eventually end up in China at a time when the tradition of both court Confucianism and Taoism were being tempered or challenged by an emergent Buddhism, a religious tradition which already had five hundred years of history behind it.

These ancient religious traditions were vibrantly alive at the precise time when Paul was writing to a minuscule community in Corinth (of perhaps a hundred people?) about Jesus making claims that on the face of it seemed outlandish. This Jesus was Lord, Son of God, Power of God, the Wisdom of God, our righteousness, sanctification, redemption, and pledge of eternal life. Those titles, gleaned from a cursory glance at the epistle, had an added dimension when Paul further stipulates that the Christ who is Wisdom is identified as the hidden wisdom of God which existed before the foundations of the world. Those claims seem so outsized when one considers the actual religious traditions of the day. What would the sages of India make of such claims?

The claims of Paul are not only audacious but they are all the more so because they were taken with such utter seriousness both in the Pauline churches and by the later generations of believers. Some of these claims were vigorously rejected by the Jewish world in which Paul was at home but the rejection of the Synagogue would be based on an intelligibility rooted in a common grammar as well as familial resemblances. The Jews who heard Paul knew what the word "messiah" meant. What sense did these claims make, however, when set against quite different and radically incommensurable religious claims coming from traditions which did not have a similar common vocabulary?

I raise this question simply because we live in a world quite different from Paul. Both modern travel and easy communications via the various forms of media make us acutely aware of our global reality. These new realities, in turn, seem to make the universal claims of Christian faith easy to relativize. It is only a matter of perspective to juxtapose Pauline claims and the exigent fact of different ancient religious traditions in Paul's day with the claims of Christianity today against a more vivid awareness of competing religious claims in the contemporary world as well as the claims of a non-religious bias deeply rooted in those cultures which are loosely described as post-industrial and postmodern. What has Jerusalem to say to Karachi or Beijing or Jakarta—to name just three cities of whose existence even an early modern like Martin Luther would not have known?

Christos Mystikos

Let me make my own position clear: I do confess Jesus as the Christ, the Icon of God, and savior. That is *my* faith and the faith of *my* community. If we do not begin there my remarks can be seen as either a cavil or an equivocation.

To make such a profession of faith, however, is not to associate that confession with those perceptions (or mis-perceptions) that people have who judge Christianity as imperious or imperialistic or, worse, self-deluding even though history tells us that Christians have been both imperious and imperialistic. The profession of faith only constitutes a beginning point for me as a theologian to look at the de facto world in which we live. Were I to make the admission that the Christian faith is just one more faith tradition alongside many others, it would allow me the luxury of so stating and then sitting down.

To profess Christ as Lord or Son of God is not to say that the sense of those titles need be affirmed as they strike the ear of the hearer. To say "Jesus is Lord" is not to say that Jesus lords it over people. It is the reality behind the christological titles (beginning with the title "Christ" itself) as well as the person who bears them that is to be discovered and recovered. That task was well summed up in Aquinas's observation that faith ends in the reality (*res*) and not in the articulation (*enuntiabile*) of that reality. It is for that precise reason that I have used in the title of this essay the phrase *Christos Mystikos* to recall the patristic understanding of *mystikos* as that which is hidden or beneath that which is experienced and grasped. *Mystikos*, in that sense, is usefully applied both to sacred scripture and to the eucharist and to the liturgy as well as to Christ himself who is that *mysterion* hidden in God before all ages (Eph 3:9). The sense in which the word "mystical" is used here indicates nothing more than this: Christ is both hidden and revealed.

The manner in which I use the term *Christos Mystikos* today is to struggle with the presence of Christ in a world which (a) does not know his name, or (b) having once heard it cannot fathom its meaning now, or (c) has only faint intimations of that name as someone or something uttered by preachers over short wave radio or cable television. This struggle for intelligibility begins with my own confession of faith against the realities which I know to be the case in the larger world in which we live.

In the remaining part of this essay some suggestions will be made about how Christ remains both hidden and revealed in this complex world described above. Please note that these reflections on hiddenness and manifestation are not to be construed as missionary remarks; nor are they meant to parallel anything like Karl Rahner's "anonymous Christians" or similar theoretical constructs. They are meant to describe how I think Christ is made present in the contemporary situation. In other words, my remarks are not crafted to elucidate anything more than how believers see the presence of Christ in a world which is decidedly, empirically, and determinedly non-Christian.

Christ Hidden and Revealed

The first and most obvious thing to be said is that the primary task of the believing community is to tell the story and enact that story in worship. The most dramatic thing that followers of Christ do to make present and reveal Christ is by doing exactly what was done in the first generation of Christianity: gather together, tell the story, and break the bread. It is only in that act of community, as the Emmaus story in Luke 24 makes transparently clear, that the One who is unknown is recognized at least for that community. At that level I find myself in agreement with the missionary strategy of those Orthodox communions who see the concrete realization of the liturgical community as the primary task of both the sustenance and spread of the Christian message which is the way Christ is, in this economy, revealed. That liturgical community, to be sure, must be one that is catholic in the theological sense of the word: neither acting as a besieged fortress protecting a remnant nor as an ethnic or tribal enclave making false discriminations about who is or is not invited to the table but as a confident community much like those of the ancient house churches in the world of Paul. To say it simply: eucharistic communities are, by their very being, hospitable communities. They grow to the degree that they are open.

Current crises in the church in the West, for example, regarding dwindling numbers of priests in certain parts of the world, rural flight to the cities, the banalization of liturgical practice, and so on, are petty intramural church squabbles if they do not get discussed in the light of the simple fact that both orthodoxy and orthopraxis as well as evangelization make sense only with the conviction—the experience as Rahner would say—that Christ is made present in these communities. It might be noted in passing that the lack of priests is not an isolated problem to be discussed at the level of canonical legislation. It is an issue intimately tied to the very meaning of Catholic Christianity: no eucharistic assembly means no church. That simple fact means, of course, that theologians need pay careful attention to the sacramental status of base communities, intentional groups, houses of non-ordained religious, etc., to ask how these communities can be eucharistic ones.

Where these communities are present or can be present they need to be supported so that they can function as a *sacramentum* of Christ's presence in the world. Making concrete the presence of believers in community does not demand, as often happened in the past, imperialistic forms of conversion (the infamous "rice Christians") or elaborate parochial structures. But believers must be seen as a *presence* which makes the church concrete and palpable. Such communities are at their best when they imitate the hospitality which was the hallmark of the Emmaus experience recounted in Luke. This strategy sometimes goes under the name of "church planting" in some quarters, but I understand that word "church" in its deepest sense of assembly or community; not the erection of structures. Perhaps the better term would be something like "community presence."

A second way in which Christ is present to the world of non-belief or unbelief is through its many gestures of care for the needy of the world. This assertion is not to be construed as some flaccid form of the social gospel; it is to say that self-forgetting service to others is a way of revealing the hidden Christ. I do not know if there are any parishes or Christian communities in Yemen today but I do know that the Missionaries of Charity have been there at the service of the handicapped children of that area and three of them lost their lives in that endeavor accused, wrongly, as being agents of Christian expansion. I know that before the rise of the Taliban in the wake of the Russian war in that sad area, Kabul in Afghanistan had a hospice run by the same sisters. Such Christian presences, hidden and resistant to impulses at proselytizing efforts in cultures where such efforts would be repulsive, have made the hidden Christ present in the most hostile areas of the world.

These efforts remind us of a truth emphasized by theologians, namely, that the scriptures are not only to be read but performed. The performance of those words of Jesus about seeing himself in the act of feeding the hungry, giving drink to the thirsty, visiting the prisoner, and so on (Mt 25:31–46) is not merely a program of social action (although social action programs may derive from those words) but, rather, a kind of evangelism—proclaiming the Good News—which, as the opening chapter of Mark indicates, advances the kingdom of God. For what does Mark say? The kingdom advances incrementally by the concrete acts reflected in the healing of Peter's mother-in-law, by accepting those who were sick with various ailments; by healing the leper by touch because, as Origen once noted in a sermon on that topic, that touch "might teach us that we should not despise any person."

Any appeal, as made above, to the witness of service to the world should not be construed as a discrete or absolute action divorced from the fundamental Christian affirmation that evangelization cannot be reduced down only to temporal amelioration. The seminal apostolic exhortation *Evangelii Nuntiandi* of the late Pope Paul VI, issued a quarter of a century ago, has a subtle discussion of the relationship between political, social, and economic liberation and evangelization[6] making the argument that such liberationist motifs cannot count as the sum total of efforts at evangelization which, even among those who are outside the Christian world, must always see the liberationist message of Christianity as allowing, in the words of the pope, for an openness to the Absolute. I would also note, but only in passing, that part of the problem with the term "evangelization" is that the word is used in different ways with quite different nuances depending on who is speaking and to what end. Evangelization in the writings of the more recent popes should not be read in the same way in which the term is used by American televangelists.

A third and far more subtle way in which the hidden Christ may be made manifest has been suggested by an issue raised by Pope John Paul II in his encyclical on missions *Redemptoris Missio* (1990) and in many subsequent documents and speeches. In that encyclical the pope raises the question of how the voice of Christ can be heard in what the pope calls the "New Areopagus." His point is simple enough. Modern mass media competes for "space" in communications to persuade across a whole spectrum of perceived needs whether those needs be commercial, social, or political. Nobody underestimates the power of the various media in the contemporary world.

John Paul's use of the term "Areopagus" (it occurs not infrequently in his writings) is a suggestive one. When one compares the early kerygmatic sermons in Acts with the famous speech of Paul in Acts 17 the difference in the tone is striking; a clear example of inculturated speech. In the former sermons there is a kind of set pattern: Jesus is the one promised by the prophets; he did mighty deeds; he suffered, died, and rose on the third day; we (i.e., the apostles) are witnesses to this. However stereotyped those sermons might have been they did all presuppose that the audience to whom they were delivered had a common vocabulary rooted in the Hebrew scriptures. By contrast, Paul, even garnishing his speech with a pagan reference, speaks to an audience who were used to philosophical discourse; hence, his sermon dealt with issues like the creation of the world; the constitution of human beings; the unity of the human race; the distinction between images of "gold, silver, or stone" or "representation by the art and imagination of man" (Acts 17:29) and the invisible God; and, finally, the ultimate destiny of human beings.

Not to put too fine a point on it: Paul's sermon was an attempt to put his faith in Christ into some kind of understandable context so that he might get a hearing in a marketplace peopled by followers of the Stoics and Epicureans. Jacques Dupuis, commenting on this speech and recognizing the exegetical problems it raises, does state both that Paul affirms that God is near to all people ("For indeed [*gar*] he is not far from each of us" 17:27) and, further, the "areopagus speech inaugurates a missionary strategy based on a positive approach to the religiosity of the Greeks."[7]

In the context of our contemporary reality we might ask how one enters this new areopagus to have one's voice heard. The answer is that the Christian community should first of all be on the side of every issue that reflects our own understanding of the human person as being made in the image and likeness of God—and image and likeness thickened and deepened by the mystery of the Incarnation. The voice of Christians ought to be on the side of life and not death; on the side of human emancipation and not slavery; on the side of human rights and not human suppression; on the side of the poor and the exploited; on the side of peace and not of war. The voice of the Christian in the areopagus ought to be a voice of risk and ought to be a prophetic voice and not one of *Realpolitik*. In those areas of social and civil discourse where there is no clear consensus even within the church the only thing one can do is to listen patiently (the church is both a "teaching church and a learning one" *ecclesia docens* and *discens*) in order to grow. History teaches us that the church has had to learn (on issues like slavery, the death penalty, etc.) slowly how to be more obedient to the Word of God.

Such a Christian voice in this new areopagus may not always be an exclusively Christian one. Such a voice might find us in solidarity with other voices but such solidarity in itself is an incarnational strategy deeply rooted in both Christian thought and practice. Although Pope John Paul II has been criticized for his assertion that Christians have the right to proclaim the Gospel everywhere in the world, it should be remembered that evangelization is not essentially aggressive. In fact, the negative reaction to the papal assertion of the right to evangelize might well derive from the way the word "evangelization" is heard.

In an audience (May 19, 1999; reported in the English language edition of *L'Osservatore Romano*, May 26, 1999) the pope asks how Christians respond to the other world religions. His answer is that apart from such technical dialogue as occurs in interreligious exchange either in academic or contemplative settings, the deepest forms of dialogue occur when people learn to live in community aiding each other; when persons exchange experiences in action when they struggle commonly for peace, education, social justice, and the amelioration of poverty; and, finally, when they are nourished by deep experiences that nourish the interior life.

How, finally, is the hidden Christ of Christianity made manifest? Such a breaking forth first occurs when Christians themselves are transformed by their own faith. That transformation, in turn, should turn them to others in whom they see the hidden face of Christ. This process, then, is a kind of sacred dance, a perichoresis. Christians, faithful to their own path of discipleship, receive glimmers of the hidden Christ in their own faith and, in that discovery, see that hidden Christ in others. Does the Other need become a Christian? Well, we believe that somehow, hiddenly, Christ is present in all of creation and in every person. We hope that that faith affirmation is not an affront to others. We would not like it to be but we must speak as Christians out of the framework of the Christian faith.

The rest is in the hands of God. However, to force Christ on the other runs the risk of idolatry since we may force, in fact, our own distorted image of who that Christ is on to the other. We must remain with the "hidden" Christ who is the subject of this meditation. Far better, it seems to me, is to stand before the face (*le visage*) of the other because our human stand of being face to face (*Face à face*) is the irreducible condition for dialogue and, as Emmanuel Levinas has brilliantly argued, all ethics.[8] It is the Christian conviction that when we look at the face of the other we see that other as made in the image and likeness of God and, further, somehow the hidden Christ, hidden to be sure, is also revealed. That revelation is not definitive until we have arrived at the *eschaton* but in the interim we take consolation in Paul's observation that in the between times "the Spirit helps us in our weakness, for we do not know how to pray as we ought but the Spirit himself intercedes for us with sighs too deep for words" (Rom 8:26).

NOTES

1. Karl Rahner, "Christian Living Formerly and Today," in *Theological Investigations VII* (New York: Seabury, 1977), 15.

2. Javier Jiménez Limón, "Suffering, Death, Cross, and Martyrdom," in *Mysterium Liberationis*, ed. Ignacio Ellacuría and Jon Sobrino (Maryknoll, N.Y.: Orbis, 1993), 714. Ellacuría himself, one of the editors, was murdered by a Salvadoran death squad.

3. At the local level, see Robert Schreiter, "Ministry for a Multicultural Church," *Origins* 29, no. 1 (20 May 1999): 1–8; for the global level: Jacques Dupuis, *Towards a Christian Theology of Religious Pluralism* (Maryknoll, N.Y.: Orbis, 1997).

4. Paul Tillich, "The Problem of Theological Method," in *Paul Tillich: Theologian of the Boundaries*, ed. Mark Kline Taylor (London and San Francisco, Calif.: Collins, 1987), 134.

5. Two recent works attempt to tell the story of the Christian East: Samuel Hugh Moffett, *A History of Christianity in Asia*, vol. 1 (San Francisco, Calif.: Harper, 1992); and Ian Gillman and Hans-Joachim Klimkeit, *Christians in Asia Before 1500* (Ann Arbor, Mich.: University of Michigan Press, 1999).

6. In *Proclaiming Justice & Peace*, ed. Michael Walsh and Brian Davies (Mystic, Conn.: Twenty Third Publications, 1991), 284–322.

7. DuPuis, *Towards a Christian Theology*, 50.

8. I borrow here from his Emmanuel Levinas, *Totality and Infinity* (Pittsburgh, Pa.: Duquesne University, 1969); see also Colin Davis, *Levinas: An Introduction* (Notre Dame, Ind.: University of Notre Dame Press, 1996), 44–62.

Contributors

James J. Buckley, Loyola College of Maryland

David Burrell, C.S.C., University of Notre Dame

Lawrence S. Cunningham, University of Notre Dame

Elizabeth A. Dreyer, Fairfield University

Claude Geffré, O.P., Professeur honoraire de l'Institut Catholique de Paris

Morna Hooker, Robinson College, Cambridge University

Kathryn Johnson, Louisville Presbyterian Seminary

George Lindbeck, Pitkin Professor of Historical Theology Emeritus, Yale University

Johann Baptist Metz, Universität Münster

Jaroslav Pelikan, Sterling Professor of History Emeritus, Yale University

Gerald O'Collins, S.J., Pontifica Università Gregoriana

Michael A. Signer, University of Notre Dame

Jon Sobrino, S.J., Centro de Reflexión Teológica, San Salvador

Index